AF541326

Cyber Threat in Global Perspective

Dr. Kapender Singh

Gaurav Book Centre Pvt. Ltd.
NEW DELHI-110002

Publisher
GAURAV BOOK CENTRE PVT LTD
4832/24, Prahlad Lane,S-207 Ansari
Road, Daryaganj, Delhi-110002
Ph.: 43570976, 23278261
Email: gauravbookcentre@gmail.com

Edition: 2024

© Author

ISBN: 978-93-83316-37-3

Laser Typesetting
JEE-VEE Graphics, Delhi

Price: 1295/-

Printed
Vikas Computers, Delhi

Contents

<u>**DEDICATED**</u>

to

my parents

KAMAL-KAPOOR

Preface

Terrorist groups have changed recently from having a clearly defined hierarchy in the organisations with designated leaders, to having multiple, semi-independent cells with no clear distinct leader in order to allow them to remain hidden. The Internet facilitates communication between cells which allows exchange of information and manuals.

The Internet is a powerful tool for terrorists, who use online message boards and chat rooms to share information, coordinate attacks, spread propaganda, raise funds, and recruit, experts say. According to Haifa University's Gabriel Weimann, whose research on the subject is widely cited, the number of terrorist sites increased exponentially over the last decade—from less than 100 to more than 4,800 two years ago. The numbers can be somewhat misleading, however. In the case of al-Qaeda, hundreds of sister sites have been promulgated but only a handful are considered active, experts say. Nonetheless, analysts do see a clear proliferation trend.

Cyberterrorism is typically defined as the use of the Internet as a vehicle through which to launch an attack. Terrorists could conceivably hack into electrical grids and security systems, or perhaps distribute a powerful computer virus. "Al-Qaeda operatives are known to have taken training in hacking techniques," Arquilla says, but the likelihood of such a cyber attack seems fairly remote. That said, Western governments have accused state and nonstate actors of infiltrating secure networks, including an alleged breach of a Pentagon system by Chinese hackers in June 2007.

A cyberterror attack on vital national infrastructure such as power facilities, transport networks and the financial sector could be imminent—and international governments are ill-prepared, cybersecurity experts have warned. "It's not easy to predict what will happen, but the worst terrorist attacks are not expected," Eugene Kaspersky, the co-founder and chief executive of global IT security firm Kaspersky Labs, told CNBC. So I am afraid that if we face this cyberterrorism, it will be very unpredictable in a very unpredictable place, but with very visible damage. Unfortunately, there are many possible victims."

In recent months, the business world and political establishment has seen an uptick in the use of debilitating digital attacks. As well as the Sony attacks, allegedly by North Korea, and the widespread hacking of international news agencies by the "Syrian Electronic Army," On Monday, Malaysian Airlines refuted that its website had been hacked by a group calling itself the "Cyber Caliphate" and claiming affiliation with the Islamic State (ISIS).

Currently, chemical, biological, radiological, and nuclear detection capabilities are modest and response capabilities are dispersed throughout the country at every level of government. Responsibility for chemical, biological, radiological, and nuclear surveillance as well as for initial response efforts often rests with state and local hospitals and public health agencies.

Defense technologists are most successful when they hone in on specific problems. The Pentagon's research agencies and their contractors were asked in 2003 to come up with ways to foil roadside bombs in Iraq and Afghanistan, and although they did not defeat the threat entirely, they did produce a number of useful detectors, jammers and other counter-explosive systems. More recently, military researchers received marching orders to help tackle the so-called "anti-access area-denial" threats, which is Pentagon-speak for enemy weapons that could be used to shoot down U.S. fighters and attack Navy ships. The next wave of national security threats, however, might be more than the technology community can handle. They are complex, multidimensional problems against which no degree of U.S. technical superiority in stealth, fifth-generation air warfare or night-vision is likely to suffice.

The book will serve as an ultimate resource book for everyone who would like to know the wide range of prospects in the emerging applications of cyber terrorism and military.

I would like to thank my teachers who made me too much capable to do work like this. Also thankful to our worthy Principal I.S. Lakhlan and all my colleagues for their valuable advices.

I will always be debted to my parents, whose inspiration and unconditional support guided me to achieve even difficult tasks. Ofcourse silent consent of my kith and kin boosted me to complete this work. At last but not least, thankful to the publisher of this book who have done better work as expected.

—Author

1

Cyber Terrorism

In the wake of the recent computer attacks, many have been quick to jump to conclusions that a new breed of terrorism is on the rise and our country must defend itself with all possible means. As a society we have a vast operational and legal experience and proved techniques to combat terrorism, but are we ready to fight terrorism in the new arena – cyber space?

A strategic plan of a combat operation includes characterization of the enemy's goals, operational techniques, resources, and agents. Prior to taking combative actions on the legislative and operational front, one has to precisely define the enemy. That is, it is imperative to expand the definition of terrorism to include cyber-terrorism.

As a society that prides itself on impartiality of justice, we must provide clear and definitive legislative guidelines for dealing with new breed of terrorism. As things stand now, justice cannot be served as we have yet to provide a clear definition of the term.

There is a lot of misinterpretation in the definition cyber-terrorism, the word consisting of familiar "cyber" and less familiar "terrorism". While "cyber" is anything related to our tool of trade, terrorism by nature is difficult to define. Even the U.S. government cannot agree on one single definition. The old maxim, "One man's terrorist is another man's freedom fighter" is still alive and well.

The ambiguity in the definition brings indistinctness in action, as D. Denning pointed in her work Activism, Hactivism and Cyberterrorism, "an e-mail bomb may be considered hacktivism by some and cyber-terrorism by others". It follows that there is a degree of "understanding" of the meanings of cyber-terrorism, either from the popular media, other secondary sources, or personal experience; however, the specialists' use different definitions of the meaning. Cyber-terrorism as well as other contemporary "terrorisms" (bioterrorism, chemical terrorism, etc.) appeared as a mixture of words terrorism and a meaning of an area of application. Barry Collin, a senior research fellow at the Institute for Security and Intelligence in California, who in 1997 was attributed for creation of the term "Cyberterrorism", defined cyber-terrorism as the convergence of cybernetics and terrorism. In the same year Mark Pollitt, special agent for the FBI, offers a working definition: "Cyberterrorism is the premeditated, politically motivated attack against information, computer systems, computer programs, and data which result in violence against noncombatant targets by sub national groups or clandestine agents."

Since that time the word cyber-terrorism has entered into the lexicon of IT security specialists and terrorist experts and the word list of mass media "professionals". One of the experts, a police chief, offers his version of definition: "Cyber-terrorism – attacking sabotage-prone targets by computer – poses potentially disastrous consequences for our incredibly computer-dependent society."

The media often use cyber-terrorism term quite deliberately: "Canadian boy admits cyberterrorism of his family: "Emeryville, Ontario (Reuter) - A 15-year-old Canadian boy has admitted he was responsible for months of notorious high-tech pranks that terrorized his own family, police said Monday"

A renowned expert Dorothy Denning defined cyber-terrorism as "unlawful attacks and threats of attack against computers, networks, and the information stored therein when done to intimidate or coerce a government or its people in furtherance of political or social objectives". R. Stark from the SMS University defines cyber-terrorism as " any attack against an information function, regardless of the means"

Under the above-mentioned definitions of cyber-terrorism one can only point to the fact that any telecommunications infrastructure attack, including site defacing and other computer pranks, constitute terrorism. It means that cyber-terrorism has already occurred and we "live " in the epoch of cyber terror.

However, another expert, James Christy the law enforcement and counterintelligence coordinator for the DIAP (Defense-wide Information Assurance Program), which is steered by the office of the assistant secretary of defense for command, control, communications and intelligence, states that cyber-terrorism has never been waged against the United States. "Rather, recent hacking events – including a 1998 web page set up by a supporter of the Mexican Zapatistas rebel group, which led to attacks on the U.S. military from 1,500 locations in 50 different countries – constitute computer crime. William Church, a former U.S. Army Intelligence officer, who founded the Centre for Infrastructural Warfare Studies (CIWARS) agrees that the United States has not seen a cyber terrorist threat from terrorists using information warfare techniques. "None of the groups that are conventionally defined as terrorist groups have used information weapons against the infrastructure" Richard Clarke, national co-ordinator for security, infrastructure protection and counterterrorism at the National Security Council offered to stop using "cyberterrorism" and use "information warfare " instead

The above-mentioned observations drive a clear line between cyber-terrorism and cyber crime and allow us to define cyber-terrorism as: Use of information technology and means by terrorist groups and agents.

In defining the cyber terrorist activity it is necessary to segment of action and motivation. There is no doubt that acts of hacking can have the same consequences as acts of terrorism but in the legal sense the intentional abuse of the information cyberspace must be a part of the terrorist campaign or an action.

Examples of cyber terrorist activity may include use of information technology to organize and carry out attacks, support groups activities and perception-management campaigns. Experts agree that many terrorist groups such as Osama bin Ladenn organization and the Islamic militant group Hamas have adopted new information technology as a means to conduct operations without being detected by counter terrorist officials.

Thus, use of information technology and means by terrorist groups and agents constitute cyber-terrorism. Other activities, so richly glamorized by the media, should be defined as cyber crime.

INTERNET AND TERRORISM

Directly after 9/11, much was made of the possibilities of a large-scale cyber-terrorism attack by the media. However, several academics in the pending years published papers focusing on the terrorist groups utilize the Internet as it was designed to be; a means to communicate and collaborate, therefore the terrorists have stronger reasons to keep it up and online. Hence the apparently impending large scale cyber-terrorist attack that would cripple the internet has not materialised although Al Qaeda has taken full advantage of this fear.

The United States in 2002 encountered cyber terrorism, John Ashcroft would violate the rights of citizens in the United States. With the passing of the USA Patriot Act in order to counter cyber terrorism, the federal government gained the power to record all electronic devices. In other words, installation of devices would be able to record all routing, addressing, signalling information with the appropriate court supervision. This act was put into law to protect the United States from cyber terrorism.

Publicity and Propaganda

As stated by Dr. Maura Conway, terrorism researcher:

"Every machine connected to the internet is potentially a printing press, a broadcasting station or place of assembly."

The internet is an un-paralleled media suite. Terrorists no longer have to have their messages diluted and edited by the media. Instead they can disseminate information of their choice to aid their causes. In most cases, this is achieved by the terrorists focusing on their grievances in order to justify why they are resorting to terrorist activities. This is usually achieved by the publication of various articles combined with pictures galleries, although this may be supplemented by video and audio files in which the terrorists themselves orally defend their actions. An example of this would be a gallery of atrocities against innocent civilians in Iraq supposedly carried out by foreign forces in order to generate local as well as international support for the terrorists.

In some cases, the terrorists choose to distribute information displaying their acts of violence or relating actions although this is not common.

Again, these can be through written articles describing the violence, but are more often videos and pictures. Examples of these would be the pre-mission pictures published on the Tamil Tigers website of the Air Tiger squadron that a few days earlier had carried out its successful inaugural air attack on Sri Lankan governmental forces. A rather more extreme example was the distribution of the beheading of the journalist Daniel Pearl by the terrorist organisation 'The National Movement for the Restoration of Pakistani Sovereignty'.

Terrorists spread their messages on sites by using symbols and imagery of victimization and empowerment. This, as we all know, rises the emotions of future supporters. On these sites, they portray the West, especially the United States, victimizing the Muslim world. The sites show images of innocent Muslims wounded and dead, the destruction of many homes, Jerusalem and of Abu Ghraib. These sites would then show images of terrorism such as US casualties, images of 9/11, etc. They would state that the Muslim world is being under attack by non believers, which are essentially the people of United States and the West.

The first type of cyber terrorism created by Al-Qaeda was the Al-Neda Centre for Islamic Study and Research which was created by the former bodyguard of Bin Laden, ShaykhYoussef al-Ayyiri. He created an Al-Qaeda propaganda video on the internet which had several audio messages from al-Ayyiri in which he stated: "In the first stage, the stage of attrition and engaging the enemy in battle, you need to make your enemy tired more than you need to kill a large number of its members. You need to scatter the enemy, demoralize it, spread it out over a large area, and cause it to get tired. If the enemy is spread out, it will need supply armies and a lot of other things. You need to make the enemy reach this stage. In this stage, you should strike, run, and disappear. Strike at the weak points." Also he wrote a book which was published on the Al-Neda Centre for Islamic Study and Research site. Thus, Ayyiri, in creating the propaganda video and the book, did, in fact, cyber terrorism acts by trying to recruit more individuals for the cause, and giving instruction for potential terrorists on attacks.

Data Mining

The Internet is a vast resource of information which anyone can tap into and terrorists are well aware of this. According to Secretary of Defence Donald Rumsfeld, speaking on January 15, 2003, an al Qaeda training manual recovered in Afghanistan tells its readers that:

"Using public sources openly and without resorting to illegal means, it is possible to gather at least 80 percent of all information required about the enemy."

The Internet allows access to highly detailed maps, schematics and various other sources of data that would allow terrorists gather information for potential targets. More importantly, once this data has been collated, it is compiled into volumes or "How to" manuals that are distributed between terrorist organisations.

Fundraising

Terrorist groups have made full use of the Internet's ability to create funds; whether legitimately or otherwise. The main methods that the terrorists achieve this is by:

Goods selling: merchandise that is directly related to the terrorist organisation, for example, CDs, DVDs and books from the LTTE.

Website and email based appeals: sending emails to sympathizers who registered interest on a group's website, posting messages on newsgroups/forums and their own websites that give directions as to how and where donations can be made.

Deception: using seemingly legitimate charities or businesses that unknown to the donator, directs the funds to terrorist organisations.

Criminal activity: Illegitimate means of gaining funds that terrorist groups are known to use include credit card fraud, online brokering and gambling.

Recruitment

Terrorist organisations are able to monitor users who browse their websites, capture their profile and information about them and if deemed possibly useful to their cause, are contacted. This grooming process starts from when the user begins to absorb the propaganda on the website, for example the often discussed "charismatic" style of delivery thatOsama Bin Laden employs on his video messages. Perhaps motivated by this video, the user seeks answers to questions and goes to internet chat-rooms and discussion boards. Possible recruits are spotted by lurking recruiters who through gradual encouragement of discussion of religious issues to gradually including more political discussions. This grooming leads the recruits to become more and more entangled in terrorist related discussions and are led through a maze of private chat-room's until personal indoctrination occurs which is often through the use of the secure software. With the proliferation of online platforms and access, terrorist organizations are also increasingly distributing propaganda aimed at encouraging extremists to "self-radicalize" and then providing them directions and suggestions for carrying out attacks in the West.

Communication & Networking

Terrorist groups have changed recently from having a clearly defined hierarchy in the organisations with designated leaders, to having multiple, semi-independent cells with no clear distinct leader in order to allow them to remain hidden. The Internet facilitates communication between cells which allows exchange of information and manuals.

The Internet also assists with internal communication within a cell particularly in relation to the planning of attacks. To avoid being detected and targeted by security forces, Messages are often sent by conspirators through emails which are often sent using public email systems such as Hotmail and Yahoo and may also be sent from public libraries and internet cafes. Chat rooms may also be used for this purpose.

In addition, steganography may be used to hide information embedded within graphic files on websites. Graphic files may also used to send very subtle messages, such as reversing the orientation of a gun graphic may indicate that the next stage of a plan is to proceed. Other methods of concealing instructions and messages may be through the use of coded language, such as that used by Mohamed Atta's final email to the other terrorists who carried out the attacks of 9/11 is reported to have read:

The semester begins in three more weeks. We've obtained 19 confirmations for studies in the faculty of law, the faculty of urban planning, the faculty of fine arts, and the faculty of engineering.

This is believed to be in reference to the four targets that the planes were planned to strike; 'architecture' being the World Trade Centre, 'arts': the Pentagon, 'law': the Capitol and 'politics': the White House.An even more secure method of communication is that which involves using one-time anonymous public email accounts; two terrorists who wish to communicate to open 30 anonymous email accounts whose usernames and passwords are known by each side. To communicate, one terrorist creates a web-based email and instead of sending it, saves it as a draft online. The "recipient" then logs onto this account, reads this message and deletes. The next day, a new account is used; this increases the difficulty of traceability of the users.

THE AUDIENCES OF THE TERRORIST WEBSITES

The first group of people that will frequent these websites are current supporters and future supporters. The websites typically include information relative to their activities, their allies, and their competitors. In addition, many websites offer items for sale.

The second group of people that will enter these websites will be members of the outside community. In hopes of appealing to people all over the world, many terrorist organizations offer their websites in multiple languages. The websites typically include historical background information and general information about the organization itself.

Only some of the websites address the enemy or citizens of a country currently under attack by terrorists. The terrorists hope weaken public support within countries and in some cases will threaten attacks if the government fails to do as they ask.

Disinformation

The use of disinformation by terrorist groups is often used to incite fear, panic and hatred by sending threats, airing videos of brutal executions, creating psychological attacks through the use of threats of cyber-terrorism. Disinformation has been used successfully to incite violence by certain militant groups. Disinformation may also be used to divert attention from an impending attack by releasing details of a hoax attack so that governmental and law enforcement agencies are side-tracked. However, this may not be wholly effective given the nature of current security climates; that is upon receiving information on a potential attack, the security level on all spectrums across a whole country is increased i.e. from black to black special or similar.

TERRORIST ORGANIZATIONS USE THE INTERNET

The Internet is a powerful tool for terrorists, who use online message boards and chat rooms to share information, coordinate attacks, spread propaganda, raise funds, and recruit, experts say. According to Haifa University's Gabriel Weimann, whose research on the subject is widely cited, the number of terrorist sites increased exponentially over the last decade—from less than 100 to more than 4,800 two years ago. The numbers can be somewhat misleading, however. In the case of al-Qaeda, hundreds of sister sites have been promulgated but only a handful are considered active, experts say. Nonetheless, analysts do see a clear proliferation trend.

Terrorist websites can serve as virtual training grounds, offering tutorials on building bombs, firing surface-to-air missiles, shooting at U.S. soldiers, and sneaking into Iraq from abroad. Terrorist sites also host messages and propaganda videos which help to raise morale and further the expansion of recruitment and fundraising networks. Al-Qaeda's media arm, As-Sahab, is among the most visible. But an entire network of jihadist media outfits has sprung up in recent years, according to a March 2008 study by Daniel Kimmage of Radio Free Europe/Radio Liberty. "The 'original' al-Qaeda led by Osama bin Laden accounts for a mere fraction of jihadist media production," Kimmage writes.

What Constitutes a 'Terrorist Website'?

Defining a terrorist website is as contentious as defining terrorism. Pentagon analysts testifying before Congress have said that they monitor some five thousand jihadi websites, though they closely watch a small number of these—less than one hundred—that are deemed the most hostile.

Terrorist sites include the official sites of designated terrorist organizations, as well as the sites of supporters, sympathizers, and fans, says Weimann. But when websites with no formal terrorist affiliation contain sympathetic sentiments to the political aims of a terrorist group, the definition becomes murky. Hoax sites can also prove a troublesome red herring for monitors of terrorist sites. For instance, in recent years a number of sites sympathetic to the Taliban have proliferated on the web. Frequent site outages, however, make it difficult to track their content and sentiment.

How effective is online terrorist propaganda? Perhaps the most effective way in which terrorists use the Internet is the spread of propaganda. Abu Musab al-Zarqawi's al-Qaeda cell in Iraq has proven particularly adept in its use of the web, garnering attention by posting footage of roadside bombings, the decapitation of American hostage Nick Berg, and kidnapped Egyptian and Algerian diplomats prior to their execution.

In Iraq, experts say terrorist propaganda videos are viewed by a large portion of society, not just those who sympathize with terrorists and insurgents. In addition to being posted online, the videos are said to be sold in Baghdad video shops, hidden behind the counter along with pornography. Evan Kohlmann, an expert in terrorists' use of the Internet, points out that propaganda films are not exclusively made in the Middle East; groups from Bosnia, Afghanistan, and Chechnya have also produced videos. Nor are videos the only form of propaganda. Some jihadi websites have even offered video games in which users as young as seven can pretend to be holy warriors killing U.S. soldiers.

What advantages does the Internet offer terrorists? "The greatest advantage [of the Internet] is stealth," says John Arquilla, professor of defense analysis at the Naval Postgraduate School. "[Terrorists] swim in an ocean of bits and bytes." Terrorists have developed sophisticated encryption tools and creative techniques that make the Internet an efficient and relatively secure means of correspondence. These include steganography, a technique used to hide messages in graphic files, and "dead dropping": transmitting information through saved email drafts in an online email account accessible to anyone with the password.

The Internet also provides a global pool of potential recruits and donors. Online terrorist fundraising has become so commonplace that some organizations are able to accept donations via the popular online payment service PayPal.

Yet some terrorism experts say while the Internet has proven effective at spreading ideology, its use as a planning and tool operational tool is minimal. For instance, the terrorists whoattacked Mumbai in November 2008 could never have carried out their strike if they hadn't received actual training in a physical camp, says terrorism expert Peter Bergen. "We talk about the Internet being important for terrorism, which I think is ridiculous. The people who did the Mumbai attack didn't sit around reading about how to do attacks on the Internet. They actually went to a training camp in Muzaffarabad for several months."

What is cyberterrorism? Cyberterrorism is typically defined as the use of the Internet as a vehicle through which to launch an attack. Terrorists could conceivably hack into electrical grids and security systems, or perhaps distribute a powerful computer virus. "Al-Qaeda operatives are known to have taken training in hacking techniques," Arquilla says, but the likelihood of such a cyber attack seems fairly remote. That said, Western governments have accused state and nonstate actors of infiltrating secure networks, including an alleged breach of a Pentagon system by Chinese hackers in June 2007.

Kohlmann suggests the established definition of cyberterrorism needs to be broadened. He says any application of terrorism on the Internet should be considered cyberterrorism. "There's no distinction between the online [terrorist] community and the real [terrorist] community." As evidence, Kohlmann recounts one extreme instance in which the Iraqi insurgent group Army of the Victorious Sect held a contest to help design the group's new website. According to Kohlmann, the prize for the winning designer was the opportunity to, with the click of a mouse, remotely fire three rockets at a U.S. military base in Iraq.

Are there any prominent online terrorists? Among the most infamous figures to emerge from the world of online terrorism in recent years is "Irhaby 007" ("Terrorist 007"). As a SITE Institute profile explains, Irhaby 007 was celebrated by other online terrorists for his hacking prowess and his ability to securely distribute information. With his assistance, terrorist organizations around the globe were able to expand the reach of their message. Irhaby 007 passed this knowledge along to other online jihadis through web postings such as his "Seminar for Hacking Websites," creating a network of technology-savvy terrorist disciples. In October 2005, Scotland Yard officers in West London arrested 22-year-old Younis Tsouli, whom they later identified as Irhaby 007. Tsouli is awaiting trial on charges that include conspiracy to murder and terrorist fundraising.

Another prominent online terrorist is Abu Maysarah al-Iraqi, who has served as the media representative for al-Qaeda in Iraq leader Zarqawi. Al-Iraqi goes online to claim responsibility for acts of terrorism, post propaganda videos, and issue statements on behalf of Zarqawi, though experts say it is unclear whether al-Iraqi is just one person or several using the same name. Al-Iraqi's current whereabouts are unclear; a March 2007 report from the Iraqi news agency Quds Press, translated by the BBC, indicated that the al-Qaeda spokesman had been released from a Mosul prison.

In November 2008, Ali Hamza Ahmad Suleiman al-Bahlul, al-Qaeda's digital media director, was convicted by a U.S. military tribunal. He is serving a life sentence at Guantanamo Bay.

How do governments respond to terrorists' online activities? There is some debate within the counterterrorism community about how to combat terrorist sites. "The knee-jerk reaction is if you see a terrorist site you shut it down," Kohlmann says, but doing so can cause investigators to miss out on a wealth of valuable information. "You can see who's posting what and who's paying for it," says Michael Kern, formerly a senior analyst at the SITE

Institutc, a Washington-based terrorist-tracking group. For instance, German officials monitoring online chatter issued early warnings prior to the Madrid train bombings in March 2004.

Shutting down a terrorist website is just a temporary disruption. To truly stop a terrorist site, experts say, the webmaster must be stopped. The ability of the U.S. National Security Agency to monitor such individuals inside the United States has been the subject of a heatedpolitical and legal debate. The United States has tried to prosecute webmasters who run terrorist websites in the West, but has run into opposition from advocates of free speech. "Sites that tell the terrorist side of the story go right up to the brink of civil liberties," Arquilla says. Sami Omar al-Hussayen, a Saudi Arabian graduate student at the University of Idaho, was charged by U.S. officials with supporting terrorism because he served as a webmaster for several Islamic groups whose sites linked to organizations praising terrorist attacks in Chechnya and Israel. Al-Hussayen was acquitted of all terrorism charges by a federal court in June 2004 under the First Amendment. Two months later, Babar Ahmad, a 31-year-old, British-born son of Pakistani immigrants, was arrested in London under a U.S. warrant.

Another approach officials have taken is to create phony terrorist websites. These can spread disinformation, such as instructions for building a bomb that will explode prematurely and kill its maker or false intelligence about the location of U.S. forces in Iraq, intended to lead terrorist fighters into a trap. This tactic must be used sparingly, says Kohlmann, or else officials risk "poisoning a golden pot [of information]" about how terrorists operate.

TERRORIST ACTIVITIES ON THE INTERNET

Terrorism and the Internet are related in two ways. First, the Internet has become a forum for terrorist groups and individual terrorists both to spread their messages of hate and violence and to communicate with one another and with sympathizers. Secondly, individuals and groups have tried to attack computer networks, including those on the Internet - what has become known as cyberterrorism or cyberwarfare.

At this point, terrorists are using the Internet more than they are attacking it. At least 12 of the 30 groups on the State Department's list of designated foreign terrorist organizations maintain Web sites on the Internet. While U.S. officials believe that some terrorists use encrypted E-mail to plan acts of terrorism, most groups appear to use the Internet to spread their propaganda. Former chief of operations at the FBI Buck Revell told *U.S. News and World Report* that "As long as they don't specifically engage in criminal acts, they can do anything they want to aid and abet their activities. This is a safe haven for them."

Most Internet sites of terrorist groups seek to advance the organization's political and ideological agenda. Immediately after the Peruvian terrorist group Tupac Amaru stormed the Japanese Ambassador's residence in Lima and held scores of diplomatic, political and military officials hostage in December 1996, Tupac Amaru sympathizers in the U.S. and Canada established several solidarity Internet sites, one of which included detailed drawings of the terrorists' plan of assault on the Japanese Ambassador's residence. Indeed, Latin American guerrilla movements are among the most electronically sophisticated extremist groups, according to a study in the *Wall Street Journal.* Mexico's Zapatista guerrillas have been rallying support online since their 1994 uprising. The Revolutionary Armed Forces of Colombia (FARC) fields press inquiries through electronic mail. The Web site of Peru's primary terrorist organization, Shining Path, contains scrolls of Marxist-Leninist propaganda.

Islamic militant organizations also use the Internet to disseminate their anti-Western, anti-Israel propaganda. Several Internet sites created by Hamas supporters, for example, carry the organization's charter and its political and military communiqués, some of which openly call for and extol the murder of Jews. Others, like the Hizb ut-Tahrir, a radical Islamic organization based in Britain, uses its Web site to provide details to the public about its regular meetings around the United Kingdom. Still others use the Internet to raise funds; Hezbollah, for example, the pro-Iranian Shiite terrorist organization based in south Lebanon, sells books and publications through its Web site. Some Israeli and U.S.

officials believe that terrorists from Hamas and Islamic Jihad use the Internet to provide specific instructions to fellow terrorists including maps, photographs, directions, codes and technical details of how to use explosives.

In addition to terrorist sites, the World Wide Web also contains dozens of sites run by domestic white supremacist and militia groups using the information superhighway to promote their radical, anti-U.S. Government agendas. Such sites are run by militias, their sympathizers, common-law "theorists" and activists as well as would-be secessionist groups such as the self-proclaimed "Republic of Texas."

Many of these sites link to other Web pages that are filled with gun-related, survival, paramilitary and pseudo-judicial information and stories of corruption and murder in the highest realms of the government. E Pluribus Unum, for example, served as the online voice of the Ohio Unorganized Militia, featuring a number of pages listing, with accompanying diagrams, the aiming points for a full man-sized target to show where to aim to hit the target in mid-chest "at various distances up to 500 yards."

Other sites actually provide information on how to build bombs as well as instructions for making dangerous chemical and explosive weapons. Many of these sites post the "Terrorist's Handbook" and "The Anarchist Cookbook" which offer detailed instructions of how to construct a wide range of bombs. The anonymous authors of such Web sites often include a disclaimer that the processes described should not be carried out.

According to the Bureau of Alcohol, Tobacco, and Firearms, Federal agents investigating at least 30 bombings and four attempted bombings between 1985 and June 1996 recovered bomb-making literature that the suspects had obtained from the Internet. Among the many examples, in February 1996, three junior high school students from Syracuse, NY, were charged with plotting to set off a homemade bomb in their school, based on plans they had found on the Internet. While many have called for laws restricting the publication of bomb-making instructions on the Internet, others have pointed out that this material is already easily accessible in bookstores and libraries.

THE INTERNET DOES NOT INCREASE TERRORISM

Terrorists are using the Internet to plot "murder and mayhem," British Prime Minister David Camerondeclared this week, as a parliamentary committee issued a report accusing Internet firms of providing a "safe haven for terrorists." Cameron and the committee were referring specifically to a brutal knife attack that killed British soldier Lee Rigby on a London street in May 2013, but the charge has been levied more broadly as well. Earlier this month, British spymaster Robert Hanniganclaimed that Silicon Valley had created "the command-and-control networks of choice for terrorists." In October, Spanish Secretary of State for Security Francisco Martinez warned that the ruthless ISIS terrorist group now dominating swathes of Syria and Iraq regards the Internet as "an extension of the battlefield," adding that they might be using it to organize an attack in the West using the Ebola virus.

Fortunately, there's good reason to believe these officials wrong. David Benson, a political scientist at the University of Chicago, argues in the summer issue of *Security Studies* that there is very little evidence that the Internet is making terrorism easier to do. While "access to the Internet has increased across the globe," he writes, "there has been no corresponding increase in completed transnational terrorist attacks."

Benson defines terrorism as "violence by non-state actors intended to terrorize or frighten a target audience." He focuses on transnational terrorism because the fear of attacks across international borders drives major changes in policy.

The Internet might benefit would-be transnational terrorists by offering anonymity, access to information, and cheap communication, which in turn increases both their capabilities and their ability to network. Anonymity blunts attempts to preempt attacks; information about how to build bombs and carry out attacks is widely available; and cheap communication makes long-distance coordination possible. In theory, all this should make it easier to carry out attacks in other lands.

But as Benson points out, analysts err when they assume that "transnational terrorists have a similar base of support as nationalist or local terror organizations." Local terrorists live among people from whom they can seek support and recruits. They can assess targets in person, and they can meet to research, plan, and prepare using local channels to communicate. Transnational terrorists, by contrast, cannot rely on local support for either recruits or operations.

Benson adds that terrorists are not really all that anonymous, since Internet activity leaves tracks that sophisticated sleuths can follow, and that the availability of bomb-building schematics is no substitute for actual weapons-making experience. Furthermore, governments and other outside groups are adept at monitoring terrorists' communications.

Benson thinks most analysts inflate the Internet's importance because they reason backwards: They look at individual attacks, then assess how the terrorists used the Internet to realize their plans. "Since the Internet is ubiquitous, it would be strange if today's terrorists did not use the Internet, just as it would have been strange if past terrorists did not use the postal service or telephones," Benson notes. The key issue is whether transnational terrorist attacks are *increasing* with the spread of the Internet.

The activities of Al Qaeda have been a focal point for public anxieties, so Benson lists the atrocities committed by Al Qaeda between 1995 and 2011. Using the number of casualties as the benchmark for assessing capabilities, Benson observes that there is a steep reduction in the number of people killed and wounded by Al Qaeda operatives after the attacks on the U.S. embassies in Kenya and Tanzania on August 8, 1998, and the September 11, 2001, barbarity. Benson argues that most of this fall off in effectiveness came as a result of losing their safe havens in Sudan and Afghanistan. Communication and instruction over the Internet is no substitute for face-to-face talk and hands-on training.

After 9/11, various local terrorists groups found value in the Al Qaeda brand and offered to become franchise operations. These franchises include Al-Shabaab in Somalia, Al Qaeda in the Arabian Peninsula (AQAP), and Al Qaeda in the Islamic Magreb (AQIM). Benson excludes Al Qaeda in Iraq and Jemaah Islamiyyah in Indonesia because their operations are almost entirely local. The others are largely local too, and when they do carry out an attack in another country it is usually in a neighboring nation. All of the "transnational" attacks done by the Algeria-based AQIM, for example, have occurred next door—in Morocco, Mauritania, Niger, Mali, and Tunisia.

Some of those countries are practically Internet-free zones. Usage rates in Mali and Niger, for example, are under three percent. Similarly, Internet penetration in Somalia, where Al Shabaab operates, is about 1.5 percent. Attacks are organized by local terrorists who meet and train together face-to-face. "Almost all of [Al Qaeda's] successful attacks following 2005 were completed by local terrorist organizations," Benson observes.

The 2014 Global Terrorism Index notes that 2013 was "the peak year in global terrorist activity not only in the early 21st century, but also for the entire period since 1970," when the statistics in the Index first begin. Deaths from terrorism increased 61 percent, rising from 11,133 in 2012 to 17,958 in 2013. But despite this dismaying increase, "The bulk of terrorist activity in the world is accounted for by militant actors that pursue relatively limited goals in local or regional contexts." Eighty-two percent of the fatalities caused by terrorism in 2013 occurred in just five countries: Iraq, Afghanistan, Pakistan, Nigeria, and Syria. (Internet penetration in those countries is 7.8 percent, 6 percent, 11 percent, 38 percent, and 27 percent, respectively. By contrast, about 87 percent of Americans have access to the Internet.)

The Index further observes that 66 percent of the claimed deaths from terrorism in 2013 are claimed by only four terrorist organizations: ISIL, Boko Haram, the Taliban, and Al Qaeda and its affiliates. Since 2000, only 5 percent of all 107,000 fatalities stemming from terrorist attacks have occurred in OECD countries—and that includes the 2,996 who died on 9/11.

Meanwhile, the same Internet used by terrorists is used by governments to gather intelligence. And as terrorists recruit online, friends and family members use social media to engage and intervene with people at risk of radicalization. So it's not as though all the Internets effects run the same way.

And often what initially looks like a transnational attack might turn out to be local after all. Consider that parliamentary report on Lee Rigby's murder. The attack was carried out by two British nationals, Michael Adebolajo and Michael Adebowale, of Nigerian heritage. The report notes that Adebowale expressed his desire to kill a British soldier in a single Facebook chat with an extremist thought to be associated with AQAP. But it adds that the British intelligence agency MI5 "told the Committee that they believe that, while Adebowale and Adebolajo were in contact with other extremists, they planned the murder of Fusilier Lee Rigby without external support, tasking or direction." In other words, the attack was a local action planned locally by local actors, not a transnational plot organized over the Internet.

As Benson argues, exaggerating the Internet's usefulness to terrorism has "egregious costs." Some officials, for example, have been calling for a "kill switch" that would allow the government to shut down the Internet in an emergency. Noting how much Americans depend upon the Net for commerce, communication, medical care, and so forth, Benson points out that "It is difficult to imagine a terrorist attack being as costly as turning off the Internet would be."

But casting the Internet as a "safe haven for terrorists" does give governments another excuse to violate our privacy in the pretense of protecting our security.

2

Cyber Security

CYBER TERRORISM AND CYBER CRIME

World in this time of enormous technological development has many challenges in fight against phenomenon of cyber threats, especially cyber crime and cyber terrorism as a new forms of asymmetric threats in 21st century.

In order to protect security system by emerging threats – cyber terrorism and cyber crime, mainly on national than regional level, is needed to be taken appropriate activities. Protection from cyber crime and cyber terrorism is related to protection on all spheres which have near points with that activities.

Reason for emerging this kind of threats is technological development, which brings certain changes in society and as a consequences are ICT penetration in all spheres in society.

Because of all previous mentioned reasons, cyber security should assist to be established mechanisms in fight against this kind of asymmetric threats not only in the region but also worldwide.

CYBER SPACE

One of the many national strategic objectives which should be written in Strategy of defense for countries in general term, it is cyber space protection in order to protect critical infrastructure and decreasing possibility of intrusion and cyber attacks but also reducing damage consequence caused by cyber attacks. Furthermore it is necessary to emphasize that government services depend on cyber space in the meaning that they "fly" in that space, because they offer services in banking, finance, healthcare, information and telecommunication services and other fields.

The US Department of Defense (DoD) defines cyberspace as "a global domain within the information environment consisting of the interdependent network of information technology infrastructures, including the Internet, telecommunications networks, computer systems, and embedded processors and controllers." (JP 1-02).

According to previously mentioned reasons, security in cyber space is most important because of permanent use of governmental services and increase of public trust in information systems. In order to accomplish aim, it is necessary to establish new level of communication and cooperation not only between governmental agencies and departments but also government and private sector (G2B).

Mentioned above affords to conclude that is necessary to protect national critical infrastructure from intrusion and cyber attacks for the reason that hackers and other intruders can firmly use critical infrastructure as tool to perform their attacks. Optimal communication in cyber space is significant in order to exchange information between linked governmental institution. High-quality connections between institutions affords accelerate detection in addition to solve IT problems, known as viruses or other types of cyber attacks.

IT infrastructure through strong control security mechanism is a "first step" to sharing information in timely, efficient and reliable manner. Security policy and strong secure mechanisms meet the requirements of sharing sensitive data which affords to government authorities to give quick answer, next make right decision and coordinated activities in critical situation.

CYBER CRIME

Cyber crime encompasses any criminal act dealing with computers and networks. Additionally, cyber crime also includes traditional crimes conducted through the Internet. For example; hate crimes, telemarketing and Internet fraud, identity theft, and credit card account thefts are considered to be cyber crimes when the illegal activities are committed through the use of a computer and the Internet.

Some attacks in cyber space do not have certain targets, because attacks against computers or group of computers are becoming more common. Home users of computers, organizations either private or governmental can and their information technology networks can be target of attackers.

Moreover, attackers using computers can cause damage to Critical National Infrastructure (CNI) that includes emergency services, energy distribution, health, finance and anything which depends of IT. Many IT systems which were isolated from the internet, now they are connected to internet and level of their violability become bigger.

There are two main ways by which computers can be involved in crime

- old crimes conducted using computers as a tool: for example storage of illegal images on a hard disk instead of in print; harassment using mobile telephones or illegal downloads of music and other forms of piracy. Another example is 'phishing': confidence tricks involving spoof emails and fraudulent websites to acquire sensitive information.
- new types of crime made possible by specific technologies. One example is denial of service attacks or DoS which prevent computer resources being available to intended users, for example by flooding web servers with more data than they can process, thus forcing websites offline. Other crimes involving attacking a computer (often by 'hacking' or gaining unauthorized access to a computer system), or writing a virus (a type of malicious software or 'malware') to delete stored data.

In (Computer Crime Definition, 2011), the probability of terrorists carrying out an electronic attack against the CNI is currently low compared with other risks such as using explosive devices, although the National Infrastructure Security Coordination Centre (NISCC) points out that threats can change quickly.

CYBER TERRORISM

Nowadays it is not unique definition related to term terrorism. Definitions in order to defining term terrorism has different origin, so that some of that definitions focuses on terrorism actors, but others on terrorism tactics and objectives and used methods. In order to fight against this kinds of terroristic acts or other forms of combat violence and crimes, national and international organization ask for defining term terrorism. Currently, one of the most often used definition about terrorism follows US legacy documents and policy.

According to US law, state secretary has obligation to get the report on Congress each year, which is put into Annual report. Terrorism is defined in a follow way:

- "premeditated, politically motivated violence perpetrated against noncombatant targets by subnational groups or clandestine agents".
- "the term "terrorist group" means any group practicing, or which has significant subgroups which practice, international terrorism"

According to Federal Bureau of Investigation (FBI), new phenomenon recognized as a cyber terrorism is defined by follow:

> *"previously planned, politically motivated attack against information, computer systems, computer programs and data that result with violence against targets that are not military (civilian) by the sub - national groups or secret agents".*

Another definition according to US Commission for Protecting Critical Infrastructure is that terrorist attacks are created in order to cause physical violence or extreme financial damage.

The cyber-terrorist is assumed to be professional, creative, and very clever. They will seek unorthodox and original methods to accomplish their goals. Individuals who are wellschooled in traditional information security techniques are not well suited to being a cyber-terrorist, simply because they have been exposed to or trained in classic security techniques and doctrine. The cyber terrorist will seek to accomplish their mission by techniques not mitigated by classic security mechanisms.

Terrorists leave traditional way of fighting with classical weapon and other weapon but also they introduce the use of sophisticated high technology which shows that they becomes "modern" warriors who take a pace with technology development. When computer terrorism is in question, nowadays there are real danger about information resources especially in global information networks, which means that if they are exploited by the terrorists, global information network can become effective weapon for cyber attacks.

Also, it give to terrorists opportunities for combating in a way which previosly they can only dream abut it.

That information infrastructure is target of terrorist groups and organization shows the fact of threats addressed from Irish Republican Army (IRA) in 1997, when the English public was shocked by the threats that besides bombs, assassinations and other forms of terrorist acts will begin using electronic attacks on commercial and government computer systems

Although terrorists are recognized as a persons with psychological profile who do not have enough high level talent and high developed computer skills, but also experience with Al-Quadå shows that members of terrorist organizations use sophisticated techniques for protecting their internet channels of communication, in a way which they continually change web locations in order to propagate their fundamentalist idea. Furthermore some terrorists who are arrested had encryption files on their computers, mobile phones and other devices for communication.

Danger of terrorist acts become bigger in a future because of high technology exploitation by terrorists to accomplish their destructive aims. They can performer that with "source of talents" who know how to provide experts or specialists capable to commit computer sabotage or espionage on a high strategic level.

As a result of previously mentioned, terrorist groups or organization undertaken tasks which made contracts or train terrorists to exploit high technology for secret operations or for strategic terrorism which has to be carried out by the disciplined and organized staff.

As a source of talents are recognized following groups:

- technological mercenaries;
- unemployed technological experts from third world countries;
- technological experts from developed west European countries;
- high level skill personnel from intelligence service as a Securitate (Romania), SPECNAZ and OSNAZ (USSR), Stasi (East Europe) and other units for special operations from ex communist countries in Eastern Europe

General conclusion related to cyber terrorism is that the time which follow, terrorists will use more and more high technology for espionage and sabotage also they will use it to propagate their idea.Likely terrorist targets can be the following:

- data banks;
- computer systems;
- government communication systems;
- automated power directed by computer systems;
- oil refineries;
- Airport infrastructure etc.

RELATION BETWEEN HACKERS AND TERRORISTS

Hacker groups are numerous and they are divide each other by the level of education in technological field. Membership in a high level educated hacker groups frequently can be limited and exclusive membership is allowed only for individuals who develop and share set of sophisticated information communication tools for hacking. This "exclusive" hacker groups make efforts to be cover and not to attract attention due to confidentiality allows them to be more effective.

Although some hacker groups can be a globally dispersed, they have similar aims as a political interest or they are connected through another basis as a religious or social ideology. Other groups can be motivated from profit which comes together with organize crime. Also it is possible to meet hacker groups which are guided from their aspiration to sell their computer skills to sponsors as a terroristic groups or countries which it is depend on emerging political interest.

As a conclusion should be stated that there are numerous reports on the above, where the actors appear as governments, companies, associations and other stakeholders. On the same manner, it should be stressed that connection between hackers, terrorist and nations that support terrorism is very hard to prove it. On other hand activities that are caused by the cyber terrorist can be detected through carefully monitoring social networks, chat, mirc and other cyber virtual location where anonymously hackers meet to exchange their information.

Nevertheless, in order to prevent and avoid damages from terrorist and crime activities are developed numerous research projects which should give contribution to find out technology, tactics, techniques and other stuff associated to cyber threats.

DIFFERENCES BETWEEN TERMS CYBER CRIME AND CYBER TERRORISM

In a present time are many definitions about cyber crime and cyber terrorism. Recently was confusion whether or not this two terms - cyber crime and cyber terrorism are synonym each other. However, some authors support definition that they two terms are synonym other authors do not support that definition and they formulate two different definitions. In a global view, the most relevant definitions are definitions which are exploited according to formulate terminology of USA.

On the other hand, to make clear distinction between terms cyber crime and cyber terrorism in a following paragraphs it is necessary to be exposed differences. Defining term cyber terrorism is crucial and the officials motivate it. Major purpose of cyber terrorism is infiltration in the system on certain institution where it can cause violence and damage (financial damage, property) in order to make destabilization and lower security in the country that is victim.

Hackers that are actors which usually cause cyber crime, and they often do it for enjoyment or they struggle between each other for bigger individual success, in addition they can do it for achieving financial or in other purposes. While hackers (cyber terrorists) who are often component of terrorist organization as a Al Qaeda, ETA, IRA etc., they make it to fulfil certain political goals.

Furthermore, some authors formulate differences about hackers that hackers who commit attacks for enjoyable reasons they can be classified in a group of simple and plain criminals while cyber terrorist should be classified in a specific rigid form of crime.

Cyber terrorist can attack on clear defined targets that are significant strategic points for certain countries but it does not means that attack is limited and cannot have a wide range in order to achieve definite aim. As a example of previous mentioned, target of cyber terrorist can be electrical plant which supply citizens with electricity who live in near that environment. Committing this type of attack, cyber terrorist can be effective in a wide range with a little resource. If chain of electricity supply is broken with this kind of attack that situation has influence on daily citizens routine to fulfilling essential needs.

Another example about cyber terrorism can be hospital computer system hacking and changing medical prescriptions and cause damage with prescribing wrong medicine to the patient. So that everyone can be a victim of this terrorist act.

As a conclusion about differences between cyber crime and cyber terrorism is that they use same weapon to commit terrorist or crime act and this weapon is computer or ICT in a wider range.

Conclusion

It is general accepted meaning that users of cyber space and their networks are not protected form cyber attacks. Moreover, it is not enough knowledge about cyber threats and risks and what kind of implication are caused to the national, regional and global security. However, mentioned above affords to conclude that are needed to do big efforts in developing mechanisms against cyber threats as new type of asymmetric threats.

Although some countries have technological advance and more experience in war against cyber threats and critical infrastructure protection in comparisons with others, however cyber crime is the most danger threat in comparison with cyber terrorism and cyber war. Addition threat is caused with lack of developed security mechanisms in terms of consequences which can influence to the individual users and possibility that gaps in cyber space to be exploited by the crime groups and terrorist. It is equally important which of this gaps will be used by the actors who have desire to cause violence or damage.

Challenges which appear in developing security mechanisms related to cyber security can be analysed from different views. First, only a few nation have developed strategy for cyber security, which should give direction in order to protect critical infrastructure. Second, decreasing financial budget per current year has influence to cyber protection. Third, for individual user are not needed security clearance in comparison with security clearance and standards that are needed for institution governmental networks and networks for private sector or corporation networks.

As a conclusion it is affordable to notice that general "mixed nature" of cyber space press on defining combined definitions and standards if cyber security is developed on national, regional and global level.

Convergence of these challenges is in correlation with technological development and desire of groups, individuals and other actors to create significant asymmetric exceptions to governments or citizens in handling with cyber threats.

Generally is accepted that international organizations should lead in developing standards which will be used in selection of activities in cyber space, but there is not clear selected international organization that should be a leader. United Nations (UN) missed chance to be leader due to they cannot build consensus and all efforts in developing standards are useless related to cyber security. So that, in near future is needed to set bigger caution by the cyber community in order to discover convenient solution to handle and fight against cyber threats.

To conclude, it is accepted that cyber security is international (global) responsibility. Each user has responsibility in cyber security depending of his/her affiliation. Due to internal connections and dependences are enormous, each user in network should contribute in strengthening security mechanisms and protection form cyber attacks. As well is needed to find solution and ideas for strengthening cyber protection and increase security in cyber space as part of global strategy in order to eliminate exceptions and neutralizing threats in a wide range as much it is possible.

CYBER-SECURITY AS SCIENCE

A science of cyber-security has to deal with a combination of peculiar features that are shared by no other area of study. First, the background on which events occur is almost completely created by humans and is digital. That is, people built all the pieces. One might have thought that computers, their software, and networks were therefore completely understandable. The truth is that the cyber-universe is complex well beyond anyone's understanding and exhibits behaviour that no one predicted, and sometimes can't even be explained well.

On the positive side, the cyber-universe can be thought of as reduced to the 0s and 1s of binary data. Actions in this universe consist of sequences of changes to binary data, interleaved in time, and having some sort of locations in space. One can speculate as to why mathematics is so effective in explaining physics, but the cyber-world is inherently mathematical. Mathematics is a natural way for reasoning about it and this point of view is a theme that appears repeatedly in this report. Second, cyber-security has good guys and bad guys. It is a field that has developed because people have discovered how to do things that other people disapprove of, and that break what is thought to be an agreed-upon social contract in the material world. That is, in cyber-security there are adversaries, and the adversaries are purposeful and intelligent.

Thus, the reasoning in cyber-security has to be both about the constructed universe and the actions and reactions of the adversaries. Definitions and concepts will shift over time in cyber-security, as in all sciences. A successfully chosen name is a bridge between scientific knowledge and common sense, between new experience and old habits. The conceptual foundation of any science consists of a complicated network of names of things, names of ideas, and names of names. It evolves itself, and its projections on reality changes.

This quote echoes the observations of a presentation to JASON by Peter Gallison of Harvard in which he compared the type of science encountered in cyber security to a "Manichaean science" or science in the presence of adversaries. Particularly important for this type of science (and indeed any branch of science) was the development of a common language so that precise arguments could be formulated that addressed directly the problems of interest. We emphasize this point because the definition of cyber-security itself is imprecise. The subject includes correctness properties like condentiality and integrity, and liveness properties such as are associated with denial-of-service attacks, together with a growing set of unpleasant surprises.

Security Degrades Over Time

We observed earlier that success in cyber-security requires constant attention. Not only do the threats and attacks change, but the old techniques tend to become less effective. Technology advances, and the properties of the security system become better understood.

Unix Passwords

The original UNIX passwords were up to 8 ASCII non-control characters. The passwords aren't stored directly. Rather hashes (some one-way function) are stored. In modern systems these hashes aren't easily read, but if a machine is compromised, then the hashes can be taken away, and one can attempt to break passwords by making up likely candidates, applying the one-way function, and seeing if the result matches any of the hashes. There are about 2 original UNIX passwords, which seemed like quite a lot at the time. Nowadays, one could imagine trying about 32 million guesses (2) per second on a single CPU core, so testing the entire space would only take about 3 days on 1,000 cores. That's not a particularly large computer, but the calculation is also embarrassingly parallel, so the 1,000 cores could be 1,000 machines in a (small) botnet. Or one could use 9,000 machines, still not a large botnet, and do the whole calculation in one night. For completeness we note that there has been a lot of work on making it harder to guess passwords; for instance, by using much slower one-way functions and much larger spaces. Another approach is to force people to use more complex passwords, but that has other sociological ramications which are unfortunately very difficult to deal with in terms of any science. An extreme version turned up in the recent Russian spy case, where "Ricci said the steganographic programme was activated by pressing controlalt-E and then typing in a 27-character password, which the FBI found written down on a piece of paper during one of its searches."

Lock Bumping

A second example of security decreasing over time comes from the common locks people use on doors. A simple technique called "lock bumping" makes all these locks quite easy to open with just a little practice. The locks were, of course, vulnerable, but it didn't much matter until the technique was popularized starting about 2005. There are plenty of explanatory videos online. The implication for cyber-security is that the nature of the attack can change over time. It will not in general be possible to anticipate all attacks. For this reason it becomes necessary to constantly survey the extant modes of attack to understand the nature of current technology as well as continually attack one's own systems in the hopes of finding heretofore undiscovered attacks.

The Role of Secrecy

All security regimes include some secrets. The TSA doesn't explain everything it is looking for; the credit card processors don't fully explain their criteria, and so on. In the computer science community, security by obscurity is generally considered bad, probably based on examples of awed cryptography. There seems to be little theoretical work on this subject. We mention a few examples of keeping (and not keeping) secrets.

Commercial anti-virus programmes, of the sort that run on your home computer, reveal some of the weaknesses of totally public defences. In principal, a malware author could just buy these, and adjust the malware until none of them detect it. The market has made this easier; there are online services that for a fee will run uploaded malware through a large number of commercial programmes, and report the result.

Game theory and economics teach us that keeping our private valuations secret sometimes adds value. Much effort has gone into auction mechanisms that get bidders to reveal their private valuations. On the other hand, under various circumstances, this "asymmetric information" can lead to lemon markets, where either no market exists, or only people who are forced to will trade in the market. Secrecy might also be required by the rules. For instance, the DoD might use logs of network trafc to tune its network defences. These logs might easily contain material that should not be made public. For these reasons, there may be some benefit in exploring the role an enhanced role for secrecy and obfuscation, particularly for DOD systems.

Finally, one might ask if keeping the source code secret adds much to security. First, there may be other reasons for keeping source code secret, such as the trade secrets incorporated in it. Certainly attackers with source code are likely to proceed differently, as they have a better chance of finding attacks based on logical errors, and this would be especially valuable for targeted attacks.

On the other hand, there seems to be no particular shortage of effective attacks when source code is unavailable. But the code owner may have no realistic alternatives to making the source available. As an example consider the following announcement: "The agreement that we signed with the FSB is an extension of Microsoft's Government Security Programme (GSP)," Microsoft said in a statement on Friday. "The purpose of the GSP is to increase trust with national governments.

In the case of the Russian agreement, GSP participation will facilitate the development of the next generation of secured solutions for Russian government agencies based on the latest Microsoft technologies and Russian cryptography."

THE FUTURE OF CYBER SECURITY

The product of human ingenuity and innovation, cyberspace now delivers a range of critical services to more citizens around the world than ever before. Yet, the online world as we know it stands at the threshold of unprecedented change.

Being invited to speak at the East West Institute's Worldwide Security Conference in Brussels this week provided an opportunity to examine the needs faced by the global security community as we prepare to meet the needs of the Internet's next billion users. The International Telecommunication Union (ITU) reported that the number of Internet users reached the two billion threshold in March of this year and according to a Boston Consulting Group report, another billion are expected to come online in the next four years, bringing the total number of Internet users worldwide to about three billion by 2015.

Planning to ensure that our online world—cyberspace—is trustworthy, resilient and secure as we move into this uncertain future, policy leaders need to consider the fundamental changes that are occurring in cyberspace, and the policy issues that these changes will likely present and that will need to be addressed. Looking towards the future of three billion users, four factors will fundamentally change the future of cyberspace security: people, devices, data, and cloud services.

The Global Online Population Expands

The emergence of the next billion Internet users will impact security in two ways. Most important will be the impact of the demographic characteristics of these users. Consider that the next billion users will (1) be younger, (2) spend more time online, (3) be more mobile, (4) see the world through social media and apps, and (5) make greater use of natural interfaces. These five factors could hasten the onset of totally digital lifestyles making connectivity seemingly as essential as oxygen. The next billion could also help foster new innovation in the development and application of technology.

Separately, however, this emerging user population also represents a greatly expanded "target rich" environment for cybercriminals that want to exploit their data, social networks, and devices via botnets or other means.

Internet of Things to Immersive Computing

These new users will require new devices. According to The Boston Consulting Group, the number of Internet-connected devices is predicted to exceed 15 billion—twice the world's population–by 2015, and to soar to 50 billion devices by 2020.

"Devices" of course refers to more than smart phones, netbooks and tablets. It also systems such as smart grids, intelligent transportation, healthcare monitoring, smart manufacturing, and environmental sensors.

The advent of powerful wireless devices that both run infrastructure and deliver infrastructure services, including providing access to cloud services, means that cybercriminals and other threat actors need not merely target traditional, and increasingly protected, commercial software and consumer applications to execute attacks with significant consequences. Attackers may well target the embedded software, firmware and hardware in these devices to attack the infrastructure or seize control of the devices and turn them into sensors that can report status, collect personally identifiable information, or conduct other espionage.

Data: Rapid increases in Understanding

The striking growth in the number of users and devices will also produce an exponential growth in the amount of data that is being generated, stored, analysed and transformed into innovation and knowledge. Analysing large data sets—so-called big data—will become a key basis of competition, underpinning new waves of productivity growth, innovation, and consumer surplus, according to research by MGI and McKinsey's Business Technology Office. However, such data sets also represent attractive targets for organized cyber criminals and other threat actors. From a security standpoint, safeguarding these huge data sets, protecting privacy and integrity, will require concerted global effort requiring collaboration among governments, the private sector, and users.

Cloud Computing: The Information Society Enabler

With an exponentially growing community of increasingly mobile users, cloud computing will commensurately grow in importance. It will fundamentally change how businesses operate, how every manner of services are delivered, and even how lives are lived. On the positive side, the security best practices implemented by an effective cloud provider may rival or surpass the measures that cloud customers might themselves be able to provide, resulting in enhanced security. Yet there are global issues that will need to be addressed in terms of transparency and jurisdiction to enable cloud services that are both secure and scalable to service the needs of this expanded user community across multiple countries.

Reducing the Cyber-attack Surface

Reducing the cyber-attack surface can be achieved by industry and government working in partnership to make the ICT infrastructure less susceptible to attack and compromise. One important way to achieve this is through concerted action to address risks in the supply chain for information and communications technology products and services.

Vendors and service providers need to build and maintain world-class approaches to secure software and hardware development methodologies. Microsoft began this journey over 10 years ago and has openly shared its Security Development Lifecycle. The nonprofit alliance SAFECode provides a platform for companies to share, both within the software development community and more broadly, information on secure software development techniques that have proven to be effective as well as those that have not. Industry needs to do more.

For their part, governments need to understand the nature of ICT supply chain risk more clearly and work collaboratively with one another and with vendors to develop a common risk management framework rooted in core principles that both address supply chain integrity concerns and preserve the fruits of global free trade. Such a system should be risk-based, transparent, flexible, and should recognize the realities of reciprocal treatment in the global economic environment.

Improving Internet Health

Improving Internet health requires a global, collaborative approach to protecting people from the potential dangers of the Internet.

Despite the best efforts at education and protection, many consumer computers host malware and may be part of a "botnet," unbeknownst to their legitimate owners.

There is currently no concerted mechanism to shield users from or help them mitigate these risks. Such infected computers do not simply expose their owners' valuable information and data; they place others at risk too. This threat to greater society makes it is essential that the technology ecosystem take collective action to combat it.

Work has been underway in industry circles to build cooperation among various stakeholder groups including ISPs, software vendors, and others; to leverage investments made in key regions of the world; and to create a future roadmap for an Internet health system.

3

Cyber Terrorism and Critical Infrastructure

CYBERTERRORISTS TO TARGET CRITICAL INFRASTRUCTURE

A cyberterror attack on vital national infrastructure such as power facilities, transport networks and the financial sector could be imminent—and international governments are ill-prepared, cybersecurity experts have warned. "It's not easy to predict what will happen, but the worst terrorist attacks are not expected," Eugene Kaspersky, the co-founder and chief executive of global IT security firm Kaspersky Labs, told CNBC. So I am afraid that if we face this cyberterrorism, it will be very unpredictable in a very unpredictable place, but with very visible damage. Unfortunately, there are many possible victims."

In recent months, the business world and political establishment has seen an uptick in the use of debilitating digital attacks. As well as the Sony attacks, allegedly by North Korea, and the widespread hacking of international news agencies by the "Syrian Electronic Army," On Monday, Malaysian Airlines refuted that its website had been hacked by a group calling itself the "Cyber Caliphate" and claiming affiliation with the Islamic State (ISIS).

'Critical Infrastructure'

Now, there are concerns that the next big attack will be against national critical infrastructure and could cripple a country's ability to function. Kaspersky told CNBC that each country needed to make a "very serious audit" of the critical infrastructure within its borders. In order of importance, he noted that the infrastructure most vulnerable was the power network, "because if the power plants and power grid don't work, then nothing else works," followed by telecommunications, financial services and transportation.

"A security strategy needs to be made for all of these components," Kaspersky said.

He warned that governments needed to allocate a good part of their budgets over the next decade to making critical infrastructure systems more secure.

"Technically it's possible to make them immune from attacks, but it's complicated, it's expensive and it will take time and budgets," Kaspersky said.

'War Games'

Budget cuts in the U.K. and Europe have undoubtedly challenged government attempts to counter cyberterrorism, but a spokesperson for the U.K. Cabinet Office told CNBC that cybersecurity was a priority.

"Cybersecurity is already a tier-one national security priority and our investment of £860 million ($1.3 billion) over five years in the National Cyber Security Programme (NCSP) supports a wide range of projects to develop the U.K.'s cyber security capabilities. This is a clear signal of just how seriously the Government is treating the threat," the spokesperson said.

Kaspersky noted that there needed to be far stronger international cooperation against cyberterrorism, including in the sharing of information, in order to relay early warnings ahead of potential attacks.

The U.K. and U.S. have already pledged to work together in a bid to remain one step ahead of terrorism groups like Islamic State that are increasingly using computers as means of attack.

In particular, there are the so-called war games involve "cybercells" of U.S. and U.K. intelligence agents staging attacks against each another, in order to test the resilience of certain sectors to cyberattacks. The first exercise will test the financial sector, with simulated attacks on the City of London, including the Bank of England, and Wall Street.

Fighting the Attacks

E.J. Hilbert, the heads Kroll's cyber unit for Europe, the Middle East and Africa, told CNBC that hundred, if not thousands attacks were already taking place—and that more attacks were coming.

"There are hundreds of attacks taking place against the U.K. and U.S. nuclear industry and financial system every day. There is this non-stop badgering of the system by hackers who are hoping that one day the system will crack," said Hilbert, a former FBI agent in the cybercrime and counterterrorism field.

He was emphatic that national governments were unprepared for a cyberattack on critical infrastructure. He said that the proposed "war games" would have limited effect in acting as a pre-warning to governments on the weaknesses of critical systems.

"These tests don't do what the bad guys are going to do, they don't go far enough. If the bad guys want to shut a system down, they'll shut it down and unless you've tested for that, you don't actually know if there's a way of bringing a system back," Hilbert said.

If an attack is so bad that all else has failed, governments can always choose to shut down their own infrastructure systems. But taking such steps can have alarming consequences, such as lack of power if power plants are shut down, lack of water if water facilities are closed, and permanent system failure.

With that in mind, Hilbert said "it might be better to fight the attack then shut down the system."

CYBER TERRORISM AND HOW IS IT DIFFERENT FROM OTHER CYBER THREATS?

Attempts to create a common terminology for cyberterroism in the United States, for example, have thus far been exceedingly difficult, with the FBI alone publishing three distinctly different terminologies and DOD, FEMA, DEA, DHS and DOJ each having their own distinct definitions. Leonard Bailey, a former member of the US National Security Division (NSD), expressed his concern stating "the area suffers from a limited lexicon…we even lack a unified definition of cyber terrorism and that makes discourse on the subject difficult." The various complexities and unknowns of cyber threats, and their relationship to acts that constitute terrorism make defining the term very difficult. What constitutes a cyber threat? When does a cyber attack become an act of terrorism rather than just a crime? These are all questions that continue to make it difficult for practitioners to navigate said threats and put policy into action to protect national security. This chapter will show how the term has evolved, and how cyberterror is distinctly different from other cyber threats.

The term cyberterrorism was originally coined in the 1980's by Senior Researcher at the Centre for Strategic and International Studies (CSIS) Barry Collin as "the international abuse of a digital information system, network, or component toward an end that supports or facilitates a terrorist campaign or action." Since that time, various scholars, government officials, and security experts have worked to refine Collins broad Postgraduate School defines the term as such:

Cyberterrorism is generally understood to refer to highly damaging computer-based attacks or threats of attack by non-state actors against information systems when conducted to intimidate or coerce governments or societies in pursuit of goals that are political or social. It is the convergence of terrorism with cyberspace, where cyberspace becomes the means of conducting the terrorist act.

Marie-Helen Maras, a professor of criminal justice at SUNY---Farmingdale elaborates even further on this terminology adding,"Cyberterroists seek to attack critical infrastructure systems (e.g., water, energy, communications) so as to intimidate or coerce a government for ideological, religious, or political reasons." In an earlier excerpt from her book *Computer Forensics: Cybercriminals, Laws and Evidence*, Maras states:

A cybertrerrorist may hack into U.S. critical infrastructure in an attempt to cause grave harm such as loss of life or significant economic damage. Such attacks are aimed at wreaking havoc on information technology systems that are an integral part of public safety, traffic control, medical and emergency services, and public works.

In this excerpt, Maras touches on very important themes that will be discussed later including the vulnerability of critical infrastructure and methods that an individual or group may employ to conduct acts of terrorism. As Maras mentions, it is important to note that not all acts that a terrorist organization may be involved in via the Internet, nor all cyber attacks writ large, constitute acts of cyberterrorism. Maura Conway at Dublin City University describes how an act of cyberterrorism must "instill terror as commonly understood (that is, result in death or large scale destruction), and they must have a political motivation." Terrorist organizations of all colors have been utilizing the Internet for various means including fundraising, planning, and recruitment since its explosive growth in the 1990's.

However, these attacks do not constitute terrorism per se as they do not directly cause large-scale death or destruction in and of themselves. As Maras explains, terrorist groups including the Liberation Tigers of Tamil Eelam (Tamil Tigers) have been responsible for conducting acts that temporarily paralyze government websites through large scale Denial of Service Attacks (DoS), but as these attacks did not cause grave and sustained harm nor loss of life, such attacks cannot be considered cyberterrorism. Thankfully, a catastrophic attack on critical infrastructure like that portrayed by Mr. Panetta and others has yet to occur. However, terrorist organizations and "lone wolves" have expressed interest in conducting such attacks and have demonstrated their proficiency on a smaller scale at quite an alarming level. If left unprotected, the critical infrastructure of nations may face an attack at a much larger scale, resulting in mass casualties and degradation of vital systems that are necessary to maintain national security.

The Threat to Critical Infrastructure: How Vulnerable are We to Cyberterrorism?

A couple dozen talented programmers wearing flip-flops and drinking Red Bull can do a lot of damage. —Fmr. Deputy Defense Secretary William Lynn

In 2007, the turbine of an electricity generator burst into smoke in the Idaho National Laboratory, ultimately causing failure of the device. Leaked to the press shortly thereafter, this incident dubbed the "Aurora Generator Test" was conducted by DHS to show just how vulnerable American critical infrastructure is to a cyber attack. In short, engineers found that by changing the operating cycle of a power generator remotely via computer, the turbines could set fire, eventually destroying the machine. By no means the first test of its kind, various scenarios have been explored by international governments to assess the vulnerabilities of critical infrastructure. However, as shown in a 2011 project conducted by global security software giant McAfee, in conjunction with CSIS, little has been done to address the large gaps in preventing such an attack from taking place. A 2013 assessment by the GAO showed that improvements have been made, but not nearly at the level necessary to safeguard critical infrastructure from cyber attack.

The Aurora Generator Test is one of the prime examples of simulations carried out to assess the vulnerabilities of Industrial Control Systems (ICS) that are used to "monitor and regulate" the majority of industrial operations (e.g., the electrical grid, water treatment, transportation). In particular, the test focused on a type of ICS called industrial Supervisory Control and Data Acquisition Systems (SCADA). In a 2003 CRS report, Dana A. Shea helps explain the role of SCADA systems and shows how they are vulnerable to attack:

"Industrial control system technologies are often employed in critical infrastructure industries to allow a single control centre to manage multiple sites. Industrial control systems were originally implemented as isolated, separate networks. They were viewed as secure systems, which protected remote locations from being physically broken into and mistreated. Control systems were originally designed to be free standing networks without Internet access. Therefore, it has been necessary to add network access systems to the original systems to integrate them into the corporate structure. This has created, in the worst cases, a labyrinth of connections, which is perhaps not rigorously constructed for cyber-security or well documented.

Unfortunately, since this report was presented to Congress in 2003, progress has been slow to put security mechanisms in place to protect SCADA and other ICS that control critical infrastructure. Although the Aurora Test and subsequent incidents such as the introduction of Stuxnet malware in 2010 have raised suspicion, companies and government have only lightly, thus far, embraced security mechanisms. For example, rather than replacing or reforming the archaic SCADA ICS, governments and corporations have altered the system to allow for increased operational efficiency at the cost of jeopardized security. The continual need for more rapid information sharing and real-time data spurred developers to step into a world that was previously closed off from the knowledge of a general computer programmer. For example, firms introduced standard computers and operating systems as well as IP based networking to allow for better control and interconnectivity so that businesses and government could run more efficiently.

These "developments," however, have come at a cost, with the GAO reporting 48,562 attacks on federal agencies alone in FY 2012 alone. Although none of these attacks have crippled infrastructure and caused terror through physical damage and loss of life, the possibility of such an attack is not without reason. As companies and governments begin to further embrace the Smart Grid System for example, critical infrastructure (primarily the electric grid) will become more reliant on a vast array of nodes that give IT systems more efficient control over the delivery of services but will undoubtedly open up further opportunities for intrusion from nefarious actors.

At this juncture it must be made clear that the majority of research for this chapter has pointed towards state actors as being the most responsible in executing the majority of cyber attacks. According to many experts, for example, the notion of cyberwar with China is not an unreal perspective. Recent criticism has come from the west towards China, blaming the country for conducting cyber espionage against the US and other international targets, stealing valuable technological secrets and financial information. These recent events have polarized the sino-US relationship with leaders on both sides calling for increased responsibility and an end to malicious actions.

Although the threat of a looming cyberwar with China and other nations should not be discredited, this chapter will continue by looking at the threat of cyberterrorism stemming from primarily non-state actors and states that directly support terrorism such as Iran. Particular emphasis will be put on the role of Iran, as groups like the Izz ad-Din al-Qassam brigades who receive direct material support form the Islamic Republic have already carried out cyber attacks. The various methods by which cyberspace *could* be used directly by a terrorist organization to achieve their goals of political or ideological change through attacks that cause terror and loss of life. In addition, we will look at particular reasons as to why terrorist groups and "lone wolf" actors pose more of a threat to transnational security than states such as China, even if they are less equipped.

Current and Future Capabilities of Cyberterrorists

Last night, the FBI received a signed threat from a very credible, well-funded, North Africa-based terrorist group indicating that they intend to disrupt water operations in 28 US cities. Because the threat comes from a credible, well known source, with an organizational structure capable of carrying out such a threat, the FBI has asked utilities, particularly large drinking water systems, to take precautions and to be on the lookout for anyone or anything out of the ordinary. —Association of Metropolitan Water Authorities, 2001

In the summer of 2012, a video from al-Qaeda's as-Sahab media outlet calling for an "electronic Jihad," was released to the FBI. The chilling video showed an unnamed al-Qaeda operative directing "covert mujahidin" to launch waves of cyber attacks against US networks including critical infrastructure such as the power grid and water supplies. The question as to what effect terrorist organizations and "lone wolfs" can have against critical infrastructure and also how could such a major cyber attack play out in the future in real time.

Terrorist organizations have demonstrated their expertize on the web in various forms for over a decade. As the recent attacks by the Tsarnaev brothers in Boston highlights, video broadcasts over social media, for example, serve as one of the many ways by which terrorist groups can recruit members and spur "lone wolf" actors to commit terrible atrocities. While dissemination of propaganda and other such activity is malicious and may eventually lead to an act of terrorism taking place, acts such as small scale hacking for financial gain, temporarily paralyzing non critical websites and spreading of propaganda, do not constitute cyberterrorism. What is worrisome, however, is that over the past 10 years in particular, trends have emerged that illustrate that al-Qaeda and other terrorists have taken an interest in directing their cyber capabilities towards directly hitting US infrastructure and causing mass damage. We have also learned, and have seen from example, that attacks can be orchestrated without massive funding, by single actors, who are not even affiliated with a terrorist group.

In her book *Computer Forensics: Cybercriminals, Laws and Evidence,* Marie-Helen Maras provides various examples of such instances where "lone wolves" were able to break into SCADA systems, and if they so desired, could have created massive damage. For example, in 2000, a Russian man hacked into an ICS that ran a natural gas pipeline and was able to control the flow of LNG. "Hypothetically, this hacker could have easily increased the gas pressure until the valves broke, causing an explosion to occur." Although many of these actors have been "lone wolves," terrorist organizations have not sat on the sidelines idly. Rather, since the new millennium, terrorist groups such as al-Qaeda, and groups supported by Iran like Hamas and Hezbollah, have been actively working towards developing a capacity to strike at the heart of the industrialized world's critical infrastructure to cause terror and havoc. Former Presidential Adviser for Cyberspace Security, Richard Clarke expresses his concern on the terrorist entrée into the world of cyberwar in a PBS Frontline special. Clarke comments:

We also found indications that members of al-Qaeda were from outside of the Unites States doing reconnaissance in the United States on our critical infrastructure. Where were railroad crossings? Where were the big natural gas depositories? Where were the bridges over rivers that also carried the fiber for the backbone on the Internet? It's possible now to do that kind of targeting, which would have, in the past, required lots of people and running around the country. It is possible to sit in the cyber café in Peshawar and do that kind of reconnaissance.

The sentiment of Clarke and others is quite telling in the sense that it not only drives home the al-Qaeda and other terrorists seek the desire to destroy US infrastructure, but that they are slowly gaining the capacity to carry out such attacks. Al-Qaeda members have been tracked seeking information on SCADA systems in the US including wastewater and water supply facilities. In 2005, the al-Farouq web forum exposed a "hacker library" with information that could aid an individual in debilitating and an electric system with a keystroke. In addition, in 2003 an al-Qaeda affiliate built upon an emerging trend in the US and developed an online university for "Jihad Sciences on the Internet," to instruct students on proper ways to fight electronic Jihad. This sustained desire to wreak havoc on the infrastructure of western nations has thankfully yet to play out. The sophistication to carry out such a large-scale attack is hard to develop and requires substantial funding. There are, however, nation states that are willing to support such ambitions.

Iran's Role in Cyberterrorism and Possibilities for Future Attack

What I worry about is that terrorists and nations that sponsor terror, such as Iran, that demonstrate cyberattack capabilities will be far more reckless than traditional adversaries. -Art Coviello, CEO of security firm RSA

The asymmetric nature of the war against terrorists can be said to transcend into the cyber realm. While al-Qaeda and other groups have been able to coordinate physical attacks with modest finances, a massive cyber operation that could debilitate US critical infrastructure would require funding and advanced technical expertise. The Islamic Republic of Iran has been known historically to fund terrorists of various stripes who oppose western interests. Even amidst an array of international sanctions, the nation still has the monetary prowess to fund one of worlds the largest military operations in which cyber strategy is a critical component. While nations like Russia and China are guilty of cyber intrusion into the institutions and systems of the United States and its allies, the majority of their operations are carried out for the sake of espionage. Also, while the US and much of the West hold normal diplomatic ties with China and the Russian Federation, the same cannot be said about Iran.

Iran has subscribed, for the most part, to a retaliatory cyber strategy against the west. The Shamoon attack in 2012 that knocked out three-quarters of the Saudi State oil firm, Aramco, and filled screens with an image of a burning US flag was traced to Iran. The regime has consistently supplied the military arm of Hamas with information and technology to carry out attacks on US financial institutions and is currently doing the same for Bashar al-Assad in Syria. These events raise important red flags on what the future may hold for terrorists groups looking to commit large-scale attacks against the United States. Not only is the transfer of information from Iran to such entities a common practice, but also powerful viruses such as Stuxnet are now readily available on the Internet, and a black market has emerged alongside offering to the highest bidder.

As the leadership of terrorists groups become younger and more tech-savvy, it is the fear that such groups will rely more heavily on a cyberterror component to achieve their ultimate goal of creating terror through destruction and death. While states like China may have the capability to carry out such acts, diplomatic and financial ties make such an occurrence unlikely. The strategic aims of the terrorist, particularly al-Qaeda and its affiliates, show that if such technology were obtained, its use would be quite certain and could be supplemented alongside a physical attack, described by secretary Panetta as a "cyber Pearl Harbor."

THE PRIVATE SECTOR, AND CIVIL SOCIETY DO TO PREVENT ACTS OF CYBERTERROR

Today, more than ever before, the world is united through the use of technology. From the systems that connect us to friends and family, to the rails and roads that bring us together, and the generators that power our homes, the security provided by era of previous isolation can no longer be seen as relevant. With the advent of the Internet and ICS systems developed to make industrial operations, commerce, and life in general easier, we have ushered in a new era of unprecedented insecurity. A clear example of this is shown in the number of cyber attacks currently facing the United States.

Between 2006-2012, the number of attacks increased by 782 percent, reaching 48,562 attacks in FY 2012. This chapter set out by reflecting briefly on the scenario of a "cyber Pearl Harbor," or surprise cyber attack that would be so devastating to the nations critical infrastructure, that the carnage could surpass that of 9/11. Although such an attack has yet to materialize, I have argued that out of the many cyber threats facing the industrialized world, actions taken by a terrorist organization or a "lone wolf," targeting critical infrastructure would prove to not only be the most catastrophic possibility, but also the most likely future event.

As the report explained, the capacity of NSA and state-sponsored terrorists have increased drastically over the years, while the goal of wreaking havoc and death to change politics and ideology have remained solid. As generations of terrorists get younger, and more adept with technology, an unforeseen cyber attack, possibly in conjunction with a physical attack may present it self. The suggestions to various government agencies, the private sector and civil society on how to prevent such an attack from taking place in the future.

Provide an Overarching Cyber Strategy, Develop Clear Cut Roles for Government Agencies, and Hold Private Industry Accountable

This recommendation reflects in part on the recent assessment by the GAO that concluded that current US government cyber strategy was to diffuse and not clearly defined. Currently, an overarching American central cyber strategy does not exist, and even the White House National Cyber Strategy contains documents piled from over a decade, with multiple layers that make priorities hard understand. The US and other governments in the same boat (the UK and Spain to name a few) must develop concise documents that designate specific roles to agencies, allow for information sharing, and set benchmarks and methods to track progress and establish best practice. In addition, the government must hold the private sector accountable for ensuring high standards of cyber security, particularly in regards to critical infrastructure.

As a 2011 report by McAfee and CSIS illustrates, in the US, UK and Spain for example, less than 20% of companies received a government audit to assess their capacity to prevent a cyber attack. In addition, 32 percent of companies had yet to design any sort of cyber strategy to deal with emerging technologies such as the Smart Grid. As these systems are critical to maintaining and regulating the nation's critical infrastructure, and an attack could jeopardize national security, it is the responsibility of the government to ensure that businesses cooperate. Such measures are already put in place in both China and Japan with high levels of interaction between business and government on various levels to guarantee operational security. The United States and its allies should learn from such approaches and hold businesses accountable in order to protect the nation from the threat of cyberterrorism.

Governments Must Engage Civil Society as Stakeholders in Increasing Cyber Resilience

Currently, populations worldwide remain untrusting of their government's ability to handle a cyber attack. While 56 percent of Chinese feel confident in the communists party's ability to thwart an attack, these numbers remain much lower for the US and Europe. While initiatives such as Cyber Security Awareness Month in the US represent a good first step, more needs to be done to create a civic culture that treats cyber security as a priority.

The attacks on 9/11 left a permanent scar on the communities affected and crafted a cultural resilience against future attack. Commercials and billboards asking citizens to report suspicious activity or to "see something, say something," are ubiquitous in New York City and have proven quite effective. Between the years of 1999-2009, of the 68 terrorist plots, aware citizens thwarted 40 percent thanks to tip offs. DHS has created an incident response and cyber education campaign titled *Stop. Think. Connect,* to inform citizens of the many threats present and encourage action to secure cyber space. More initiatives like this should be created and well funded. Governments should disseminate such initiatives via social media, traditional canvasing, and through radio and television and begin joint programs with public education to begin stressing the importance of cyber security at an early age.

Establish International Norms for Governance on the Web and Crackdown on International Black Market

No one entity, government body, or international organization, can or should have complete control over the Internet. However, in order to prevent malicious actors such as terrorists from disseminating information, recruiting, funding, and executing cyber attacks, more could be done on behalf of the international community. For example, in 2012, the International Telecommunication Union (ITU), an arm of the United Nations, convened in Dubai to discuss ways to revise a treaty known as the International Telecommunications Regulations (ITR) in order to open a space for discussion on how to best secure cyberspace. While some of the delegates, including the US ambassador, expressed reservations, believing that such a treaty could allow for government suppression of civil liberties in cyberspace, this discussion is a necessary first step in preventing future cyber attack. The UN has put into place various universal instruments to battle international terrorism including an overarching plan to battle global terrorism. However, amendments should be added to incorporate the role of the internet in such strategy. Ratified on October 13, 2010, GA resolution A/RES/62/272 fails to mention the role the Internet as part of the terrorist arsenal. Although working groups on the topic have since been convened, clear legislation needs to be put in place, especially considering the role of state actors such as Iran in directly funding terrorism and cyber attack across the globe.

THE UNITED STATES IS VULNERABLE TO CYBERTERRORISM

The Danger is Real, and the Country must Prepare

Today's battlefields transcend national borders. Cyberspace adds an entirely new dimension to military operations, and the ubiquitous dependence on information technology in both the government and commercial sectors increases exponentially the opportunities for adversaries as well as the potential ramification of attacks.

To understand cyberterrorism fully, it is necessary first to understand the cyberspace environment and its particular attributes. The various components of the cyberterror anatomy reveal the answers to the basic questions about who, what, how, where, why and when.

It is not difficult to imagine a scenario where the global media is buzzing with reports of U.S. military systems under relentless electronic assault from computers in the Middle East. An unknown adversary controls military logistics, transportation and administration systems essential to deploying troops to the Persian Gulf. Many of the largest U.S. commercial Web sites are flooded with connection requests, paralyzing significant portions of the Internet. Deadly viruses begin to infect computers around the world, including many military systems. More than 60 million computers are affected, costing billions of dollars.

Consider other scenarios. People around the globe join in electronic attacks simply by clicking on a Web site to begin flooding campaigns. Osama bin Laden calls for a cyber Jihad on an Afghanistan-hosted Web site. Computers at U.S. infrastructure sites such as dams are infiltrated, and more than a million liters of raw sewage are released into coastal waters.

Agents tied to al Qaida buy useful information to penetrate U.S. Defense Department computer networks. Power grids in California are infiltrated and held captive for weeks. The stock market closes early because of computer problems after a record-setting one-week loss. Americans are alarmed at the devastation, and the cost of these cyberattacks comes on the heels of a major attack on U.S. soil. The competitive media help spread the cyberterrorism panic throughout the world.

Each of these situations is 100-percent plausible because each one has occurred. Fortunately, they took place at different times during the past several years. However, they could occur in an orchestrated fashion in a short time frame in the future.

Cyberspace is a unique environment. It is ageographic and borderless, and attacks can be asymmetric and clandestine. Attacks have virtually unlimited range and speed. Massive results can be achieved without massing forces. These attacks are fast, easy and relatively inexpensive. Many regional conflicts have cyberspace dimensions where battles are fought by hackers on both sides with their own rules of engagement. This occurred in Bosnia, Kosovo and several Middle Eastern countries. Cyberspace security is an international challenge that is not constrained by national boundaries.

The diversity of information system adversaries ranges from individuals to nation-states. Enemies of the United States are conducting information operations against the nation daily. Hackers are probing while well-organized and well-financed foreign intelligence collection organizations are performing intelligence preparation of the cyberbattlefield to gain unauthorized knowledge and access to Defense Department systems.

Over time, the level of sophistication required to hack into an information system has decreased dramatically. At the same time, the quantity and availability of hacking tools have increased substantially, and the quality has improved greatly. This creates an environment where even teenagers can successfully infiltrate Defense Department and other U.S. government systems, in turn creating a dangerous target-rich and low-risk combination.

Cyberattacks are rising exponentially, and several factors contribute to this equation. The growth of the Internet raises the number of both attackers and targets. Vulnerabilities of new software versions continue to grow. Sophisticated hacking tools are easily accessible.

The weapons of cyberwar are available for download on the Internet. Unlike the weapons of conventional warfare, the tools of this trade require no long-term acquisition, training or fielding to mount an attack. As the typical PC has become more powerful and easier to use, so has the sophistication of the weapons that information adversaries have at their disposal. An adversary with minimal technology, funding, training, staff and defense infrastructure can employ these limited resources as weapons on short notice from anywhere in the world. An intruder could take countless specific actions after gaining access to an information system; however, these acts can be grouped into four general categories: modification, fabrication, interception and interruption.

For years, the world has witnessed unauthorized intrusions and Web hacks from a myriad of actors, including teenagers, industrial espionage experts, hacker groups and nation-states. Newcomers to this area have infiltrated very sensitive systems with relative ease. These people use many tactics, techniques and procedures, such as polymorphic viruses or polymorphic code, worms, software vulnerability exploits, other viruses and denial-of-service attacks.

The challenge is that all critical infrastructures must be defended. The President's Commission on Critical Infrastructure Protection divided U.S. infrastructures into five sectors: information and communication, physical distribution, energy, banking and finance, and vital human services. In an asymmetric world, terrorists look for alternative methods to spread terror. The cyberworld may prove to be the simplest and quickest alternative to traditional physical attacks. The motives of cyberterrorists in this realm likely will be the same as those that incite physical attack. They generally seek financial gain, disruption, decreased military capability, fear/panic, publicity and news impact, decreased confidence in critical infrastructures/psychological operations, great physical damage and even loss of life. The dilemma in the cyberworld is not only to detect attackers but also to understand why they are attacking.

Cyberattacks, whether stand-alone or coordinated, occur at the time and choosing of the adversary. They are inherently stealthy and can be used at critical periods such as when U.S. forces deploy, at a crucial point in a war or at high-profile events. They can be used as retaliation for trials or sentencing. Terror attacks are often randomly timed and sporadically targeted to maximize the aspect of surprise, and cyberattacks have the same characteristics.

It is likely that cyberattacks will accompany physical attacks to enhance the impact and reduce U.S. response capabilities. Combining physical attacks with cyberattacks magnifies their impact and limits first responders and other assistance. This type of attack will serve as a force multiplier for terrorists.

Today, al Qaida is America's primary terrorist adversary. The organization already operates within the cyberworld. The television network al Jazeera reported that Osama bin Laden's senior aides transmitted the instructions for the attacks on September 11, 2001, to Mohammed Atta via encoded e-mail. Al Qaida terrorists are using the Internet to research infrastructure information about U.S. water and wastewater systems. Federal Bureau of Investigation bulletins say that U.S. law enforcement and intelligence agencies have received indications that al Qaida members have sought information on supervisory control and data acquisition (SCADA) systems available on multiple SCADA-related Web sites. SCADA systems allow utility and transportation companies to monitor and direct equipment at unmanned facilities from a central location. The computers of bin Laden associates were found to include structural engineering data and programs related to dams and other water retaining structures.

Ramzi Yousef, the first World Trade Centre bomber, stored detailed plans to destroy U.S. airliners in encrypted files on his laptop computer. Terrorist groups also are using the Internet to recruit like-minded people to their cause. "Hacktivists" is a term that has recently emerged to describe those who carry out cyberprotests, e-mail floods, denials of service and hacks for a political cause. These actions undertaken immediately following real-world events also are on the rise.

Al Qaida has not been known to use cyberattacks in the past. However, bin Laden has suggested that he has the expertise to use the computer as a weapon. After the September 11 attacks, he was quoted in the newspaper Ausaf as saying that hundreds of young men had pledged to him that they were ready to die and that hundreds of Muslim scientists were with him who would use their knowledge in chemistry and biology as well as in areas ranging from computers to electronics against the infidels. This statement implies that bin Laden is threatening computer attacks against the United States. The Central Intelligence Agency (CIA) is already alert to the possibility of cyberwarfare by al Qaida and describes this group as becoming more adept at using the Internet and computer technologies. Al Qaida is believed by some government officials to be developing cyberterrorism plans. The Washington Post and CBS News have reported that al Qaida prisoners have informed interrogators about their intent to use cyberattack tools. Captives have said al Qaida is on the threshold of using the Internet as a direct instrument for bloodshed.

Terrorists must go beyond Web page defacements, simple hacks or pranks. To gain publicity for their cause, cyberterrorists must cause widespread damage, destruction, or death. An example of how this could be accomplished already has occurred. In 1998, a 12-year-old hacker broke into the SCADA computer systems that run Arizona's Roosevelt Dam. Federal authorities said the hacker had complete control of the dam's massive floodgates. This dam holds back as much as 489 trillion gallons of water above a flood plain inhabited by more than a million people. More than 3 million SCADA devices are in use today.

Members of Congress have expressed concern. "There is a 50 percent chance that the next time al Qaida terrorists strike the United States, their attack will include a cyberattack," Rep. Lamar Smith (R-TX) said. Al Qaida has the capabilities, has the intention, has a history of gathering reconnaissance and has targeted the United States. This makes the organization a very serious cyberthreat.

A June 2002 survey of technology industry experts revealed that 74 percent thought it was nearly certain that there would be a cyberattack against the United States within one year. Nearly 60 percent said they expect a major cyberattack against the federal government within one year. A February 2002 CIA memorandum indicates that al Qaida had far more interest in cyberterrorism than previously believed and had contemplated the use of hackers for hire to speed the acquisition of capabilities.

As a relatively new dimension of warfare, the cyber environment must be thoroughly studied and analysed. The events of September 11 caught the United States by surprise. Unless appropriate steps are taken to protect the country against cyberattacks now, it surely will suffer tragic cyberterrorist attacks that could include loss of life. Terrorists are pursuing this capability. Major cyberterror attacks against the United States will occur. It is a matter of when, not if.

CYBER THREAT MOVING TO CRITICAL INFRASTRUCTURE

The cyber threat is moving from data breaches to global critical infrastructure, an insurance industry commissioned study shows. Technology running the world's critical infrastructure is increasingly at risk of cyber attack, according to in-depth research by Lloyd's of London insurer Aegis London.

The study, conducted by BAE Systems, covers the evolution of cyber risk in the energy sector and its impact on critical infrastructure businesses in the UK, Europe, US and Canada. Researchers found that state-sponsored cyber attacks are a serious and evolving threat to power and utility companies.

A survey of energy and utility companies showed that most respondents believe a cyber attack of major significance and impact on critical operational infrastructure is highly likely. The study revealed that power companies are better prepared to deal with cyber threats to their operational technology than many recent media reports have indicated.

STATE-SPONSORED CYBER ATTACKS

The researchers said these organisations have a good understanding of the cyber threats they face, and one of the biggest challenges energy companies and utilities face are constraints outside their control. These include things like a lack of adequate and mature technology systems.

Cyber Insurance

In response to the findings, Aegis London has introduced a new breed of cyber insurance for operational technology and critical infrastructure, in addition to cover for data protection and privacy issues. The company's CyberResilience product is designed to cover critical operational technology and assets, before and after a cyber attack. The product combines liability, business interruption and terrorism coverage with a service-based offering that consists of cyber underwriting assessment, risk management consultancy, loss control, threat analysis, incident response and vulnerability management. This combination of cover and services is important in the light of recent concerns that critical infrastructure suppliers are looking for insurance without taking adequate steps to protect data.

Some representatives of the security industry have accused utility companies of making security trade-offs due to a lack of security expertise and/or inadequate resources to address security. "Cyber attacks are no longer focused solely on IT environments," said Alan Maguire, chairman of Aegis London. "Cyber terrorists have turned their attention to operational technologies and the critical infrastructure they support, so we have expanded our coverage accordingly."

The insurance cover is offered in conjunction with specialised pre- and post-attack services provided by cyber security partners who focus on the critical infrastructure industry. "Now, for the first time, businesses can obtain secure and reliable cyber insurance cover and service-based offerings for both operational and information technology," said Maguire.

David Croom-Johnson, active underwriter at Aegis London, said: "We believe that vulnerabilities in and threats to operational technology have the potential to lead to business interruption or significant loss of operating capability and availability. "These represent some of the most acute organisational risks currently facing critical infrastructure, which is why we developed CyberResilience. However, this is only our first step in evolving a complete suite of products and services around global critical infrastructure cyber security," he said.

Rick Welsh, head of cyber insurance at Aegis London, said cyber risks are one of the biggest challenges the insurance industry faces today. "Improving the security posture of critical infrastructure industries such as the energy sector is paramount," he said. According to Welsh, the insurance product acknowledges the need to understand and underwrite the relationship between industrial control systems and enterprise networks without disregarding the impact of data security and privacy liability.

'CYBER-TERROR IS GROWING THREAT' TO INFRASTRUCTURE SYSTEMS

The online world is a mystery to many people, especially adults, according to Eugene Kaspersky, head of the anti-virus and cyber protection firm that bears his name. "We're all immigrants in the new world of cyberspace," Kaspersky said at a roundtable discussion with some of Israel's top IT managers. "Our children who will one day replace us are, on the other hand, cyber-natives," and it shows in myriad ways.

But understanding cyber issues – especially cybersecurity – isn't as complicated as many believe, if you think about it the right way, Kaspersky said at the event, held on the sidelines of the Third Annual International Cyber Security Conference of Tel Aviv University's Yuval Ne'eman Workshop, taking place this week. The roundtable was conducted by the Israel Internet Society.

Some two dozen speakers from countries around the world, as well as many Israeli information technology security people, gathered to discuss cybersecurity policy issues, better ways to protect critical systems from hackers, and how to build cooperation between institutions and governments in other countries, said Professor Yitzhak Ben Yisrael, chairman of the Yuval Ne'eman Workshop, and a chief architect of the Prime Minister's National Cyber Committee.

"Cyberspace is a reflection of the real world," Kaspersky said, and once you start thinking about it in those terms, many of the solutions to problems the world faces become obvious. "Many people bristle at the idea of an online ID card, but I think it's essential for the future of the Internet. If you were to go to a real-life bank, you would have to present your ID card, and in newer biometric ID systems, your palm or fingerprint, in order to get money. Why should the online world be any different?

The last time Kaspersky was in Israel (for the 2012 edition of the Conference) he astounded conference attendees by announcing that "the end was near." Kaspersky presented evidence of the existence of the Flame virus, the malware that wreaked havoc with computer infrastructure systems used by Iran in its nuclear program, and said that it could represent "the end of interconnected world as we know it. Like a germ on a rampage, Flame, he said, could end up infecting power stations, air control systems, government computers, and a thousand and one other systems that make 21st century life possible. "The world is just so interconnected today, and the viruses that attack one power plant put them all at risk," Kaspersky said, warning of dire consequences if IT personnel did not take immediate safety precautions.

Kaspersky did not come bearing such dramatic news this year, but said that he was worried nonetheless. "I have been in the IT security business for 25 years, and I am paranoid because of the things that I have seen." Although he had plenty of stories about security breaches, with some published in the media, "there are a lot stories I can't share," he said – and if he did, listeners would be just as fearful of the cyber-future as he is.

On the other hand, Kaspersky said, he is optimistic – because the lessons on how to protect organizations, businesses, governments, and infrastructure seem to be getting through. There is much more awareness of the need for cybersecurity by private enterprise and governments, even if the pace of implementing protection can be slow.

"Cyber, of course, operates at the speed of cyber, but governments operate at the speed of governments, meaning that there are committees, discussions, and votes," he said. But things are getting better; for example, after years of discussions, international law enforcement organization Interpol will next year open up a department specifically geared to dealing with cyber-threats, to be called CyberPol. "It will make life much more difficult for cyber-criminals," the hackers who break into bank accounts to transfer money, and the like, said Kaspersky. But there are much more serious threats in the cyber-world that have barely begun to be addressed, Kaspersky said. "Cyber-espionage is a much greater threat than cyber-crime today, but even that can be detected and controlled. What's really worrying is cyber-terror, where an entity sends out an 'Internet missile' to search out and destroy critical infrastructure."

Many of the "famous" viruses that have been unveiled in the past year – like Red October – were designed to steal information, and there are plenty of other viruses that are doing the same thing. "Just last week, the leaders of the United States and China sat down to discuss espionage and hacking, a major issue involving China."

But it's not just China; every country in the world is cyber-spying on both enemies and friends. "It's just so easy to do, I would be shocked if there were a major country with an educated population – including Israel and the United States – were not cyber-spying. Even Sweden, a paragon of democracy, monitors Internet traffic coming from Russia," Kaspersky said.

What really should be worrying everyone is cyber-terror, where rogue groups attack infrastructure and critical systems. In order to protect society, those systems need to be locked down. The problem is that many were designed years ago, before cyber-threats were even thought of. The systems running electricity, water, gas, public safety, and other systems needs to be upgraded, but it can only be done incrementally, Kaspersky said, since no country is going to close down its electrical grid or other infrastructure to allow for a lengthy system and equipment upgrade. (Speaking at the same conference three days ago, Prime Minister Benjamin Netanyahu said Israel was under relentless hack attack.)

The question, of course, is how to prevent these, and less serious attacks. According to Kaspersky, the answer is far less complicated than people think. Following his simile of real life and cyber-life, Kaspersky advocates things like fingerprint readers to allow access to financial and other Web sites. In addition, there should be standards for security systems, agreed to and implemented by everyone; for example, if one country suspected hacking activity aimed at it was being conducted in another country, the host of that hacking would be obligated by international agreement to root out the hackers.

"If you were to build a bridge, for example, you would have to comply with all sorts of rules and regulations," said Kaspersky. "That's what the cyber-world needs, as well," and such standards should be worked out among nations. "Or we can do what is usually done – wait for the United States to come up with standards, and have everyone else adopt them." Until that time, Kaspersky has some suggestions for organizations hoping to prevent damage from cyber-attacks (preventing attacks is too much to ask for, he said; the best anyone can hope for is mitigation). "We need to increase awareness and education on cybersecurity matters, especially in universities, in order to train IT security workers, who are in very short supply." There are few universities that teach those skills, said Kaspersky – although Tel Aviv University is set to become one of them, Ben-Yisrael said, offering majors and minors to all students in cyber-related disciplines.

Along with that, Kaspersky said, organizations needed to educate members and workers on the dangers of the Internet. Many cyber-attacks have their roots in "social engineering," where users receive a message to submit information or click on a link that will install malware.

"We have a presentation that we provide to clients that is shown to their workers," said Kaspersky. "It's all about real-life stories of workers who clicked on the wrong link, jeopardizing their organizations. Once they see that presentation they become as paranoid as me." It's a fear tactic, without question, but the consequences of a cyber-attack are a lot scarier.

CYBER SECURITY AND CRITICAL INFRASTRUCTURE PROTECTION IN INDIA

Cyber Security of India is an essential part of National ICT Policy and Strategy of India. Despite some very good suggestions and critical evaluations, the Government of India (GOI) has not considered it necessary to take some action in this regard. There has been repetitive wake up calls given to the GOI but it seems the GOI is in indefinite sleep.

On the other hand, the International Community is stressing really hard to make cyber security an essential part of their day to day lives. Dartmouth's Institute for Information Infrastructure Protection (I3P) has recently provided its cyber security research recommendations.

They are in the form of a set of recommendations for advancing research in cyber security that can be implemented in the next five to 10 years. The report recognises four areas of need that emerged during the forum:

(1) A coordinated and collaborative approach is needed.

(2) Metrics and assessment tools must be developed.

(3) An effective legal and policy framework for security must be created.

(4) The human dimension of security must be addressed.

It may be a coincidence that similar suggestions were provided by Mr. Praveen Dalal, Managing Partner of Perry4Law to the Government of India. He has also provided the Indian Policies and Strategies for Critical ICT Infrastructure Protection and Management in India. The stress upon Legal Enablement of ICT Systems in India is very important to make Cyber Law of India strong and effective.

There are lot of Problems through which the present Cyber Law of India is passing through. A good account of the same can be found at this nice piece of work.

The problem still remains the same. In India we don't have a dedicated resource that is taking care of Techno-Legal Laws of India in a holistic manner. Of course, we have a Cyber Law Database of India.

We also have a Techno-Legal ICT Regulations Database in India. These two resources are tracing back the history of cyber law in India. However, we need a resource that can trace both history of cyber law in India as well as its current position and the prospective future of the same.

The task is very difficult but it has been successfully achieved by Mr. Praveen Dalal, Managing Partner of Perry4Law. He has successfully come out with a "Dedicated Resource" on cyber law in India. The same is titled "Legal Enablement Of ICT Systems in India" and is the exclusive, most comprehensive and holistic web resource in India dealing with Techno-Legal ICT Laws and Regulations in India. All the cyber law observers can now access information about cyber law in India and the changes that are proposed or actually made from time to time. The resource is very futuristic and promising in nature and it would be good idea if the Government of India (GOI) consults the same while making, amending or reformulating techno-legal laws in India.

One of the important aspects of this resource is that it is the exclusive resource that is providing a "Constitutional Analysis" of the present as well as proposed techno-legal laws in India. Therefore all of the "Civil Liberty Crusaders" keep a close eye upon this resource for issues like Privacy Rights, Life and Liberty, Right to Speech and Expressions, etc.

For instance, surveillance has become a controversial issue since the Information Technology (Amendment) Bill, 2008 has been proposed. Surprisingly some people are justifying these wide and unregulated powers as justified under the garb of security that does not exists at all in India. There is only one answer to the pro surveillance argument and it is a Benjamin Franklin quote: Those who would give up essential liberty to purchase a little temporary safety deserve neither liberty nor safety.

E-Surveillance should not be a substitute for cyber security and cyber forensics capabilities. Privacy Rights must be respected and followed in both letter and spirit in India. He Bill, 2008 has seriously compromised these Fundamental Rights. So friends, wake up and be a vigilant and legally aware citizens. We will keep on spreading the "Cyber Law Awareness" in India so that we may have an informed citizenry.

Security and Systems Design

Most current real-world computer security efforts focus on external threats, and generally treat the computer system itself as a trusted system. Some knowledgeable observers consider this to be a disastrous mistake, and point out that this distinction is the cause of much of the insecurity of current computer systems - once an attacker has subverted one part of a system without fine-grained security, he or she usually has access to most or all of the features of that system. Because computer systems can be very complex, and cannot be guaranteed to be free of defects, this security stance tends to produce insecure systems. The 'trusted systems' approach has been predominant in the design of many Microsoft software products, due to the long-standing Microsoft policy of emphasizing functionality and 'ease of use' over security.

Since Microsoft products currently dominate the desktop and home computing markets, this has led to unfortunate effects. However, the problems described here derive from the security stance taken by software and hardware vendors generally, rather than the failing of a single vendor. Microsoft is not out of line in this respect, just far more prominent with respect to its consumer marketshare.

It should be noted that the Windows NT line of operating systems from Microsoft contained mechanisms to limit this, such as services that ran under dedicated user accounts, and Role-Based Access Control (RBAC) with user/group rights, but the Windows 95 line of products lacked most of these functions. Before the release of Windows 2003 Microsoft has changed their official stance, taking a more locked down approach.

On 15 January 2002, Bill Gates sent out a memo on Trustworthy Computing, marking the official change in company stance. Regardless, Microsoft's operating system Windows XP is still plagued by complaints about lack of local security and inability to use the fine-grained user access controls together with certain software (esp. certain popular computer games).

Financial Cost

Serious financial damage has been caused by computer security breaches, but reliably estimating costs is quite difficult. Figures in the billions of dollars have been quoted in relation to the damage caused by malware such as computer worms like the Code Red worm, but such estimates may be exaggerated. However, other losses, such as those caused by the compromise of credit card information, can be more easily determined, and they have been substantial, as measured by millions of individual victims of identity theft each year in each of several nations, and the severe hardship imposed on each victim, that can wipe out all of their finances, prevent them from getting a job, plus be treated as if they were the criminal. Volumes of victims of phishing and other scams may not be known.

Individuals who have been infected with spyware or malware likely go through a costly and time-consuming process of having their computer cleaned. Spyware and malware is considered to be a problem specific to the various Microsoft Windows operating systems, however this can be explained somewhat by the fact that Microsoft controls a major share of the PC market and thus represent the most prominent target.

Reasons

There are many similarities (yet many fundamental differences) between computer and physical security. Just like real-world security, the motivations for breaches of computer security vary between attackers, sometimes called hackers or crackers. Some are teenage thrill-seekers or vandals (the kind often responsible for defacing web sites); similarly, some web site defacements are done to make political statements. However, some attackers are highly skilled and motivated with the goal of compromising computers for financial gain or espionage. An example of the latter is Markus Hess who spied for the KGB and was ultimately caught because of the efforts of Clifford Stoll, who wrote an amusing and accurate book, The Cuckoo's Egg, about his experiences. For those seeking to prevent security breaches, the first step is usually to attempt to identify what might motivate an attack on the system, how much the continued operation and information security of the system are worth, and who might be motivated to breach it. The precautions required for a home PC are very different for those of banks' Internet banking system, and different again for a classified military network. Other computer security writers suggest that, since an attacker using a network need know nothing about you or what you have on your computer, attacker motivation is inherently impossible to determine beyond guessing. If true, blocking all possible attacks is the only plausible action to take.

Vulnerabilities

To understand the techniques for securing a computer system, it is important to first understand the various types of "attacks" that can be made against it. These threats can typically be classified into one of these seven categories:

Exploits

Software flaws, especially buffer overflows, are often exploited to gain control of a computer, or to cause it to operate in an unexpected manner. Many development methodologies rely on testing to ensure the quality of any code released; this process often fails to discover extremely unusual potential exploits. The term "exploit" generally refers to small programs designed to take advantage of a software flaw that has been discovered, either remote or local. The code from the exploit program is frequently reused in trojan horses and computer viruses. In some cases, a vulnerability can lie in certain programs' processing of a specific file type, such as a non-executable media file.

Eavesdropping

Any data that is transmitted over a network is at some risk of being eavesdropped, or even modified by a malicious person. Even machines that operate as a closed system (i.e., with no contact to the outside world) can be eavesdropped upon via monitoring the faint electro-magnetic transmissions generated by the hardware such as TEMPEST. The FBI's proposed Carnivore program was intended to act as a system of eavesdropping protocols built into the systems of internet service providers.

4

Prepare to Prevent or Respond to Catastrophic Terrorist Attacks

DEFENDING AGAINST CATASTROPHIC THREATS

The expertise, technology, and material needed to build the most deadly weapons known to mankind-including chemical, biological, radiological, and nuclear weapons-are proliferating. If our enemies acquire these weapons, they are likely to try to use them. The consequences of such an attack could be far more devastating than those we suffered on September 11-a chemical, biological, radiological, or nuclear terrorist attack in the United States could cause large numbers of casualties, mass psychological disruption, and contamination, and could overwhelm local medical capabilities.

Currently, chemical, biological, radiological, and nuclear detection capabilities are modest and response capabilities are dispersed throughout the country at every level of government. Responsibility for chemical, biological, radiological, and nuclear surveillance as well as for initial response efforts often rests with state and local hospitals and public health agencies. Today, if a natural disaster or terrorist attack causes medical consequences that exceed local and state capabilities, the Department of Health and Human Services would coordinate the deployment of medical personnel, equipment, and pharmaceuticals among the Departments of Agriculture, Defense, Energy, Justice,

Transportation, Veterans Affairs, the Environmental Protection Agency, the Federal Emergency Management Agency, General Services Administration, National Communications System, U.S. Postal Service, and the American Red Cross.

While the government's collaborative arrangements have proven adequate for a variety of natural disasters, the threat of terrorist attacks using chemical, biological, radiological, or nuclear weapons with potentially catastrophic consequences demands new approaches, a focused strategy, and a new organization. Our country has already expanded capabilities and improved coordination among federal agencies, but more can be done to prepare and respond.

Major Initiatives

Prevent terrorist use of nuclear weapons through better sensors and procedures. Our top scientific priority must be preventing terrorist use of nuclear weapons. Under the President's proposal, the Department of Homeland Security will implement a new system of procedures and technologies to detect and prevent the transport of nuclear explosives toward our borders and into the United States. The Department of Homeland Security would develop and deploy new inspection procedures and detection systems against the entry of such materials at all ports of entry in the United States and at major overseas cargo loading facilities. The Department-in cooperation with the Department of Transportation, state and local governments, and the private sector-would develop additional inspection procedures and detection systems throughout our national transportation structure to detect the movement of nuclear materials within the United States. It will also initiate and sustain research and development efforts aimed at new and better passive and active detection systems.

The Departments of State, Energy, and Defense are already working with foreign states possessing nuclear programs to ensure continued strict security for the global inventory of nuclear weapons and materials, consistent with domestic and international legal obligations (including the Treaty on Non-Proliferation of Nuclear Weapons). These Departments will also work with foreign governments to improve their capabilities to detect the movement of nuclear materials or weapons and to respond appropriately. They will work with foreign governments, for example, to assess their need for enhanced radiation detection capabilities at borders, seaports, and airports and, where appropriate, will coordinate the provision of detection equipment to countries where the threat from the movement of nuclear weapons and materials is significant.

Detect chemical and biological materials and attacks. The federal government, with due attention to constraints such as the need for low operating costs, will develop sensitive and highly selective systems that detect the release of biological or chemical agents. The Environmental Protection Agency, for example, is evaluating the upgrading of air monitoring stations to allow for the detection of certain chemical, biological, or radiological substances. The federal government will also explore systems that can detect whether an individual has been immunized against a threat pathogen or has recently handled threat materials.

The ability to quickly recognize and report biological and chemical attacks will minimize casualties and enable first responders to treat the injured effectively. Local emergency personnel and health providers must first be able to diagnose symptoms. In addition to existing state laws mandating the reporting of threat diseases by physicians, veterinarians, and public health laboratories, rapid diagnosis of diseases of concern and communication form the cornerstone of a robust response. The Department of Homeland Security, under the President's proposal, will improve infectious disease and chemical terrorism surveillance by working with the Centers for Disease Control and Prevention (CDC) and the Department of Veterans Affairs in concert with local and state public health jurisdictions. These entities will work to develop a national system to detect biological and chemical attacks. This system will include a public health surveillance system to monitor public and private databases for indicators of biological or chemical attack. National research efforts will pay particular attention to recognizing harmful dual-use industrial chemicals.

The CDC will continue its vital role in detecting, diagnosing, and addressing bioterrorist threats. Its Epidemic Intelligence Service will be expanded and modernized to better train local and state officials in recognizing biological attacks. Under the President's proposal, the Department of Homeland Security will also provide resources to state and local jurisdictions with a population of 500,000 or more to hire skilled epidemiologists. The recently established Epidemic Information Exchange System will allow the sharing of disease information in a secure information system. Public health databases will be linked nationwide through the National Electronic Disease Surveillance System to recognize patterns of disease occurrence and to identify potential regional or national outbreaks. The Laboratory Response Network will improve laboratory technology and infrastructure to increase the speed and precision of diagnoses and confirmation of biological attacks. The Department would build the capacity to gather data from all these systems and sensors, quickly assess the extent of any attack, and recommend response options to policymakers.

The Department of Homeland Security, working with the Department of Agriculture, would also strengthen our parallel system for monitoring agricultural outbreaks. Since animals can serve as important sentinels signalling a biological attack against humans or be targets themselves, the Department of Homeland Security would collaborate closely with the Department of Agriculture and the Food and Drug Administration's Food and Animal Health program.

Improve chemical sensors and decontamination techniques. Private industry and the military routinely use sensors that can detect and identify toxic chemicals. Sensors with medical applications have also reached the market. Affordable, accurate, compact, and dependable sensors, however, are not available. The Department of Homeland Security would therefore fund and coordinate a national research program to develop, test, and field detection devices and networks that provide immediate and accurate warnings. The Department would also support research into decontamination technologies and procedures.

Develop broad spectrum vaccines, antimicrobials and antidotes. In many cases, our medical countermeasures cannot address all possible biological agents or may not be suitable for use by the general population. The Departments of Health and Human

Services and Homeland Security, and other government and private research entities, will pursue new defenses that will increase efficacy while reducing side effects. For example, they will explore the utility of attenuated smallpox vaccines and of existing antivirals modified to render those vaccines more effective and safe. Furthermore, the federal government, in collaboration with the private sector, will research and work toward development of broad spectrum antivirals to meet the threat of engineered pathogens aimed at both humans and livestock.

Short-and long-term efforts will expand the inventory of diagnostics, vaccines, and other therapies such as antimicrobials and antidotes that can mitigate the consequences of a chemical, biological, radiological, or nuclear attack. Development of safer smallpox vaccines and antiviral drugs will lower the risk of adverse reactions experienced with the traditional vaccine. The goal of protecting a diverse population of all ages and health conditions requires a coordinated national effort with a comprehensive research and development strategy and investment plans.

Harness the scientific knowledge and tools to counter terrorism. We will harness America's resources to fight against the most pressing chemical, biological, radiological, or nuclear challenges. In consultation with the Department of Health and Human Services, the Department of Homeland Security would leverage the expertise of America's cutting-edge medical and biotechnological infrastructure to advance the state of knowledge in infectious disease prevention and treatment, forensic epidemiology, and microbial forensics. Substantial research into relevant medical sciences is necessary to better detect, diagnose, and treat the consequences of chemical, biological, radiological, or nuclear attacks. The President has proposed a National Biological Weapons Analysis Centre in the Department of Homeland Security to address some of these issues and conduct risk assessments. This Centre, with input from the public health sector, will identify the highest priority threat agents to determine which countermeasures require priority research and development. The federal government will also consider and address the potential impact of genetic engineering on the biological threat.

The Food and Drug Administration (FDA) ensures the availability of medical products (drugs, vaccines, and devices) in the event of the intentional use of chemical, biological, radiological, or nuclear agents. Recently, the FDA adjusted its new drug and biological product regulations so that certain human drugs designed for emergency responses can be quickly introduced based on animal rather than human tests.

Implement the Select Agent Program. Research laboratories can also counter bioterrorism through prevention, and by tracking and securing dangerous biological agents. Under the President's proposal, the Department of Homeland Security will oversee the Select Agent Program to regulate the shipment of certain hazardous biological organisms and toxins. Through the registration of more than 300 laboratories, the Select Agent Program has significantly increased oversight and security of pathogens that could be used for bioterrorism. The CDC is also training public health officials in every state to assist in accurately interpreting biosafety containment provisions and select agent procedures.

EMERGENCY PREPAREDNESS AND RESPONSE

We must prepare to minimize the damage and recover from any future terrorist attacks that may occur despite our best efforts at prevention. Past experience has shown that preparedness efforts are key to providing an effective response to major terrorist incidents and natural disasters. Therefore, we need a comprehensive national system to bring together and command all necessary response assets quickly and effectively. We must equip, train, and exercise many different response units to mobilize for any emergency without warning. Under the President's proposal, the Department of Homeland Security, building on the strong foundation already laid by the Federal Emergency Management Agency (FEMA), will lead our national efforts to create and employ a system that will improve our response to all disasters, both manmade and natural.

Many pieces of this national emergency response system are already in place. America's first line of defense in the aftermath of any terrorist attack is its first responder community-police officers, firefighters, emergency medical providers, public works personnel, and emergency management officials. Nearly three million state and local first responders regularly put their lives on the line to save the lives of others and make our country safer. These individuals include specially trained hazardous materials teams, collapse search and rescue units, bomb squads, and tactical units.

In a serious emergency, the federal government augments state and local response efforts. FEMA, which under the President's proposal will be a key component of the Department of Homeland Security, provides funding and command and control support. A number of important specialized federal emergency response assets that are housed in various departments would also fall under the Secretary of Homeland Security's authority for responding to a major terrorist attack. Because response efforts to all major incidents entail the same basic elements, it is essential that federal response capabilities for both terrorist attacks and natural disasters remain in the same organization. This would ensure the most efficient provision of federal support to local responders by preventing the proliferation of duplicative "boutique" response entities.

Americans respond with great skill and courage to emergencies. There are, however, too many seams in our current response plans and capabilities. Today, at least five different plans-the Federal Response Plan, the National Contingency Plan, the Interagency Domestic Terrorism Concept of Operations Plan, the Federal Radiological Emergency Response Plan, and a nascent bioterrorism response plan-govern the federal government's response. These plans and the government's overarching policy for counterterrorism are based on a distinction between "crisis management" and "consequence management." In addition, different organizations at different levels of the government have put in place different incident management systems and communications equipment. All too often, these systems and equipment do not function together well enough.

We will enhance our capabilities for responding to a terrorist attack all across the country. Today, many geographic areas have little or no capability to respond to a terrorist attack using weapons of mass destruction. Even the best prepared states and localities do not possess adequate resources to respond to the full range of terrorist threats we face. Many do not yet have in place mutual aid agreements to facilitate cooperation with their neighbors in time of emergency. Until recently, federal support for domestic preparedness efforts has been relatively small and disorganized, with eight different departments and agencies providing money in a tangled web of grant programs.

Major Initiatives

Integrate separate federal response plans into a single all-discipline incident management plan. Under the President's proposal, the Department of Homeland Security will consolidate existing federal government emergency response plans into one genuinely all-discipline, all-hazard plan-the Federal Incident Management Plan-and thereby eliminate the "crisis management" and "consequence management" distinction. This plan would cover all incidents of national significance, including acts of bioterrorism and agroterrorism, and clarify roles and expected contributions of various emergency response bodies at different levels of government in the wake of a terrorist attack.

The Department of Homeland Security would provide a direct line of authority from the President through the Secretary of Homeland Security to a single on-site federal coordinator. The single federal coordinator would be responsible to the President for coordinating the entire federal response. Lead agencies would maintain operational control over their functions (for example, the FBI will remain the lead agency for federal law enforcement) in coordination with the single on-site federal official. The Department would direct the Domestic Emergency Support Team, nuclear incident response teams, National Pharmaceutical Stockpile, and National Disaster Medical System, as well as other assets.

Create a national incident management system. Under the President's proposal, the Department of Homeland Security, working with federal, state, local, and non-governmental public safety organizations, will build a comprehensive national incident management system to respond to terrorist incidents and natural disasters. The Department would ensure that this national system defines common terminology for all parties, provides a unified command structure, and is scalable to meet incidents of all sizes.

The federal government will encourage state and local first responder organizations to adopt the already widespread Incident Management System by making it a requirement for federal grants. All state and local governments should create and regularly update their own homeland security plans, based on their existing emergency operations plans, to provide guidance for the integration of their response assets in the event of an attack. The Department of Homeland Security will, under the President's proposal, provide support (including model plans) for these efforts and will adjust the Federal Incident Management Plan as necessary to take full advantage of state and local capabilities. State and local governments should also sign mutual aid agreements to facilitate cooperation with their neighbors in time of emergency. Starting in Fiscal Year 2004, the Department would provide grants in support of such efforts.

Improve tactical counter terrorist capabilities. With advance warning, we have various federal, state, and local response assets that can intercede and prevent terrorists from carrying out attacks. These include law enforcement, emergency response, and military teams. In the most dangerous of incidents, particularly when terrorists have chemical, biological, radiological, or nuclear weapons in their possession, it is crucial that the individuals who preempt the terrorists do so flawlessly, no matter if they are part of the local SWAT team or the FBI's Hostage Rescue Team. It is also crucial that these individuals be prepared and able to work effectively with each other and with other specialized response personnel. Finally, these teams and other emergency response assets must plan and train for the consequences of failed tactical operations.

The Department of Homeland Security, as the lead federal agency for incident management in the United States, will, under the President's plan, establish a program for certifying the preparedness of all civilian teams and individuals to execute and deal with the consequences of such counter terrorist actions. As part of this program, the Department would provide partial grants in support of joint exercises between its response assets and other government teams.

Enable seamless communication among all responders. In the aftermath of any major terrorist attack, emergency response efforts would likely involve hundreds of offices from across the government and the country. It is crucial for response personnel to have and use equipment, systems, and procedures that allow them to communicate with one another. Under the President's proposal, the Department of Homeland Security will work with state and local governments to achieve this goal.

In particular, the Department would develop a national emergency communication plan to establish protocols (i.e., who needs to talk to whom), processes, and national standards for technology acquisition. The Department would, starting with Fiscal Year 2003 funds, tie all federal grant programs that support state and local purchase of terrorism-related communications equipment to this communication plan and require all applicants to demonstrate progress in achieving interoperability with other emergency response bodies.

Prepare health care providers for catastrophic terrorism. Our entire emergency response community must be prepared to deal with all potential hazards, especially those associated with weapons of mass destruction. Under the President's proposal, the Department of Homeland Security, working with the Departments of Health and Human Services and Veterans Affairs, will support training and equipping of state and local health care personnel to deal with the growing threat of chemical, biological, radiological, and nuclear terrorism.

It would continue to fund federal grants to states and cities for bioterrorism preparedness. It would use the hospital preparedness grant program to help prepare hospitals and poison control centers to deal specifically with biological and chemical attacks and to expand their surge capacity to care for large numbers of patients in a mass-casualty incident. These efforts would enhance training between public health agencies and local hospitals and seek improved cooperation between public health and emergency agencies at all levels of government.

A major act of biological terrorism would almost certainly overwhelm existing state, local, and privately owned health care capabilities. For this reason, the federal government maintains a number of specialized response capabilities for a bioterrorist attack. The National Disaster Medical System, a federal/private partnership that includes the Departments of Health and Human Services, Defense, Veterans Affairs, and FEMA, provides rapid response and critical surge capacities to support localities in disaster medical treatment. Under the President's proposal, the Department of Homeland Security will assume authority over the System as part of the federal response to incidents of national significance. The System is made up of federal assets and thousands of volunteer health professionals that are organized around the country into a number of specialty teams such as Disaster Medical Assistance Teams, National Medical Response Teams, and teams trained in caring for psychological trauma. In addition, the Department of Veterans Affairs operates a vast health care, training, and pharmaceutical procurement system with facilities in many communities nationwide. The Department of Defense provides specialized skills and transportation capabilities to move these teams and evacuate casualties.

The Department of Homeland Security, working with the Department of Health and Human Services, would lead efforts to test whether illnesses or complaints may be attributable to chemical, biological, radiological, or nuclear exposure; establish disease/exposure registries; and develop, maintain, and provide information on the health effects of hazardous substances. The Environmental Protection Agency will continue to provide a laboratory diagnostic surge capacity for environmental samples during crises.

Augment America's pharmaceutical and vaccine stockpiles. The National Pharmaceutical Stockpile ensures America's ability to respond rapidly to a bioterrorist attack or a mass casualty incident. This program, which the Department of Homeland Security will operate in consultation with the Department of Health and Human Services under the President's proposal, maintains twelve strategically located "Push Packs" containing 600 tons of antibiotics, antidotes, vaccines, bandages, and other medical supplies. The federal government can transport these packs to an incident site in less than 12 hours for rapid distribution by state and local authorities. This system performed extremely well in the aftermath of the September 11 attacks, delivering a "Push Pack" to New York City in seven hours. Additional deployments followed the anthrax attacks of October 2001.

Prepare for chemical, biological, radiological, and nuclear decontamination. The Department of Homeland Security would ensure the readiness of our first responders to work safely in an area where chemical, biological, radiological, or nuclear weapons have been used. The Department would begin requiring annual certification of first responder preparedness to handle and decontaminate any hazard. This certification process would also verify the ability of state and local first responders to work effectively with related federal support assets.

Under the President's proposal, the Department of Homeland Security will help state and local agencies meet these certification standards by providing grant money (based on performance) for planning and equipping, training, and exercising first responders for chemical, biological, radiological and nuclear attacks. It would launch a national research and development effort to create new technologies for detection and clean-up of such attacks. After a major incident, the Environmental Protection Agency will be responsible for decontamination of affected buildings and neighborhoods and providing advice and assistance to public health authorities in determining when it is safe to return to these areas.

Plan for military support to civil authorities. The armed forces were an integral part of our national response to the terrorist attacks of September 11. The Department of Defense currently uses a "Total Force" approach to fulfil its missions overseas and at home, drawing on the strengths and capabilities of active-duty, reserve, and National Guard forces. In addition to response from the active-duty forces, Air National Guard fighters took to the air on September 11 to establish combat air patrols. New Jersey and New York guardsmen and Navy and Marine Corps reservists provided medical personnel to care for the injured, military police to assist local law enforcement officials, key asset protection, transportation, communications, logistics, and a myriad of other functions to support recovery efforts in New York City. Maryland Army National Guard military police units were brought on duty and dispatched to provide security at the Pentagon. President Bush asked governors to call up over seven thousand National Guard personnel to supplement security at the Nation's 429 commercial airports. Guardsmen also reinforced border security activities of the Immigration and Nationalization Service and the U.S. Customs Service.

The importance of military support to civil authorities as the latter respond to threats or acts of terrorism is recognized in Presidential decision directives and legislation. Military support to civil authorities pursuant to a terrorist threat or attack may take the form of providing technical support and assistance to law enforcement; assisting in the restoration of law and order; loaning specialized equipment; and assisting in consequence management.

In April 2002, President Bush approved a revision of the Unified Command Plan that included establishing a new unified combatant command, U.S. Northern Command. This Command will be responsible for homeland defense and for assisting civil authorities in accordance with U.S. law.

As in the case with all other combatant commanders, the commander of Northern Command will take all operational orders from and is responsible to the President through the Secretary of Defense. The commander of Northern Command will update plans to provide military support to domestic civil authorities in response to natural and man-made disasters and during national emergencies. The Department of Homeland Security and the Department of Defense would participate as appropriate in homeland security training that involves military and civilian emergency response personnel.

Build the Citizen Corps. Under the President's proposal, the Department of Homeland Security will maintain and expand Citizens Corps, a national program to prepare volunteers for terrorism-related response support. If we can help individual citizens help themselves and their neighbors in the case of a local attack, we will improve our chances to save lives.

Implement the First Responder Initiative of the Fiscal Year 2003 Budget. Before September 11, the federal government had allocated less than $1 billion since 1995 to help prepare first responders for terrorist attacks. A range of federal departments provided funding for training and equipment, technical assistance, and other support to assist state and local first responders. These disparate programs were a step in the right direction but fell short in terms of scale and cohesion.

In January 2002, President Bush proposed the First Responder Initiative as part of his Fiscal Year 2003 Budget proposal. The purpose of this initiative is to improve dramatically first responder preparedness for terrorist incidents and disasters. This program will increase federal funding levels more than tenfold (from $272 million in the pre-supplemental Fiscal Year 2002 Budget to $3.5 billion in Fiscal Year 2003). Under the President's Department of Homeland Security proposal, the new Department will consolidate all grant programs that distribute federal funds to state and local first responders.

Build a national training and evaluation system. The growing threat of terrorist attacks on American soil, including the potential use of weapons of mass destruction, is placing great strains on our Nation's system for training its emergency response personnel. The Department of Homeland Security will under the President's proposal launch a consolidated and expanded training and evaluation system to meet the increasing demand. This system would be predicated on a four phased approach: requirements, plans, training (and exercises), and assessments (comprising of evaluations and corrective action plans). The Department would serve as the central coordinating body responsible for overseeing curriculum standards and, through regional centers of excellence such as the Emergency Management Institute in Maryland, the Centre for Domestic Preparedness in Alabama, and the National Domestic Preparedness Consortium, for training the instructors who will train our first responders. These instructors would teach courses at thousands of facilities such as public safety academies, community colleges, and state and private universities.

Under the President's proposal, the Department of Homeland Security will establish national standards for emergency response training and preparedness. These standards would provide guidelines for the vaccination of civilian response personnel against certain biological agents. These standards would also require certain coursework for individuals to receive and maintain certification as first responders and for state and local governments to receive federal grants. The Department would establish a national exercise program designed to educate and evaluate civilian response personnel at all levels of government. It would require individuals and government bodies to complete successfully at least one exercise every year. The Department would use these exercises to measure performance and allocate future resources.

Enhance the victim support system. The United States must be prepared to assist the victims of terrorist attacks and their families, as well as other individuals affected indirectly by attacks. Under the President's proposal, the Department of Homeland Security will lead federal agencies and provide guidance to state, local, and volunteer organizations in offering victims and their families various forms of assistance including: crisis counseling, cash grants, low-interest loans, unemployment benefits, free legal counseling, and tax refunds. In the case of a terrorist attack, the Department would coordinate the various federal programs for victim compensation and assistance, including the Department of Justice's Office for Victims of Crime and FEMA's Individual Assistance programs.

5

Threats and Effect of Cyber Terrorism

CYBER TERRORISM: COMPLEXITIES AND CONSEQUENCES

While a terrorist using the Internet to bring down the critical infrastructures the United States relies on makes an outstanding Hollywood plot, there are flaws in the execution of this storyline as an actual terrorist strategy. Conway (2011) calls out three limitations on using cyber-related activities for terrorists: Technological complexity, image, and accident.

Each is important to consider. While critical infrastructures may make a tempting target and threat actor capabilities are certainly increasing, it is a complicated process to attack something of that magnitude. It is precisely the interconnectedness of these two disparate parts that make them a target, however.

ETHICAL HACKING TRAINING – RESOURCES (INFOSEC)

Nyugan (2013) calls them cyber-physical systems (CPS): "A physical system monitored or controlled by computers. Such systems include, for example, electrical grids, antilock brake systems, or a network of nuclear centrifuges".

In Verton's (2003) imaginary narrative, the target of the Russian hackers, the SCADA system, is a CPS. However, Lewis (2002) argues the relationship between vulnerabilities in critical infrastructures (such as MAE-East) and computer network attacks is not a clear cut as first thought (p. 1). It is not simply a matter of having a computer attached to a SCADA system and thus the system is can now be turned off and society goes in a free fall of panic and explosions and mass chaos.

The first idea Conway (2011) posits reduces to the notion that information technology is difficult in most cases. There are reasons it takes veritable armies of engineers and analysts to make these complex systems interact and function as intended. However, there are a limited number of terrorists with the necessary computer skills to conduct a successful attack.

Immediately the argument turns to hiring external assistance from actual computer hackers (as most journalists and Hollywood scriptwriters do). Conway (2011) dismisses that idea, correctly, as a significant compromise of operational security (p. 28).

The US Department of Defense as defines operational security, or OPSEC:

A process of identifying critical information and analyzing friendly actions attendant to military operations and other activities to: identify those actions that can be observed by adversary intelligence systems; determine indicators and vulnerabilities that adversary intelligence systems might obtain that could be interpreted or pieced together to derive critical information in time to be useful to adversaries, and determine which of these represent an unacceptable risk; then select and execute countermeasures that eliminate the risk to friendly actions and operations or reduce it to an acceptable level (US Department of Defense, 2012).

In the context of this chapter, letting outside profit-motivated technicians into the planning and execution phase of a terrorist plot would be risky for conservative-minded individuals such a religious terrorists. As the number of people who are aware of a plot increases, the potential number of people who can leak operational details of the plot increases exponentially.

It is for this reason Verton's (2003) scenario is most improbable.

The second concern Conway (2011) notes is one of audience. Recalling the definition of terrorist put forth by Hoffman (2006), terrorists need to generate publicity to achieve their goals: they need to create a climate of fear through violence or the threat of violence. Simply attacking something and having no one notice it is not an operational success for a terrorist. Terrorists need to have their grievances known.

The terrorist act needs to be witnessed, such as the planes crashing into the World Trade Centre or the hostage taking in Munich. in order to generate the necessary level of discourse to affect the goals the terrorist has in mind. Unfortunately, injecting code into a DNS server or shutting down Amazon.com does not generate the required intensity of chaos modern terrorists require (Conway, Against Cyberterrorism, 2011, p. 28).

This leads to Conway's (2011) third point: the accident. The United States relies heavily on computer and information systems. However, if a system goes offline in today's world, users are just as likely to suspect a system failure or accident as anything else is (p. 28).

As stated previously, this would be unacceptable to the terrorist organization. In order to generate a sufficient amount of concern on the part of the population, aseries of cascading cyber-attacks would have to occur. Recalling Conway's (2011) first concern about complexity, multiple system attacks of the necessary intensity and frequency are unlikely.

While this might appear as merely an academic exercise, a review of the Global Terrorism Database maintained by the National Consortium for the Study of Terrorism and Responses to Terrorism at the University of Maryland shows only two incidents under the search term "cyber" (Global Terrorism Database Search Results).

The first involved two men in Morocco who got into an argument at an Internet café with the café owner about viewing bomb-making materials. During the altercation, an actual bomb strapped to one of the men accidentally exploded killing the would-be bomber and wounding three others.

The second involved a pay phone in Hong Kong that was wired with explosives and detonated. A search of telecommunications facilities as targets in the database showed similar results: Explosions or arson, not the use of computers as a weapon system.

There are side effects of the mischaracterization of cyberterrorism by the media and popular culture. In the United States, the Uniting (and) Strengthening America (by) Providing Appropriate Tools Required (to) Intercept (and) Obstruct Terrorism Act of 2001, or PATRIOT Act, was passed in the immediate aftermath of the September 11, 2001 attacks.

It has two key provisions designed to counter potential cyberterrorist activity and increase the punishment for computer crimes (US Government, 2001). Section 814 of the PATRIOT Act enumerated specifically the goals of deterring and preventing cyberterrorism.

It increased the minimum prison terms for unauthorized access to a computer system, regardless of activity once in the system i.e. mixing criminal activity and cyberterrorism under a cyberterrorism section heading.

Additionally, the law amended "the Federal sentencing guidelines to ensure that any individual convicted of a violation of section 1030 of title 18, United States Code, can be subjected to appropriate penalties, without regard to any mandatory minimum term of imprisonment".

In other words, simply being convicted of unauthorized access to a computer system allowed a federal judge (who most likely was not familiar with the nuances of cyber threats and threat + actors) to assume the worst and lock someone up for a very long time. Outside of the United States, others have made similar decisions regarding cyber threats and the law.

In the United Kingdom, Parliament changed its Terrorism Act so that using a computer system or threatening to use a computer system that interferes or disrupts another computer system is now considered terrorism (Conway, Cyberterrorism: Hype and Reality, 2007, p. 91).

Of concern of course is who makes the determination as to what constitutes disruption. Right now, that falls to Scotland Yard. That leaves a sour taste and no small amount of anxiety for human rights workers and other civil libertarians (p. 91).

Since the advent of the Internet, life has changed remarkable for citizens of the United States and the world. Unfortunately, this pace of change brings fear. When the legitimate danger terrorists create is married to our dependence on technology, it is understandable how people become concerned. This new sense of panic is the fear of terrorists using the computer systems we depend on against us.

Fortunately, the evidence of cyberterrorism very limited thus far. Of course, an assumption is made that cyberterrorism is properly defined as a non-state organization that creates politically motivated destruction to information, computer systems and/or computer programs leading to violence or the threat of violence.

Any implication of state-sponsorship of cyber-attacks is outside the scope of this chapter and could constitute an act of war. An analysis of the issue has demonstrated that cyberterrorism as a strategy for actual terrorists has been over-hyped through the media, academia, and popular literature.

This exaggeration of capabilities has led to several instances of questionable law made by people who do not understand the intricacies involved in launching a cyberterrorist attack. Rather, they acted out of fear and doubt.

More cybersecurity professionals need to counter such sentiments by public and public officials to ensure actual threats are mitigated and unsubstantiated ones are given less priority and fewer resources. Only then can the more important threats be dealt with.

CYBER-TERRORISM: THE EMERGING THREAT

A number of economies were thrown into disarray with the recent financial turmoil. Opinions remain divided on which way the road ahead leads to. But even when household names and industry heavyweights were being brought down to their knees, technology remained steadfast. In fact, technology today has so inconspicuously become a business enabler that it's almost easy to overlook.

The United Nations telecommunications agency warns that the next world war could well be in cyberspace. This should come as no surprise. Wars have often included attacks on installations or facilities that are critical to the enemy, delivering a crippling blow to gain the higher ground. Considering the sheer magnitude of dependence that the modern world places on technology, it would logically make a fine target if a war were to ensue.

Cyber-Terrorism

A new page in the information warfare book comes in a sinister form. Cyber-terrorism involves highly targeted efforts made with the intention of terrorism. It is an emerging threat that has the potential to cause serious damage. While we'd often associate terrorism with loss of life, we cannot overlook important results like intimidation or coercion that can be brought about by cyber-terrorism.

A prolonged and targeted terrorism campaign against a country has the potential to render it weak in the long-run. Given the varied economic, financial, and even psychological effects such a campaign could have, cyber-terrorism poses a significant hurdle in times to come. Technology is the backbone of most countries in the world today. A hard hit on such a critical backbone would be an ideal strategy for attackers.

Non-Tech? Think Again!

The long-held belief that terrorists are unorganized and non-technical has been clearly shattered in modern times. The most recent example of this could be seen in the 2008 terror attacks in Mumbai (India), where satellite phones using VoIP technology, complex GPS systems, and, allegedly, even Google Earth were all used to aid the acts of terror.

As far back as 1998, the, now-exterminated, terrorist organization in Sri Lanka, known as the Tamil Tigers, overloaded Sri Lankan embassies with more than 800 e-mails per day for two weeks. In more recent times, cyber attacks directed at India from terrorist organizations and others with similar malicious intentions is commonplace. Israel has significant threats from organizations such as Hamas and Hezbollah.

Today, terrorists share information by embedding it in image files and sharing these images over e-mail. The image with embedded information is strikingly similar to the original and does not appear to be different by just looking or comparing visually. This technique is commonly classified under what is known in the security world as "steganography". There are free tools available on the Internet to do this.

While the bleak prospect of having an image embedded with information being intercepted even exists, another method allows terrorists to plot without even sending e-mail. By saving e-mails as drafts and never sending them, terrorists effectively communicate with each other without even really sending an e-mail. The communicating parties simply share the password to the e-mail account. No e-mail sent means no e-mail intercepted.

Why should you care? As a direct or indirect victim of a cyber-terror attack, you could be left groping around in the dark if you aren't reasonably well-prepared. The impacts are pretty much the same as any other hacker attack on an organization, except that you'll be a pawn in a broader terrorist agenda.

Another significant reason lies in the fact that we don't live in a vacuum. Cyber threats can have the same impacts as real world threats. The economic and political impacts alone are enough causes to worry, and cyber-terror attacks are not limited to geographic borders or reach. The world is much smaller due to technology. When the very technology that enables this is attacked, it may not matter which part of the world you're in when an attack takes place if the objective and magnitude of the attack is large enough.

Countering Cyber-Terrorism

Preparing against the threat of cyber-terrorism requires the same level of planning and preparation to survive an economic or financial crisis.

One of the biggest concerns that organizations have when protecting against an emerging threat is the cost associated with it. In fact, the costs associated with countering cyber-terrorism are not new costs at all. Your existing information security strategy need only be tweaked and adapted to be well-prepared.

Responsible Attitude

To be able to counteract the threat posed by cyber-terrorism, the first need would be to take it seriously. Even if you were to believe that the threat will never materialize, being prepared for it is the responsible thing to do. You do not want to be caught unaware.

Program, Policies, and Procedures

Your existing information security program should already provide a guideline on how to deal with information security threats. You need only add guidelines on how to specifically approach the threat of cyber-terrorism. Ensure that policies and procedures guide the organization to know when to activate the incident response mode. Switching to this mode could be expensive, so ensure that the guidelines are accurate, clear, and well-documented.

Incident Response

An organization's incident response capability will be severely tested in the event of a cyber-terror attack. A good incident response plan is critical to address the threat adequately. Ensure that the plan includes steps on monitoring, prevention, communication, and escalation. Testing should be performed on a periodic basis with documented test results and future improvement steps. It is also important to interface and interact with advisories such as the CERT to keep abreast with current events and happenings.

Technical Security Assessments

Technical assessments such as external and internal penetration tests, audits, vulnerability assessments, social engineering engagements, and application hacking engagements are generally performed by many organizations. While these could arise from regulatory requirements, they greatly benefit the organization's information security posture as a whole. Technical security assessments, if performed thoroughly and accurately, can transform an organization into an impenetrable fortress. While the regulatory compliance will be a pleasant by-product, your secure organizational information is of utmost importance to protecting your assets.

Business Continuity Planning

Business continuity is another vital ingredient in preparations to counter the threat of cyber-terrorism. The business continuity plan ensures that your organizational operations will continue to run profitably even in the event of a cyber-terror attack. Although real-world terrorist attacks are often included in business continuity plans, it is a good idea to include virtual-world terrorist attacks as well. Ensure on regular data backups and full-recovery testing.

Awareness Training

Generating awareness of emerging threats is critically important. The information security industry is one that is ever changing and evolving. Hence, training and awareness efforts need to keep pace. The employees of an organization are the ultimate implementers of information security and so training them correctly should be considered vital to a secure and profitable business operation. The best awareness training efforts utilize a variety of approaches in order to avoid monotony. Such methods include seminars, newsletters, intranet forums, awareness posters, and many others. The key is to keep it interesting.

Moving Forward Sensibly

Borders between countries have been greatly diminished in modern times, in large part due to technology. Real-world terrorism is arguably the biggest challenge faced by the world today, and perhaps the best opportunity for committed terrorists. When this translates into the virtual-world, the impacts could be disastrous and debilitating. Recent trends suggest that this migration to cyber-terrorism has already begun.

Being mindful of the emerging threat of cyber-terrorism when protecting your organization's information will enable a wholesome approach to information security. As the world strides into the future, sensible organizations will be wary of the threat looming large at the horizon and take precautions to ward against potential threats.

UNDERSTANDING CYBERTERRORISM

Without a doubt, cyberterrorism poses a real threat to governments, organizations and individuals around the globe. In today's high-tech world, all types of computer networks are logical targets for all sorts of adversaries. In fact, according to a figure from U.S. officials, an astounding 60,000 new malicious computer programs are identified every day.

But how does one exactly define cyberterrorism? In a 2000 testimony before the Armed Services Committee of the U.S. Representatives, Dorothy Denning of Georgetown University coined a still-popular definition of cyberterrorism: "the convergence of terrorism and cyberspace...generally understood to mean unlawful attack and threats of attack against computers, networks and the information stored therein when done to intimidate or coerce a government or its people in furtherance of political or social objectives."

While that may be a mouthful, it does seem to sum it up. Depending on who you ask, however, cyberterrorism can have a somewhat surprising variety of meanings. Why this ambiguity? Well, since cyberterrorism is a relatively new term and is a product of the technological age in which we currently live, its definition is naturally still evolving. And as the technology surrounding cyberterrorism itself changes, the definition of the term will continue to change as well.

"It's hard to define something that's so intangible, so shifty, so below the radar of an otherwise law-abiding society," said Carmi Levy, an independent technology analyst and journalist. "It's also hard to define something most of us would rather shunt out of sight. This is typical behavior, and nothing we haven't seen with earlier forms of anomalous technology-related threats, such as viruses and malware."

The other hurdle he sees is our collective unfamiliarity with the threat. "It's hard to define something until the majority of society agrees it's a problem and has seen enough of it to merit actual recognition," said Levy. "Unfortunately, we're not there yet. Until it touches more of us in a more direct manner, expect it to remain difficult to pin down."

Perhaps the thorniest issue is that the term's root word is something society still struggles to define. "The simpler term 'terrorism' itself can have a variety of definitions, and 'cyber' just adds layers of complexity and misunderstanding to the issue," said Kurt Baumgartner, a senior security researcher at Kaspersky Lab, a Moscow-based computer security company.

As the terms "terrorist" and "freedom fighter" have been debated in the past, when it comes to cyberattacks, there can be a fine line between activism and terrorism. And which side of that line an event falls on often varies depending on your perspective. In today's digital world, some see the progression from activist to "hacktivist" as a natural one.

"It's pretty easy to imagine past activist heroes might well have engaged in some type of hacktivism depending if they'd had access to the technology," said John Kindervag, a security expert and principal analyst at Forrester, a research company in Cambridge, Massachusetts.

Kindervag also wonders if defacing a website or bringing down an ecommerce portal, like the 2011 disruption of Sony's Play Station Network, an online video game platform, is actually terrifying or merely inconvenient. "For me, the issue is if individual lives are in jeopardy at the moment of the action," said Kindervag. "Disrupting the air-traffic control system to make planes crash would definitely be cyberterrorism. The Sony Play Station Network attack would not be."

What Kind of Damage Can Cyberterrorism Do?

Since cyberterrorism is such a new brand of crime, we as a society do tend to be somewhat complacent when it comes to cybersecurity. However, in the near future, we can only expect to hear more about both cyberterrorism threats and actual incidents.

"The threat will only grow with the passage of time," said Levy. "And it's up to everyone to begin treating it as it deserves to be treated: with respect." Currently, the most frightening potential attacks are those that come from all angles. Baumgartner envisions a scenario in which cyberterrorists simultaneously disrupt communications systems, infrastructure controls and financial markets. Such a wide-net strike would be difficult to pull off, but the resources may exist—for the right price.

"It somewhat depends on the attackers' goals and capabilities," he said, "but capabilities are for sale."

In terms of actually inciting terror, most rightfully fear bombings and explosions more than anything else. But the damage caused by cyberterrorism attacks can induce a different brand of fear since they are orchestrated by a faceless evildoer.

"Tangibly, we can all relate: a power plant could be taken offline, a company's finances could be wrecked and a region's ability to communicate wiped out," said Levy. "Intangibly, the psychological impact could be even greater and longer-lasting, as cyberterrorism strikes at the very heart of what makes us feel safe in a supposedly safe society."

This can lead to a feeling of helplessness. "It allows enemies to easily bypass the traditional barriers of military and geography, and it allows them to get at the soft underbelly of day-to-day society," said Levy. "Fear of these types of attacks, in many respects, is just as debilitating as the overt effects might be."

While definitive, public accounts of large-scale acts of cyberterrorism can be difficult to come by, there have been some comparatively smaller-scale examples of cyberattacks in the recent past. The hacker group Anonymous, for example, has launched multiple attacks against authorities. Founded in 2003, this group of loosely associated hackers is extremely opposed to any type of internet surveillance and censorship.

"These attacks illustrate the broadly disruptive impact of a distributed, focused campaign to take down resources controlled by forces they deem the enemy," said Levy. "Chicago's police department, for example, was taken down earlier this year, and law enforcement agencies in Ontario had usernames and passwords published by hackers claiming to be affiliated with Anonymous."

While groups with agendas similar to Anonymous will likely continue to carry out attacks regardless of the day's political climate, social factors have driven other hacktivists to action. "The Occupy movement as well as the Arab Spring spawned an upsurge in this type of activity," said Levy.

With respect to governmental organizations, Stuxnet, a malicious computer "worm" designed to interfere with the nuclear program in Iran, was accidentally discovered in 2010 when the virus left the digital perimeter of Iran's Natanz plant and reached the wider internet. According to the *New York Times,* this malicious code was developed by both the United States and Israel. Since then, two new versions of this worm have been discovered.

In May 2012, another piece of malware, a virus called Flame, was uncovered. This virus infiltrated the computers of high-ranking officials in Iran with the goal of collecting information. Flame appeared to be approximately five years old when it is was found, and the *Washington Post* has reported that it was designed by the United States; publicly, U.S. officials have not stated that they were responsible for creating this particular virus.

During April and May of 2007, Estonia was the victim of violence, riots and cyberattacks after officials moved a memorial commemorating the Soviet liberation of Estonia from the Nazis during World War II. Hackers shut down government ministry websites, two important banking websites and political party websites. They even disabled the email server for the Estonian parliament. Officials in Estonia accused the Russian government of orchestrating the denial-of-service attacks, but NATO and the European Commission were unable to find concrete evidence to prove these allegations.

In 2011, researchers from various high-tech companies uncovered a Trojan horse called Sykipot. This cyberweapon attempted to obtain documents from high-ranking executives, mainly those in the defense field at companies that developed unmanned drone planes. Officials believe that these attacks are coming from an established group located in China.

While we all like to hope that our government infrastructure is infallible, such attacks show that 100% protection is likely impossible. "Every system has areas of vulnerability, and there is no such thing as an inviolable or impenetrable solution," said Levy. "Like conventional crime, military and quasi-military threats, it's foolish to think we'll ever be 100% safe. The world has simply never worked that way, and it isn't about to start now."

How Do We Stop Cyberterrorists?

While no amount of improvement will ever ensure society is cyberattack-free, experts say that governments and organizations should be proactive when it comes to investing in preventative measures. As technology continues to move forward at an alarming rate, so too must the laws regarding cyberactivities. Because currently, neither civilian nor government officials are truly able to combat this new and ever-changing threat. "Traditional law enforcement tools and processes need to be updated or replaced entirely," said Levy.

Baumgartner feels similarly. "It is important to get past the short-term political gimmicks and silliness that we have seen and get down to business," he said. "Addressing the problem effectively is a complex and difficult task, and overburdening defenders with ineffective tasks that waste time instead of necessary solutions is a difficult balance."

To reach the proper balance, Levy recommends that law enforcement officials and business leaders strive for improved task forces, specialized training, and a re-prioritization of resources toward this class of crime. This, he believes, will greatly reduce the risk of attack and lower the severity and impact if an attack does occur.

"They can raise the vulnerability bar sufficiently high to discourage the lesser-skilled and motivated attackers, and make life sufficiently difficult on the true pros," said Levy.

Unfortunately, in his view, those who built the last-generation standards of policing the digital world may not be up to the task without extensive and expensive retraining. And even then, they may not be able to adapt their capabilities to this new reality.

"The existing culture within law enforcement may be inadequate," said Levy. "No one project or initiative will be enough to adapt. Nothing short of a wholesale rebuild of government and law enforcement best practices will do."

THE CYBER THREAT AND FBI RESPONSE

We face cyber threats from state-sponsored hackers, hackers for hire, global cyber syndicates, and terrorists. They seek our state secrets, our trade secrets, our technology, and our ideas— things of incredible value to all of us. They seek to strike our critical infrastructure and to harm our economy.

Given the scope of the cyber threat, agencies across the federal government are making cyber security a top priority. We and our partners at the Department of Homeland Security (DHS), the National Security Agency, and other U.S. Intelligence Community and law enforcement agencies have truly undertaken a whole-of-government effort to combat the cyber threat. Within the FBI, we are prioritizing high-level intrusions—the biggest and most dangerous botnets, state-sponsored hackers, and global cyber syndicates. We are working with our counterparts to predict and prevent attacks, rather than simply react after the fact.

FBI agents, analysts, and computer scientists use technical capabilities and traditional investigative techniques—such as sources and wiretaps, surveillance, and forensics—to fight cyber crime. We work side-by-side with our federal, state, and local partners on Cyber Task Forces in each of our 56 field offices and at the National Cyber Investigative Joint Task Force (NCIJTF). Through our 24-hour cyber command centre, CyWatch, we combine the resources of the FBI and NCIJTF, allowing us to provide connectivity to Federal cyber centers, government agencies, FBI field offices and legal attaches, and the private sector in the event of a significant cyber intrusion.

We also exchange information about cyber threats with the private sector through partnerships such as the Domestic Security Alliance Council, InfraGard, and the National Cyber Forensics and Training Alliance (NCFTA).

In addition, our legal attache offices overseas work to coordinate cyber investigations and address jurisdictional hurdles and differences in the law from country to country. We are supporting and collaborating with newly established cyber crime centers at Interpol and Europol. We continue to assess other locations to ensure that our cyber personnel are in the most appropriate locations across the globe.

We know that to be successful in the fight against cyber crime, we must continue to recruit, develop, and retain a highly skilled workforce. To that end, we have developed a number of innovative staffing programs and collaborative private industry partnerships to ensure that over the long term we remain focused on our most vital resource—our people. As the committee is well aware, the frequency and impact of cyber attacks on our nation's private sector and government networks have increased dramatically in the past decade and are expected to continue to grow. Since 2002, the FBI has seen an 80 percent increase in the number of computer intrusion investigations.

Recent Successes

Over the past several months, the FBI and the Justice Department have announced a series of separate indictments of overseas cyber criminals.

In an unprecedented indictment in May, we charged five Chinese hackers with illegally penetrating the networks of six U.S. companies. The five members of China's People's Liberation Army allegedly used their illegal access to exfiltrate proprietary information, including trade secrets.

Later that month, we announced the indictments of a Swedish national and a U.S. citizen believed to be the co-developers of a particularly insidious computer malware known as Blackshades. This software was sold and distributed to thousands of people in more than 100 countries and has been used to infect more than half-a-million computers worldwide.

In June, the FBI announced a multi-national effort to disrupt the GameOver Zeus botnet, the most sophisticated botnet that the FBI and its allies had ever attempted to disrupt. GameOver Zeus is believed to be responsible for the theft of millions of dollars from businesses and consumers in the U.S. and around the world. This effort to disrupt it involved notable cooperation with the private sector and international law enforcement.

GameOver Zeus is an extremely sophisticated type of malware designed specifically to steal banking and other credentials from the computers it infects. In the case of GameOver Zeus, its primary purpose is to capture banking credentials from infected computers, then use those credentials to initiate or re-direct wire transfers to accounts overseas that are controlled by the criminals. Losses attributable to GameOver Zeus are estimated to be more than $100 million.

Just last month, a federal grand jury indicted Su Bin, a Chinese national, on five felony offenses stemming from a computer hacking scheme that involved the theft of trade secrets from American defense contractors, including The Boeing Company, which manufactures the C-17 military transport aircraft. Su is currently in custody in British Columbia, Canada, where he is being held pursuant to a provisional arrest warrant submitted by the United States. The charges carry a total maximum statutory penalty of 30 years in prison. The investigation in this case was conducted by the Federal Bureau of Investigation and the Air Force Office of Special Investigations.

The Blackshades and GameOver Zeus indictments are part of an initiative launched by the FBI Cyber Division in April 2013 to disrupt and dismantle the most significant botnets threatening the economy and national security of the United States. This initiative, named Operation Clean Slate, is the FBI's broad campaign to implement appropriate threat neutralization actions through collaboration with the private sector, DHS, and other United States government partners, as well as our foreign partners. This includes law enforcement action against those responsible for the creation and use of the illegal botnets, mitigation of the botnet itself, assistance to victims, public service announcements, and long-term efforts to improve awareness of the botnet threat through community outreach. Although each botnet is unique, Operation Clean Slate's strategic approach to this significant threat ensures a comprehensive neutralization strategy, incorporating a unified public/private response and a whole-of-government approach to protect U.S. interests.

The impact of botnets has been significant. Botnets have been estimated to cause more than $113 billion in losses globally, with approximately 375 million computers infected each year, equaling more than one million victims per day, translating to 12 victims per second.

Another Operation Clean Slate success came in January 2014, when Aleksandry Andreevich Panin, a Russian national, pled guilty to conspiracy to commit wire and bank fraud for his role as the primary developer and distributor of the malicious software known as Spyeye, which infected more than 1.4 million computers in the United States and abroad. Based on information received from the financial services industry, more than 10,000 bank accounts had been compromised by Spyeye infections in 2013 alone. Panin's co-conspirator, Hamza Bendelladj, an Algerian national who helped Panin develop and distribute the malware, was also arrested in January 2013 in Bangkok, Thailand.

In addition to these recent investigative successes against cyber threats, we are continuing to work with our partners to prevent attacks before they occur.

One area in which we have had great success with our overseas partners is in identifying and targeting infrastructure we believe has been used in distributed denial of service (DDoS) attacks and preventing that infrastructure from being used for future attacks. A DDoS attack is an attack on a computer system or network that causes a loss of service to users, typically the loss of network connectivity and services by consuming the bandwidth of the victim network.

Since October 2012, the FBI and DHS have released more than 170,000 Internet Protocol addresses of computers that were believed to be infected with DDoS malware. We have released this information through Joint Indicator Bulletins (JIBs) to more than 130 countries via DHS's National Cybersecurity and Communications Integration Centre (NCCIC), where our liaisons provide expert and technical advice for increased coordination and collaboration, as well as to our legal attaches overseas.

These actions have enabled our foreign partners to take action and reduced the effectiveness of the botnets and the DDoS attacks. We are continuing to target botnets through this strategy and others.

In 2013, for example, the FBI created FBI Liaison Alert System (FLASH) reports and Private Industry Notifications (PINs) to release industry-specific details on current and emerging threat trends and technical indicators to the private sector. To date, the FBI has disseminated 40 FLASH messages, 21 of which dealt with threats to the financial industry. These PIN and FLASH messages were created to proactively deliver timely, actionable intelligence to potential victims and law enforcement partners at the international, state, and local levels.

Next Generation Cyber Initiative

The need to prevent attacks is a key reason the FBI has redoubled our efforts to strengthen our cyber capabilities while protecting privacy, confidentiality, and civil liberties. The FBI's Next Generation Cyber Initiative, which we launched in 2012, entails a wide range of measures, including focusing the Cyber Division on intrusions into computers and networks—as opposed to crimes committed with a computer as a modality hiring additional computer scientists to assist with technical investigations in the field; and expanding partnerships and collaboration at the NCIJTF. In addition, after more than a decade of combating cyber crime through a nationwide network of interagency task forces, the FBI has evolved its Cyber Task Forces in all 56 field offices to focus exclusively on cyber security threats.

At the NCIJTF—which serves as a coordination, integration, and information sharing centre for 19 U.S. agencies and several key international allies for cyber threat investigations—we are coordinating at an unprecedented level. This coordination involves senior personnel at key agencies. NCIJTF, which is led by the FBI, now has deputy directors from the NSA, DHS, the Central Intelligence Agency, U.S. Secret Service, and U.S. Cyber Command. In the past year, three of our Five Eyes international partners joined us at the NCIJTF: Australia embedded a liaison officer in May 2013, the U.K. in July 2013, and Canada in January 2014. By developing partnerships with these and other nations, NCIJTF is working to become the international leader in synchronizing and maximizing investigations of cyber adversaries.

Private Sector Outreach

In addition to strengthening our partnerships in government and law enforcement, we recognize that to effectively combat the cyber threat, we must significantly enhance our collaboration with the private sector. Our nation's companies are the primary victims of cyber intrusions, and their networks contain the evidence of countless attacks. In the past, industry has provided us information about attacks that have occurred, and we have investigated the attacks—but we have not always provided information back.

To remedy that, the Cyber Division has established a Key Partnership Engagement Unit (KPEU) to manage a targeted outreach program focused on building relationships with key private sector corporations. The unit works to share sector-specific threat information with our corporate partners.

We have provided a series of classified briefings for key sectors, including financial services and energy, to help them repel intruders.

Through the FBI's InfraGard program, the FBI develops partnerships and working relationships with private sector, academic, and other public-private entity subject matter experts. Primarily geared toward the protection of critical national infrastructure, InfraGard promotes ongoing dialogue and timely communication among a current active membership base of more than 25,000.

InfraGard members are encouraged to share information with government that better allows government to prevent and address criminal and national security issues. Active members are able to report cyber intrusion incidents in real-time to the FBI through iGuardian, which is based on our successful counterterrorism reporting system known as Guardian.

Just last month, the FBI deployed a malware repository and analysis system called Malware Investigator to our domestic and foreign law enforcement partners and members of the U.S. Intelligence Community. The system allows users to submit malware directly to the FBI and quickly receive technical information about the samples to its users so they can understand how the malware works. It also enables the FBI to obtain a global view of the malware threat. Beyond technical reporting, Malware Investigator identifies correlations that will allow users to "connect the dots" by highlighting instances in which malware was deployed in seemingly unrelated incidents.

The FBI's Cyber Initiative and Resource Fusion Unit (CIRFU) maximizes and develops intelligence and analytical resources received from law enforcement, academia, international, and critical corporate private sector subject matter experts to identify and combat significant actors involved in current and emerging cyber-related criminal and national security threats. CIRFU's core capabilities include a partnership with the National Cyber Forensics and Training Alliance (NCFTA) in Pittsburgh, Pennsylvania, where the unit is collocated with CIRFU. NCFTA acts as a neutral platform through which the unit develops and maintains liaison with hundreds of formal and informal working partners who share real-time threat information and best practices and collaborate on initiatives to target and mitigate cyber threats domestically and abroad.

The FBI recognizes that industry collaboration and coordination are critical in our combating the cyber threat effectively. As part of our enhanced private sector outreach, we have begun to provide cleared industry partners with classified threat briefings and other information and tools to better help them repel intruders.

Counterterrorism and Other Threats

Though the cyber threat is one of the FBI's top priorities, combating terrorism remains our top investigative priority. As geopolitical conflict zones continue to emerge throughout many parts of the world, terrorist groups may use this instability to recruit and incite acts of violence.

The continuing violence in both Syria and Iraq and the influx of foreign fighters threatens to destabilize an already volatile region while also heightening the threat to the West. Due to the prolonged nature and the high visibility of the Syrian conflict, we are concerned that U.S. persons with an interest in committing jihad will be drawn to the region. We can address this issue more fully in the closed session.

CYBERCRIME & CYBERTERRORISM: INDUCING ANXIETY & FEAR ON INDIVIDUALS

"Cyberterrorism is also clearly an emerging threat. Terrorist groups are increasingly computer savvy, and some probably are acquiring the ability to use cyber attacks to inflict isolated and brief disruptions of US infrastructure. Due to the prevalence of publicly available hacker tools, many of these groups probably already have the capability to launch denial-of-service and other nuisance attacks against Internet-connected systems. As terrorists become more computer savvy, their attack options will only increase."

This is what Robert Mueller, FBI Director, testified on 11 February 2003 before the US Senate on a hearing about *War On Terrorism* against Al-Qaeda and other terrorist organizations. The US and global media organizations picked up this testimony and begun speculating on the possibility of a large-scale Cyberterrorist attack. So far, such an attack has not materialised. At the same time a similar term, Cybercrime, is used to describe criminal activities on the Internet such as identity theft, copyright infringement and bank fraud, but many times these two terms (Cybercrime and Cyberterrorism) end up been used inter-changeably and their meaning, especially to the public, becomes blurred and unclear. Governments, policy networks and the media around the globe have engaged in an effort to build defences against Cyberattacks, bring new regulations in effect while maintaining an almost mythological atmosphere over the threats and risks of potential Cybercrime and Cyberterrorist attacks.

This essay will explore the concepts of Cybercrime and Cyberterrorism, how such acts are portrayed in the media and the government policies that come in effect. The focus will be on*how all these processes affect people's psychology* in regards to induced feelings of anxiety and fear and *not* the illegal activities themselves. In essence the essay aims to investigate Furedi's statement that "what we already fear can now thrive in the new space provided by the Internet".

Firstly, the terms *Cybercrime* and *Cyberterrorism* will be analysed and defined, in an effort to identify how they have been used over the past years, what are their similarities, differences and incorrect usages. Secondly, the two terms will be analysed in regards to real events of Cybercrime and Cyberterrorism and how such events lead to new government policy. The third part investigates how all these affect the psychology of the public and look into how individuals and groups have reacted in such cases. Finally, the last part aims to identify some potential solutions to the problem.

Defining Cybercrime and Cyberterrorism

As the global reach of the Internet keeps growing, its effect on all areas of online human endeavour becomes more pervasive. Individuals or groups can exploit the anonymity afforded by cyberspace to engage in illegal or illicit activities that aim to intimidate, harm, threaten or cause fear to citizens, communities, organizations or countries. The virtual and physical distance between the attacker and the victim and the difficulty in tracing back the attack to an individual minimizes the inherent threat of capture to the attacker. But how are such activities defined? What is a Cybercrime and what are its characteristics? How can a Cyberterrorist be identified and what are his or her differences from a Cybercriminal? So far, the definitions for Cybercrime and Cyberterrorism in literature, government documents and everyday use have been highly varied, context-specific and emotionally loaded, which makes discourse on the subject difficult. The FBI alone has published three distinct definitions of Cyberterrorism: "Terrorism that initiates...attack[s] on information" in 1999, to "the use of Cyber tools" in 2000 and "a criminal act perpetrated by the use of computers" in 2004.". Cybercrime and Cyberterrorism have been used to describe online acts such as:

- o Black-hat hacking / Cracking
- o Child sex offences (pornography and grooming)
- o Crimes in virtual worlds
- o Cyberactivism / Hacktivism
- o Virus writing and malware
- o Cyberstalking
- o Identity theft / Fraud
- o Illegal financial transactions / Money laundering
- o Copyright infringement
- o Serious acts of cyberbullying
- o Denial of service attacks
- o Rogue bot-nets

Cyberterrorism usually has a stronger meaning than Cybercrime, describing acts that have similar characteristics to real-world terrorism attacks, but not always. On the other hand,

Cybercrime is often used as a catch-all term to describe illegal, harmful and/or hostile activity on the Internet (including Cyberterrorism). Furthermore, other terms are sometimes used to describe similar illicit online acts, which complicate things even more, and their use is typically dependant on the context or the person/organisation that uses them. For example, a spokesperson within the military is likely to use the term Cyberwarfare to describe hostile online acts between two countries and/or acts of terrorism that originate from another country and are manifested online (instead of using the term Cyberterrorism).

Before attempting to define Cyberterrorism and Cybercrime one has to reflect on the validity of the two terms. Taipale (2010) has argued that "Cyberterrorism, whatever it is, is a useless term" and he believes that, "terrorists will use any strategic tool they can" so Cyberterrorism is no more important than other forms. A similar argument could be made for Cybercrime, as Wall (2008) says, "Cybercrime is relatively meaningless by itself because it is mainly a fictional construction that has no original reference point in law, science or social action.". However, the term is gradually gaining ground in formal legal discourse due to new legislation in many countries such as Australia (Cybercrime Act 2001), Nigeria (Draft Cybercrime Act), the United States (proposed Cybercrime Act 2007) and the UK (the Home Office introduced its Cybercrime Strategy in March 2010). An additional layer of complexity is added when one looks at the legal systems of different countries and their varied definitions of unlawful acts. It is not unusual for what one country defines as a criminal offence to merely be a civil wrong in another. The problem arises when an individual is the receiver of news about a Cyberterrorist attack in a foreign country, that would only be characterised as a hacking attempt or an Cyberactivism protest in his or her own country, and vice versa. It is thus likely that a person can manifest unwarranted feelings of fear, insecurity, anxiety or panic, along with a general confusion on how to interpret the news.

Recent History

Until the late nineties, interest on Cyberterrorism was quite low with Cybercrime making the news sparingly, mainly on accounts of computer hacking and cracking incidents. As 2000 approached, catastrophic scenarios based on the *millennium bug* (a flaw in the way computers used to store dates) started to circulate in the news and there was some activity on the state level to prevent any unwanted side-effects from the bug. Although the millennium bug did not turn out to be as devastating as many were speculating at the time, it did introduce a new kind of fear into people's minds. The fear that technology and manipulation of technological means (the Internet) by mal-intended individuals or groups can have a negative impact in their livelihoods. No matter how significant the millennium bug's impact was on people's lives, it pales in comparison to the aftermath of the terrorist attacks in the United States on September 11, 2001.

Shortly after the attacks, the US government announced its plan to initiate a *War on Terror*, (including war on Cyberterrorism). The mainstream media made extensive use of these two peculiar words (*war* and *terror*), for an effort that was supposedly aiming to help citizens feel safer, on a daily basis in order to inform citizens on the new potential threats. Such alleged threats included large scale Cyberattacks that would use computer networks to infiltrate critical infrastructures, aiming to endanger human lives or disrupt financial transactions and bring the country to a halt. Although, again, the front on Cyberterrorism has failed to materialise an attack of this magnitude, the *War on Terror* campaign was the point in time when Cyberterrorism was established as a new potential threat into the minds of people, mainly in the US, but also across the world. With the attention that War on Terror got from the public, the level of speculation on potential Cyberterrorism scenarios grew significantly to a point where some authors claimed that even nuclear meltdowns or chemical plant explosions were possible. Such claims are built on the basis of non-falsifiability, meaning if a predicted catastrophe fails to materialize it does not falsify the theory but merely shows that any security measures taken thus far are effective and/or that it is only a lucky coincidence and it is a matter of time for something unfortunate to happen. Such threats can be perceived as abstract, incomprehensible and uncontrollable, and generate longstanding fears in the public consciousness.

The Lipman Report (2010) states that "During 2009, a series of cyber attacks were launched against popular government Web sites in the United States and other countries, effectively shutting them down for several hours" and claims that "most disturbing is the possibility that this limited success may embolden future hackers to attack critical infrastructure, such as power generators or air-traffic control systems — with devastating consequences for the United States economy and national security". It is interesting to observe how a very trivial *Denial of Service* (DoS) attack is described as the predecessor of attacks on critical infrastructure, without any previous evidence to support the claim. Such attacks are placed under the heading "Cyber Warfare" in the report. The report goes on to describe Cyberterrorism threats that could possibly originate from Al Qaeda. In regards to Cybercrime the report claims that the annual cost of criminal activity is estimated at $1 trillion, but without providing relevant evidence. In essence, the report makes bold claims, presents huge numbers in dollars and goes from DoS attacked to Al Qaeda.

Such is the current state of affairs regarding Cyberterrorism and Cybercrime, that it is non-trivial for someone to fully understand the scope and implications of each term. This makes the public discourse on the subject and the process of legislation complicated for the stakeholders, the decision makers and for the public.

Policies, Regulations and Legal Actions towards Cybercrime and Cyberterrorism

Following the Cyberterrorism and Cybercrime incidents of the past two decades, there is now a push for stricter control and regulation on cyber activity. This push originates mainly from the United States but more countries are joining in the effort. In the following paragraphs some of the most recent acts aiming to combat Cybercrime and Cyberterrorism will be presented. In June 25th 2010, the United States government released to the public a draft version of an upcoming policy against Cybercrime, titled *National Strategy for Trusted Identities in Cyberspace: Creating Options for Enhanced Online Security and Privacy* (Department of Homeland Security, 2010). The draft reads:

"One key step in reducing online fraud and identity theft is to increase the level of trust associated with identities in cyberspace. While this Strategy recognizes the value of anonymity for many online transactions (e.g., blog postings), for other types of transactions (e.g., online banking or accessing electronic health records) it is important that the parties to that transaction have a high degree of trust that they are interacting with known entities."

Fundamentally, this policy will enable the US government to create verified online identities for its citizens in a closed identity ecosystem that will be backed by private corporations such as Verizon, Google, PayPal, Symantec and AT&T. Users will then be able to use one login to sign in to many websites that implement this functionality and their personal details will be retrieved from a central location maintained by the government. This proposed policy has created controversy over its effect on issues of privacy and anonymity on the web. The security of data is also crucial, as the personal information of all the participating citizens could be subject to a hacking attack. A similar attempt has been made by China with its *China Wide Web,* a country-wide intranet that is closed to outsiders.

Another Cybercrime-related effort of governments across the world is the shutting down of websites that link to or host copyrighted content using file sharing and peer-to-peer technologies. The most popular website that was involved in such a case is *The Pirate Bay,* a site that lets its users share files using the popular *torrent*technology. Legal activity against such sites is usually initiated by the music and movie industry and their methodology varies. In the Pirate Bay's case, the music industry moved against the owners of the site that are Swedish citizens. After a lengthy legal process in the Swedish courts, the website is still in operation and its owners although losing the first trials they are currently appealing an unfavourable for them court decision. But besides the outcome of that particular case, it is still unclear if the music industry will reap any benefits over the possible closure of the website or by imposing significant fines to its founders. Right after the move against the Pirate Bay many other new file sharing sites came to existence, while the view of many site users towards the music industry became quite negative.

Similar actions against torrent websites are going on across the world coming either by private firms or by governments, prompted by representatives from the music and movie industry.

Beyond the tactic of targeting the owners of popular file sharing site, a recent trend is the creation of private law firms that represent copyright owners and go after Internet Service Providers (ISPs) and individual users, trying to make them stop sharing files or face significant fines. By sending mass lawsuits the copyright holders are trying to obtain the personal details of Torrent users who allegedly shared their material online. Once this information is handed over, they then offer the defendant the opportunity to settle the case for a few hundred dollars, thereby avoiding a full trial. This policy has been characterised as remarkable and unprecedented, as the business model behind this practice is to make money simply by threatening people to "pay up or else". Significant controversy has been raised over this issue and courts in the UK have questioned the way such firms operate, as in the case of ACS Law.

There have been many incidents where innocent individuals have been targeted and been sent warning letters, in essence putting them in defence where they have to prove their innocence and not the other way around. As in the case of the Pirate Bay and besides the fact that people might share copyrighted material in an illegal way or not, it is worth noting the effect that such acts have on the psychology of individuals. How people's online behaviour is affected and whether they choose to conform or protest is a matter that has to be further studied and investigated.

Until recently, it was understood that when an organisation of government body wanted to take action against a website that used to facilitate illegal activity, they moved legally against the owner(s) of the website, its ISP or its users. Recently, the United States homeland security, in an unprecedented move, took back ownership of many.com domain names that were used to host sites that facilitated illegal activity. Domain names ending in.com are regulated by the US-based Internet Corporation for Assigned Names and Numbers (ICANN) organisation. In November 2010 the U.S. Immigration and Customs Enforcement (ICE) seized 82 website domains involved in selling counterfeit goods as part of *Cyber Monday crackdown* operation (U.S. Immigration and Customs Enforcement, 2010), and made the following announcement on their website:

"As of today – what is known as 'Cyber Monday' and billed as the busiest online shopping day of the year – anyone attempting to access one of these websites using its domain name will no longer be able to make a purchase. Instead, these online shoppers will find a banner notifying them that the website's domain name has been seized by federal authorities (U.S. Immigration and Customs Enforcement, 2010)."

This action created uproar in the file sharing community and lead to various reactions from users and site owners. Many file sharing websites simply changed their domain name from one that ends in.com to others that end in.me,.tv and.info that are regulated by other countries in order to avoid having their website seized by the US government. Some website owners that had their site seized, started a legal process against that action. The question still remains on how effective such aggressive measures are and what is their effect on the behaviour of individuals.

Psychology of Individuals

According to a 2007 study commissioned by security software makers AVG of more than 1,400 regular Internet users, Cybertheft is the UK's most feared crime, outranking burglary, assault and robbery. The study found that 87% of the participants were worried about the threat of Cybertheft, 33% were not convinced they had adequate measures in place to protect themselves, while 25% said there was not enough information available on Cybertheft to protect themselves effectively.

That leaves a significant percentage of people (62%) that although can find enough information to protect themselves, they are still inherently worried about the threat of Cybertheft. Furedi (2002) and others have portrayed the general culture of fear as a type of psychological fear of fear (Phobophobia), which can lead to stress, intense anxiety and unrealistic and persistent public fear of crime and danger, regardless of the actual presence of such fear factors. Garland (2002) describes this phenomenon as the *crime complex,* a societal state where public anxiety about crime is the norm and has been imprinted in people's everyday lives as an established and expected societal aspect.

News reporting by the mainstream media has a tendency to feed the sensation seeking public with shocking information, while also feeding off it. Baudrillard describes this as a "dizzying whirl of reality", the continuous desire for sensationalism that blurs reality with rhetoric; reality being 'what is actually happening' and rhetoric being 'what could happen'.

To this extend, relatively insignificant events can sparkle significant reactions and have a considerable impact upon public perception, even more so when they trigger panics and moral panics. Such irrational social inferences are documented in the field of Social Psychology as the base-rate fallacy or base-rate neglect.

"Base-rate information is general information, usually factual and statistical, about an entire class of events". In the case of media reporting on Cybercrime or Cyberterrorism, individual reported incidents tend to be perceived as a stereotypical representation of the current status quo in Cyberspace and are not taken within the context and scope that they occurred.

In a 2003 survey 49% of US citizens said that they were afraid of Cyberassaults on key parts of the US economy. Lack of control over a situation that is perceived as threatening or dangerous gives rise to feelings of emotional distress, fear and insecurity. Such strong emotions can inhibit flexible thinking and lead to irrational behaviour or other equally strong reactions. The effects of Cybercrime and Cyberterrorism related discourse and the induced fear in the public can be seen by acts such as the need more laws to protect them against illegal cyber activity and the giving away of their own privacy in exchange for better security. In a 2001 survey of United States citizens, such trends were identified. 62% of the respondents said that new laws need to be written just for the Internet to protect their email and online activities, and 57% approved the Federal Bureau of Investigation (FBI) to intercept email over the Internet to and from people suspected of criminal activities. At the same time 62% of the citizens surveyed said that they trust their government to do what is right only *some* of the time. When asked how much, if at all, have they heard about an existing computer system known as *Carnivore,* which allows the FBI to intercept email messages sent or received by people suspected of criminal activities, 77% said that they knew nothing at all.

The Way Forward

Cybercrime and Cyberterrorism are two issues that are likely to continue to exist for many years to come and they surely must be dealt with. But this process needs to be done in a way that will ensure the growth of the Internet in an inclusive and open way, maintaining the fundamental principles that it has been built upon. One of the principal issues is the disambiguation of the terms Cybercrime and Cyberterrorism. Government bodies, policy networks, scholars, the media and the people need to engage in a global conversation that will help demythologize Cybercrime and define what constitutes a Cybercrime and how Cybercriminals should be dealt with.

Cyberterrorism should be decoupled from Cybercrime and be specified in realistic terms, as to what are the probable threats of a Cyberterrorist act and to what extend society should go to face such effects. After these two terms have been clearly and unambiguously defined, people will be much better equipped to receive and comprehend related news and policies, and will be able to engage in a meaningful discourse over the subject. This will help alleviate unwarranted fears while at the same time enable individuals to make informed decisions when considering a new proposed policy by weighing its pros versus the cons and its effects on multiple levels, long and short term, instead of giving-in to fear and forfeiting their privacy and online freedom for better security.

The role of the media (television, blogs, online news outlets and more) is critical in the process of educating the public and engaging in a conversation, as they will be the mediators and curators of information and discourse on the issue. Thus, a concise and sensible approach, devoid of fear-mongering and shock practices, should be followed. Since this is an international issue, governments and policy networks across the world have to come together and discuss openly on what is better for their citizens. Scholars and academics can provide valuable expertise on technological, psychological, ethical and other issues, while highlighting any misgivings by those involved in the process.

The people in their local communities, families and social networks should help and train each other to increase their peers' level of Internet literacy and highlight the advantages of the web. A higher Internet literacy level can help people protect themselves even better by taking simple security measures, such as using anti-virus software and identifying potential risks or scams in their online financial transactions.

6

Cyber Crime in Global Perspective

CYBER-CRIME AND LEGAL PROBLEMS OF USAGE NETWORK THE INTERNET

The most significant social changes during the last decades have occurred in the sphere of new social relations - informational. The essence of transfer from the industrial to informational society is the aggregate of processes related to automated processing, search, storage and transmission of increasing flow of information into all spheres of social life.

This has increased the need in legal regulation of relationship in the sphere telecommunication systems in order to speed up the processes of informatization of Ukrainian society and catching up to other countries.

Together with the development of global Internet network and formation of new economic technologies (trading through virtual stores, broker operations, cyber-banks, etc.) the new types of crime have appeared (cyber-crime). Cyber-crime and its sequences are the new form of anti-social behavior, which only recently has been acknowledged as phenomenon, which is dangerous for safety and normal functioning of the society. According to the domestic and foreign specialists' assessments, the resolution of the problems of prevention and investigation of crimes of this type is rather complicated task for the law enforcement agencies, because only 10% of disclosed crimes in the sphere of computer information can be detected in time, and 90% are detected accidentally. The indicated data evidences high level of latency of such types of crimes. The state and commercial structures affected are not inclined to announce the sequences of such acts. Partially, this is confirmed by statistic data in our country. According to the data of the Department of Operative Information of MIA of Ukraine in 1997 under the article 198. On Violation of the Work of Automated Systems» of the Criminal Code of Ukraine (CC) 12 criminal cases were opened, and in 1998 - 15. The indicated data witnesses complication of this category of crimes investigation, as well as imperfection of organization-legal protection of information in computer systems.

Term "cyber-crime" is young and created by combination of two words: cyber and crime. The term "cyber" means the cyber-space (terms "virtual space", "virtual world" are used more often in literature) and means (according to the definition in "New hacker vocabulary" by Eric S. Raymond) the informational space modeled through computer, in which defined types of objects or symbol images of information exist – the place where computer programs work and data is processed. The term "cyber-crime" is not by chance put in quotes and its further use requires certain explanation. The thing is, that cyber-crime is not covered by CC of Ukraine currently in force, therefore this term will be used without quotes as social phenomenon well-known all around the world.

From the moment of announcement of Ukraine state independence the national system of the laws and normative legal acts is being created for legal regulation of social informational relationship and informatization process, taking into account the speed of its development and penetration into different spheres of social activity.

In order to regulate the informational relationship on the state level it is necessary to determine the most important legal norms of its participants acts, including preventing and combating the offences, related to use of the global Internet network. In turn, this conditioned the necessity of separating and establishing the section in the national law, named today as "computer law", which goal is to implement the state policy in the conditions of stabilization and development of the country's informatization: creation of information resources, their turn over and distribution, consuming, storage and protection, etc.

Term "computer law" appeared in industrially developed countries in the middle of our century in connection with wide introduction of calculation machinery means and other related technical means into different spheres of social activity, private life and formation of the relationship, which appear in the production process and using of new information technologies.

The appropriate legislation is developed quite quickly, trying to take into account the development of the computer technology and telecommunication systems, but, naturally, is not catching up due to reasonable conservatism, which anticipates appearing of new legal mechanisms upon accumulation of certain "critical mass" of legal relationship requiring regulation.

In Ukraine similar legislation is named "legislation in the sphere of informatization", which covers — according to different assessments — from 50 to 250 normative acts (including acts providing for creation of branch or specialized automated systems).

Analysis of domestic normative-legal base directed to regulation of the relationship in the sphere of informatization and endurance of information protection, allows to conclude that it is on its initial stage. The regime of legitimacy is also on the stage of establishing in this sphere of normative – legal regulation. The establishment of legitimacy regime in this case means the aggregation of socially conditioned processes related to development and adoption of legal norms as well as implementing means for its accurate and steady execution and adherence.

For further analysis of these problems, let's consider certain legal aspects of using global Internet network. In contemporary conditions Internet is catalyst for many negative phenomenon, the social danger of which requires additional attention and research. Besides that, if consider Internet from legal point of view, we can conclude that the subjects of these new social relations face the range of legal issues, which require prompt resolution. Among basic generally theoretic issues, it is necessary to determine the problems of network jurisdiction, legal relations between the subjects, which distribute and consume information within the network, as well as the problem of determining the time and place of action within Internet.

Analyzing the mechanisms of Internet action and ways of presenting and distributing information the unique special legal problems appear, which does not have any analog. First of all, these are problems of electronic commerce regulation. They include concluding contracts through Internet, advertising, problem of Internet entrepreneurs' taxation, etc.

The next group of legal problems is copy right problems, which appear when the issues of using information or referring to information received through the network are interpreted by different ways under Ukraine legislation and legislation's of other foreign countries.

The trade marks issue is also disputable, including well-known dilemma: trade mark – domain name, as well as the issue of abuses upon domain registrations (cybersquatting). Currently, a lot of court cases are opened (in Western countries) on this network problem.

Very important Internet problem is to define the liability of providers and site owners for content of information, located on their servers. Several countries have already adopted certain specific normative acts regulating such relationship, and law enforcement practice has obvious national differentiation, which is contradictory to international character of the Internet.

Another group of legal relationship reflecting peculiarity of the problem is many-sided issues of information protection, which include coding, data access protection, privacy protection. This group is related to issues of moral and censorship (of private and network social groups, as well as state and organizations).

It can, therefore, be concluded that currently in Ukraine and in the entire world as well, the new branch of the law is being established – the law of using the global informational Internet network.

Of course, the objects of legal regulation of Internet are, first of all, social relationships related to copy right, patent right, trade marks and personal non-property rights, to the extent to which the information, located in the Internet can affect it, then, the objects of legal regulation are other property relationship, realized through Internet (for instance, those, related to international contracts conclusion or settlements of international disputes through Internet) — all of it, to our opinion, can be determined as information, which use is regulated by the law. The detailed description of the objects of legal regulation in the Internet is the same as list of all types of social relationship realized through Internet.

Nowadays, when people realize the importance of possession of accurate and actual information for the work in any sphere, the information industry related to modern information technologies is coming foreground. Using Internet now it is possible to get access to official as well as scientific resources through official sites. The Organization of United Nations and European Union provide direct access to officially published documents of these organizations, information notes and bulletins, not depending on where the user is located. Teleconferences open absolutely new opportunities to exchange opinions and obtain information directly from the source in the regime of real time. There is now new branch of production – information industry, which is developed according to general rules, but also has certain peculiarities. Besides that, generally accepted human rights and freedoms, which do not depend on pertaining to certain country, are becoming more important as well as endurance of these human rights.

As practice shows, in Ukraine there is lack of attention to the issues of legal regulation of using the telecommunication systems in general and the Internet related law in particular. This is conditioned by low level of development of technical communication means, telecommunication infrastructure and enterprises of this sphere. However, the interest to this branch of the law is continuously increasing together with willing to implement and use new information technologies.

The legal relationship in the sphere of telecommunication is new and quite wide term. This sphere is regulated by the state law as well as international norms. Upon development of technique, the information systems of different states start to contact each other and, therefore, the part of international legal regulation should increase, so the international cooperation is necessary in the sphere of transmission and distribution of information.

The issue of legal regulation of telecommunication systems using occupies one of the important places abroad. As an example, let's consider the Internet pages (as of today they are the most accessible object for research) the general, popular, as well as specific legal resources, always contain telecommunication section.

Article 19 of the General Declaration of Human Rights provides for freedom of search, obtaining and distribution of information and ideas by any means and not depending on state borders. Meaning of this provision is difficult to overestimate. Recently, when information technologies provide more opportunities, the people's need in information becomes as much important as need in property and other benefits. That is why the provisions of Declaration should be considered as starting point for international regulation of relationship, connected to transmission of the information between the states. The main task of the international legal regulation in this sphere is organization of cooperation between the states and coordination of their efforts in global information exchange.

In order to resolve many issues of the international legal regulation in this sphere, it is necessary to conduct the scientific research of the telecommunication systems international law problems when as an aggregate of legal principles, norms and rules regulating the relationship between the states and international organizations. The issue of the international legal regulation of telecommunications in its nature and content is an integral part of the international law. It is created by the subjects of the international law in accordance to general rules of creation of international law norms taking into account the peculiarities of the new information technologies and information exchange needs of the society.

Legal regulation of telecommunications is quite wide term, which is used in different scientific spheres, sometimes in different meanings. However, for international legal regulation it is necessary to give general meaning of telecommunication systems.

On our opinion, the definition given in the Law of Ukraine "On the National Informatization Program" is appropriate: information – telecommunication system includes high-speed and ordinary communication channels, distributed and local networks of different level and purpose, which gives the possibility to realize wide range of information technologies, provides for operative and reliable cooperation of all levels of management in resolution of interagency level issues, as well as provides wide range of information services to population, state and commercial organizations, foreign users..

With development of the international law the discussions about systemizing always occur, touching the grounds of separation of branches of the law and their precise frames and characteristics. Within the branch framework the sub-sections and legal institutions are separated. In this respect there is an issue arising about the place of telecommunication international law in the international law system in general. At present moment it is, perhaps, necessary to describe the telecommunication international law as legal institution, which includes the norms of different branches of the international law: international space law, international sea law,international air law (related to joint use of the resources); international economic law, regulation of scientific-technical progress (related to international cooperation on economic and technical development). However, in the future, taking into consideration the development of technical progress and cooperation in communication sphere, it is absolutely possible that telecommunication international law will be separated as independent branch of the law.

Considering this problem, it should be mentioned that there are different – traditional and new, revolutionary for us, as well – approaches to this branch abroad. Example of such approach is the work of Darrell Mente, where he considers the result of telecommunication development as new reality, which should influence development of the law system, including international law. We consider, that such research deserve attention, first of all, because they come beyond practice and take into account new achievements of industrially developed countries technology. The essence of approach described in Darrel Mente's work is the following:as the result of creation of telecommunication network and their active use the unified global information space will be created. Significant problems appear in connection with determination of states' jurisdiction within this information space. In order to overcome these problems the international legal regulation of this telecommunication space is necessary. Discussing these problems there is made parallel with legal regime of Arctic and Antarctic, which do not belong to any country, with other international resources. Therefore, it is impossible to mention only one general problem, which is reflected by international law.

Considering criminal – legal aspects of using the Internet, related to appearing and expansion of the new types of crimes, it is necessary to note, that their analysis allows to divide them into two groups. First of which is related to participation of the employees of most affected organizations in criminal activity.

The second group includes attempts of unauthorized access to telecommunication systems from outside, using remote attacks and other methods. In these cases, cyber – criminals can attack the system only from generally accessible global networks and use methods which are difficult to combat without their knowledge. However, neither in domestic nor in foreign literature available for public, the analysis of concrete cases of penetration into computer systems, unfortunately, was not properly described. The reasons of that are: organizations which face the thief of means, damage or disclosure of their data, and cases of blocking their services as the result of cyber – criminal acts, are not interested in disclosing or publication of such reports.

Cyber – crimes that became transnational, force the research of adequate ways of combating. The increase of these negative phenomenon is, on our opinion, conditioned by the following unsettled issues:

- vulnerability and dependence of computer systems within global Internet network. With increased dependence of the society on computer technique and telecommunications systems, the risk of damage of the new technology as the result of criminal acts is significantly increasing. The expansion of computer viruses and program bookmarks once more underlining this danger. However, these cases are just symptoms of serious disease;

- transnational character of cyber - crimes, effective means, directed to endurance the integrity of computer systems became vitally important for economic and social interests of developing countries as well as industrial countries;
- absence of liability. Many aspects cyber – crime in most cases is rather the sequence of week information protection than offenders acts. Therefore, it is necessary to give more information about vulnerability of computer systems and necessity of effective protection means;
- ineffectiveness of the Civil Code. Criminal laws should be supplemented with appropriate civil sanctions, because court cases on cyber – crime are the most responsible procedure due to difficulty of proving and may not fall within traditional legal frames;
- imperfection of the legislation and absence of international cooperation. Great use of Internet significantly surpass the level of development of the national and international social and legal norms, which regulate the sphere of information protection;
- enforcement of criminal sanctions does not ensure the success in combating the cyber - crime, because the laws currently in force does not have precise classification and difficulty of interpretation and application of articles restrict the law enforcement agencies activity. The necessary mechanism of ensuring activities and cooperation of the law enforcement agencies for proper detection and punishment of cyber – crime is not yet developed.

The absence of certain international agreements affects the normal functioning of the law enforcement agencies, taking into consideration the following:

- criminal cases related to cyber – crime may fall within several jurisdiction. Proving that the crime has been committed stays the most difficult component of investigation, since experienced offenders cover their tracks, going through the justice system, especially in those countries which refuse to cooperate while collecting evidences;

- even if quite reliable elements of crime where detected in separate country, i.e. evidence exists, this country may not have the necessary jurisdiction to prosecute the offender;
- the country having jurisdiction may appear not properly authorized in prosecution of the offender, if s/he lives in the other country, which does not have legislation which provides for extradition of offenders in such cases;
- even there, where prosecution of offenders succeeded, the courts makes nominal sentences.

Complex resolution of the indicated problems is current urgent need, their resolution will allow to overcome most risks, and will condition the prevention, detection and criminal prosecution of virtual offenders.

Notwithstanding the fact that in our country there are many other urgent problems necessary to resolve, the problem of combating the cyber – crime can not be put out of attention.

It is necessary to develop methodological, theoretical and practical basis for information protection within global Internet network.

Almost all relationship between the subjects of the information society will base on consuming and exchange of information. In this case the issue of information protection will became priority. Development of the legal regulation of using Internet in our country must be directed to foreign experience as well as national interests of Ukraine in informational sphere.

Special attention should be attracted to detection and research of defects in order to avoid them further in law-making and law enforcement activity and to prevent negative sequences of informatization. This should be realized by way of scientific approach, involving wide circle of domestic specialists, who possess knowledge of legal theory and practice of Ukraine and foreign countries as well having certain background in the sphere of information technology and information protection.

ORGANIZATION-LEGAL PROBLEMS PREVENTION OF TRANSNATIONAL COMPUTER CRIME

The global network Internet, comprising mullions of computers, Internet, provides unheard-of opportunities to communicate and obtain information and is increasingly used for criminal purposes.

The advent of electronic money and virtual banks, exchanges, and shops, which, however, supply real services and commodities, is just one factor promoting new crime - "transnational computer crimes". Today, together with traditional activity, law-enforcement agencies face new types of crime – "cyber crimes".

Cyber crimes is a new and unusual concept to law-enforcement agencies, but criminal activities, involving Internet are the most dangerous to society. And it many states already have understood.

The transnational nature of network crime suggests that the development of common policies on key issues should be part of any control strategy. Such common policies are important to prevent the occurrence of "legal havens" in jurisdictions where certain activities have not been criminalized, for example.

In the United States, for example, Presidential Decision Directive 63 (a white paper on critical infrastructure protection) states, "Addressing these vulnerabilities will necessarily require flexible, evolutionary approaches that span both the public and private sectors, and protect both domestic and international security. ... The Federal Government shall encourage international cooperation to help manage this increasingly global problem".

In the Decree of the President of Ukraine [1] 928/2000 from July 31, 2000 Is told, that an overall objective of development of a national global network Internet in Ukraine is the decision of tasks of information safety of our state and perfection of legal regulation of activity of the subjects of the information relations, amplification of the responsibility for computer crimes.

Certainly, as all other types of offences, cyber crime presents great threat for people and the extent of such threat, to our opinion, is not fully recognized and evaluated by the society. However, that insignificant existing experience in this sphere, not to mention the experience of leading countries of the world, obviously shows the doubtless vulnerability of any state. Moreover, the transnational computer crime is not limited by state borders and criminal is equally capable to threat the information systems located practically in any place of the world.

This crimes, as a rule, are extraordinary and often present irresolvable problem for legislation in force. Special concern is problem of investigation the crime, which tracks and evidences have been erased or terminated by computer criminals. Other peculiarity of cyber crime, making its investigation even more difficult, is the use of small-sized satellite systems communications, so such crime may be committed significantly far from the object of offence within seconds. However, investigation of such crimes may take weeks, even months, giving criminal the destroy traces of a crime and to avoid punishment.

For the last few years transnational crimes have achieved menacing measures. As professor Louisa Shelley mentioned, "Transnational organized crimes will become one of the main problems governments will face in the 21st century. It will be the crucial problem for the 21st century, as the cold war for the 20th and colonialism for the 19th centuries".

In the Viennese declaration "About criminality and justice: the answers to the challenges of the 21st century" which was adopted in Vienna at the Tenth Congress of the Organization of the United Nations, 10-17 April,2000, there was also expressed concern about transnational organized crimes and intercoupling between various kinds of them.

Due to the prompt development of information technologies on the basis of Internet network the geographical obstacles which for a long time restrained the growth of crimes of this kind have disappeared. Today, transnational crimes connected with the use of the global Internet network occupy a significant share in the total volume of criminal offences. Their growth and development are promoted by the very nature of this kind of crimes characterized by availability of the Internet network and impunity of the offences because of inadequate preparation of law-enforcement agencies in investigating such crimes.

To a certain extent, one of the factors promoting the increase of this new kind of crimes is the absence of proper interaction within law-enforcement agencies while preventing and investigating such crimes.

The efficiency of prevention and investigation of cyber crimes depends much on co-ordinated international approach to the problem at different levels. At the state level there is required a well prepared staff, as well as modification of national legislation aimed at creating legal base to provide with law-enforcement agencies as well as judicial authorities dealing with offences in information sphere and transnational computer crimes. At the interstate level investigation of cyber crimes requires coordinated efforts of national centers dealing with cyber crimes with similar international centers in other countries.

In order to regulate informational relations at the state level, there appeared a demand to set legal norms for their participants so that to make it possible to confront crimes related to global Internet network.

While interested countries have considered the problems arising from cyber crimes, there has not been much attention paid to it at the interstate level. Reasons for the lack of attention to cyber crimes may include relatively low levels of participation in international electronic communication, low levels of law-enforcement experience and low estimations of the damage to society expected to occur from electronic crimes.

In global computer Internet network, the criminal policy of one State has a direct influence on the international community. Cyber criminals may direct their electronic activities through a particular State where that behaviour is not criminal and thus be protected by the law of that country.

Even if a State has no particular national interest in criminalizing certain behaviour, it may consider doing so in order to avoid becoming a "legal root" and isolating itself internationally. The harmonization of substantive criminal law with regard to cyber crimes is essential if international cooperation is to be achieved between law-enforcement and judicial authorities of different States.

One of significant steps directed on settlement of this problem was the adoption by the Council of Europe, April 24, 2000 of "Draft Convention On Cyber Crime".

Time has come to take action, and the Council of Europe released a Draft Convention to deal with crime in cyberspace. This document provisionally entitled "Draft Convention On Cyber Crime" (further "Draft") will be the first international treaty to address criminal law and procedural aspects of various types of similar misuse. The draft provides, among others, for the coordinated criminalization of computer hacking and hacking devices, illegal interception of data and interference into the work of computer systems connected with fraud and forgery.

Considering organization-legal aspects of struggle with cyber-crime, it is possible to give some tentative estimation of this document and his international importance for the decision of the problem. Conscious of the profound changes brought about by the digitalization, convergence and continuing globalization of computer Internet network, the effective fight against cyber-crime requires increased, rapid and well-functioning international co-operation in criminal matters. One by of the main conclusions, which is possible to make at the analysis of "Draft" it that, a common understanding has developed about which behaviour in relation to computer systems and networks should be criminalized.

First this providing for the criminalisation of such conduct, as described in this Convention, and the adoption of powers sufficient for effectively combating such criminal offences, by facilitating the detection, investigation and prosecution of such criminal offences at both the domestic and international level.

Secondly adoption Article 14 - "Search and Seizure of Stored Computer Data" enable one party to achieve conservation of the important information necessary for investigation of a crime, which is found in jurisdiction of other party. As far as know Internet service providers usually have traffic date from past communications, generated by equipment that records details including the time, duration and date of any communications, the parties involved and type of service or activity. Such data are generally kept for a limited period of time, depending of the commercial needs of the provider and legal or commercial requirements for privacy protection. Many national Laws allow law enforcement authorities or judicial authorities to order the collection of traffic data of future communications. In cases where traffic data is part of the communications, such as the "header information" of e-mail messages, however, the collection of such traffic data may be considered an interception of the communications itself and subject to legal restrictions on that basis.

Important the provision of "Draft" which enables shall take such legislative and other measures as may be necessary to empower its competent authorities to seize or similarly secure computer data, which are available at Internet service providers and are necessary for criminal investigation. The provisions of Article 16 – "Expedited preservation of data stored in a computer system" and Article 17 – "Expedited preservation and disclosure of traffic data" enables the law-enforcement agencies, for the purpose of criminal investigations or proceedings, the expeditious preservation of data that is stored by means of a computer system, at least where there are grounds to believe that the data is subject to a short period of retention or is otherwise particularly vulnerable to loss or modification.

Undoubtedly from the legal point of view the large importance have also common principles, concerning international cooperating. This questions of extradition cyber criminals, and basis in order to ensure the provision of immediate assistance for the purpose of the investigation of criminal offenses related to the use of computer systems and data, or for the collection of electronic evidence of any criminal offense.

To sum it up it should be emphasized, that with the extension of electronic networks, it is becoming less likely that all elements of a cyber crime will be restricted to a single national territory state. In investigations, law-enforcement authorities of different states will need to cooperate, both formally, mutual legal assistance in the frameworks of structures such as Interpol, and informally, by providing potentially useful information directly to the authorities of another State. Additional problems may arise with respect to legal assistance in the investigation international cyber crime. If a party has not provided specific powers to search for evidences in electronic environments under domestic law, it may not be able to respond to request for assistance. For this reason the harmonization of coercive powers is an important condition for international cooperation.

In spite the variety of issues, related to different aspects prevention of transnational computer crimes, on our opinion, the following basic problems could be defined, which should be immediately addressed within the framework of international cooperation:

1. Imperfection of the legislation in the sphere of combating transnational computer crime. Criminal sanctions on national and international level do not ensure good protection from computer crime, because of absence of precise clarification of computer crime in the laws or because difficulty of interpretation andapplication of these laws restricts the law enforcement activity. Therefore, policy and law makers should perform consequent activity on development of the new legal norms and relevant sanctions, creating necessary mechanism for law enforcement, judge and prosecution activity, which could prosecute and punish the guilty in computer crime.
2. Weak specialized professional training for officers of law enforcement agencies, related to prevention and investigation of transnational computer crime. Conducting the investigation measures, related to search, seizure and arresting the computer machinery has certain peculiarities. First, specially trained personnel able to duly conduct these actions is required.

   Second, upon the arrest of information the possibility of its modification and termination should be excluded. These actions should be conducted within minimum period of time, taking into account the speed of receiving the information. Third, careful analysis of the records about connections to Internet of the computer system should be made prior to arrest of this system. This is necessary for full procedure of conducting the measures on arrest and seizure of evidences. Therefore, conducting investigation and operative – search measures upon investigation of computer crime has certain range of peculiarities and requires special background.

3. There are no specialized response teams similar to CERT on the territory of Ukraine. The creation of special response teams on the territory of Ukraine is a most important task. If it is not solved in the nearest future, both informational networks of Ukraine and other countries may suffer.
4. Non-availability the coordinated criminalization of computer hacking and hacking devices, illegal interception of data and interference into the work of computer systems. Therefore the acceptance of " Convention On Cyber Crime" offered by the Council of Europe - will promote strengthening of the international cooperation in the prevention of transnational computer crimes.

   National limitation of legislation as well as the lack of a single international legal base can be considered as on of the main reasons of prompt increase of transnational computer crimes.

The growth of cyber crimes parallel with the weak legal over them turn into a certain vicious circle which could only be broken by the proper unity of criminal law strategies of struggle with crimes of this kind. And international cooperation should become an important constituent part of such strategy as it is obvious that it is practically impossible to control of transnational computer crimes at a level of separate states. These are problems to be urgently solved by international community in the sphere of struggle with cyber crimes on the threshold of the 21st century.

7

The Importance of Military Information Security in the East and the West

Make no mistake; information security is one of the most important military issues of the 21st century. Heavy reliance on computers by the U.S. and its allies for communications, vehicle control, surveillance, and signal processing makes it imperative for U.S. military forces to keep data secure from nations and groups hostile to our national interests.

Just to be clear, information security concerns the ability for the U.S. military to keep its computers and data networks safe from outside attempts to steal, eavesdrop, or corrupt vital defense and security information. It also refers to technologies designed to avoid the accidental corruption of mission-critical data, as well as maintaining U.S. ability to penetrate enemy information technologies in times of war.

Let's put information security in perspective. Almost every era has its defining military systems that help maintain a huge edge over adversaries. Many of the crucial battles of history involve the first or most decisive clashes of these leading-edge military systems.

Two of the defining weapon systems of World War I, for example, were the armored battleship and the machine gun. The battles of Jutland and the Somme chillingly demonstrated the capabilities of these weapon systems and the advantages they brought to those who used them. Later, World War II saw the aircraft carrier and the atomic bomb. The Battle of Midway, and the attack on Hiroshima, Japan, showed the significance of these weapon systems. Such crucial enabling military technologies and platforms can be traced back through history, and include the rifled musket of the American Civil War era, all the way back to the stirrup of ancient times that enabled humans for the first time to fight from horseback and wreak havoc on the soldiers who still fought only on foot. Today, the precision-guided munition and the unmanned vehicle perhaps are the defining military technologies of this era.

Now let's take a look forward. I believe the computer and the data network will be the aircraft carrier and atomic bomb of the future. If a nation can exploit its enemies' computers and data networks, then it clearly has the upper hand. Conversely, a nation that cannot safeguard its own computers and data networks has little chance of prevailing.

The criticality of U.S. information security was driven home early last month with reports of Chinese military technicians hacking into a Pentagon computer network. These computer incursions, which allegedly happened last June, were called some of the most successful cyber attacks ever on the U.S. Department of Defense.

Pentagon leaders admitted that they had to shut down part of the computer system serving the office of Defense Secretary Robert Gates to contain the damage. Reports place blame for the attack on the Chinese People's Liberation Army. There is little doubt that China will be among the chief military adversaries to the U.S. and its allies in the early to mid 21st century. U.S. intelligence reports made public last June indicate that China is covertly supplying large quantities of small arms and weapons to U.S. terrorist enemies in Iraq and Afghanistan. China, moreover, repeatedly demonstrates to the world that it is deadly serious about building and perfecting its capabilities in offensive and defense information warfare.

A clear cyber threat exists from a powerful nation that shows itself to be hostile to U.S national interests, and the U.S. has to be ready to meet this threat. This nation, moreover, must be better prepared to wage and defend information warfare with better capability than it has now.

Fortunately, U.S. military leaders are not standing still, and the U.S. Air Force is taking the lead. Sometime this fall Air Force leaders are expected to activate Air Force Cyberspace Command (AFCC), which will be attached to the 8th Air Force at Barksdale Air Force Base, La.

Military leaders define cyberspace as using electronics and the electromagnetic spectrum to store, modify, and exchange data via networked systems and related physical infrastructures. "Cyberspace is a domain that we need to defend, just like the air, land, and sea," says Lt. Gen. Robert J. Elder Jr., who will be the AFCC commander. The new Cyberspace Command will start with personnel from the 67th Network Warfare Wing, and receive support from the 8th Air Force. The intent is to create a major command that stands alongside Air Force Space Command and Air Combat Command to help preserve freedom of access and commerce where computers and computer networks are concerned.

The new command "is a recognition that what we do in the cyber realm is no longer an enabler for other operations; it actually is an operation itself," Elder says. "We'll be taking roles that are traditionally viewed as support functions, and those people will become the operators in cyberspace."

The Air Force has other information security projects in the works, as well. At Langley Air Force Base, Va., the Air Force has established the Global Cyberspace Integration Centre to serve as a test bed to evaluate software and information systems for their vulnerability to cyber attack.

The Air Force's initiatives in information security and information warfare are a solid start, but all the military services need to step up and take cyber security just as seriously as does the Air Force. The next large global conflicts will be unlike anything we've seen before, and information warfare will be a large-perhaps defining-component. U.S. military forces most likely will not have a second chance to get themselves ready.

INFORMATION TECHNOLOGY SECURITY

Security is a basic human concept that has become more difficult to define and enforce in the Information Age. In primitive societies, security was limited to ensuring the safety of the group's members and protecting physical resources, like food and water. As society has grown more complex, the significance of sharing and securing the important resource of information has increased. Before the proliferation of modern communications, information security was limited to controlling physical access to oral or written communications.

The importance of information security led societies to develop innovative ways of protecting their information. For example, the Roman Empire's military wrote sensitive messages on parchments that could be dissolved in water after they had been read. Military history provides another more recent example of the importance of information security. Decades after World War II ended, it was revealed that the Allies had gained an enormous advantage by deciphering both the German and Japanese encryption codes early in the conflict. Recent innovations in information technology, like the Internet, have made it possible to send vast quantities of data across the globe with ease. However, the challenge of controlling and protecting that information has grown exponentially now that data can be easily transmitted, stored, copied, manipulated, and destroyed.

Within a large organization information technology generally refers to laptop and desktop computers, servers, routers, and switches that form a computer network, although information technology also includes fax machines, phone and voice mail systems, cellular phones, and other electronic systems. A growing reliance on computers to work and communicate has made the control of computer networks an important part of information security. Unauthorized access to paper documents or phone conversations is still an information security concern, but the real challenge has become protecting the security of computer networks, especially when they are connected to the Internet. Most large organizations have their own local computer network, or intranet, that links their computers together to share resources and support the communications of employees and others with a legitimate need for access. Almost all of these networks are connected to the

Internet and allow employees to go "online."

Information technology security is controlling access to sensitive electronic information so only those with a legitimate need to access it are allowed to do so. This seemingly simple task has become a very complex process with systems that need to be continually updated and processes that need to constantly be reviewed. There are three main objectives for information technology security: confidentiality, integrity, and availability of data. Confidentiality is protecting access to sensitive data from those who don't have a legitimate need to use it. Integrity is ensuring that information is accurate and reliable and cannot be modified in unexpected ways. The availability of data ensures that is readily available to those who need to use it.

Information technology security is often the challenge of balancing the demands of users versus the need for data confidentiality and integrity. For example, allowing employees to access a network from a remote location, like their home or a project site, can increase the value of the network and efficiency of the employee. Unfortunately, remote access to a network also opens a number of vulnerabilities and creates difficult security challenges for a network administrator.

MILITARY NETWORK SECURITY

Defense Data Network

In 1975, the Defense Communication Agency (DCA) took over operation of the ARPANET as it became an operational tool instead of a research project. In 1983, plans for a new generation of the Automatic Digital Network (Autodin II) were canceled. Instead, a separate network to connect military installations called MILNET was split off the ARPANET. The ARPANET would be used as an Internet backbone for researchers, but be slowly phased out. Both networks carried unclassified information, and were connected at a small number of points which would allow total separation in the event of an emergency. The DCA used the Defense Data Network (DDN) as the program name for these network programs.

As a large-scale, private internet, the DDN provided Internet

Protocol connectivity across the United States and to US military bases abroad. Throughout the 1980s it expanded as a set of four parallel military networks, each at a different security level. These networks transitioned to become the NIPRNET, SIPRNET, and JWICS networks in the 1990s.

The four DDN subnetworks were:

- Military Network (MILNET) for Unclassified traffic
- Defense Secure Network One (DSNET 1) for Secret traffic
- Defense Secure Network Two (DSNET 2) for Top Secret traffic
- Defense Secure Network Three (DSNET 3) for Top Secret/ Sensitive Compartmented Information (TS/SCI)

MILNET and DSNET 1 were common user networks, much like the public Internet, but DSNET 2 was dedicated to supporting the Worldwide Military Command and Control System (WWMCCS) and DSNET 3 was dedicated to supporting the DOD Intelligence Information System (DODIIS).

DDN-NIC

DDN-NIC or Network Information Centre (NIC) was located at the DDN Installation and Integration Support (DIIS) program office in Chantilly, Virginia. It provided general reference services to DDN users via telephone, electronic mail, and U.S. mail. It was the first organization responsible for the assignment of TCP/IP addresses and Autonomous System numbers.

MILITARY INFORMATION TECHNOLOGY

Arabian sands had no safe haven for U.S. troops during Operation Iraqi Freedom. Dotting the barren Kuwaiti and Iraqi frontier, soldiers and airmen routinely found themselves targets of enemy rocket attacks and frontline probing actions.

Seasoned combat troops might expect such dangers, but not reservists in the 335th Theater Signal Command, who built, secured and maintained the American and coalition forces' IT networks. Firewalls and IDSes kept enemy hackers off their systems, but they relied on nearby Patriot batteries to keep Saddam Hussein's Ababil-100 missiles at bay.

It has been a year since U.S. troops pushed across the Kuwaiti border in their drive toward Baghdad. In the weeks leading up to the war and those tumultuous two months of heavy fighting, the network and security specialists supporting the combat divisions found that there are worse things than a bad day at the office.

"Everything is relative," says Tom Lantzy, a major in the U.S. Army Reserve who recently returned to his job as an infrastructure project manager for CocaCola. "If you've never been in a situation where someone is shooting at you, it may be that the server crash is the biggest problem you've ever dealt with."

Modern armed forces depend on high technology. Military intelligence, battle plans, troop movements and the availability of supplies are just some of the information that's converted into digital form and transmitted over cables, radio and satellites. Leave even a single crack and an enemy with access to computers and trained experts (hardly in short supply these days) could tap your entire command and control infrastructure. In other words, a breach could cost lives.

"Computer network defense issues and challenges in the commercial world and the military world are similar," says Lt. Col. Thomas Michelli, a Virginia National Guardsman deployed in Kuwait, where he oversees the Southwestern Asia CERT. "Except that the risks — mission-critical systems equal human lives — are much higher in the military world."

Marching Orders

The hurdles faced by the 335th dwarfed those of the civilian world, where mortar fire and missiles don't rain down. Creating and managing network systems — which link all U.S. units with those of 30 nations contributing troops or logistical support — was equivalent to integrating the complete IT systems for eight to 10 medium-sized corporations. The 335th rolled out the systems in just two months, an operation Lantzy estimates would have taken a full year in the corporate world.

"We moved more than 250,000 soldiers, Marines and coalition forces into a very small country about the size of Massachusetts," says Maj. Gen. Rip Dettamore, commander of the 335th and head of communications for all land forces in the Middle East.

Military units had to be plugged into the infrastructure that would connect them to their lifeblood — supplies, intelligence and instructions. Although there was a secure backbone for units already stationed in Kuwait, the 335th had to scale the infrastructure from 10 routers to approximately 600. Network bandwidth had to jump from 16 Mbps to nearly 200. Every unit needed a satellite link, IDS, router and other hardware and software.

The mission was immeasurably difficult because different services used different systems and standards. Even the various parts of the U.S. Armed Forces using the same equipment would configure them differently. Then, there was the need to integrate different databases and OSes to provide unified views of theater operations.

Another aggravating factor was that responsibility for critical IT jobs was split among different organizations because the total task was larger than the Army, the Air Force or the Marines could handle individually. For instance, the Army would install IDSes, but the Air Force would run them.

"I'm going to send this airman out, who is going to put in this new intrusion detection sensor, and you're going to have to reengineer the data package, maybe change the IP subnetting, which influences the way the routers work," Lantzy says.

While much of the equipment is off the shelf, important elements of the infrastructure are specific to the military and make securing the network easier. The Army uses one unsecured network that's connected to the Internet, and two closed satellite- and microwave-based networks for all critical information, as well as voice communications and video teleconferencing. Frequency-hopping and NSA Type-1 encryption are standard issue. All traffic and networks are protected with layers of firewalls, IDSes, proxy servers and tightly configured routers.

Hostile Environment

The climate was as hazardous and unwelcoming to the equipment as it was to the IT soldiers. In the first days of the war, the worst sandstorms in decades kicked up, leaving foot-deep drifts overnight and driving sand everywhere. Soldiers venturing into the open had to completely cover themselves to avoid getting burned by the blasting particles. The weather became a concern for the 335th, which had to keep shifting and blowing sand from tearing apart the infrastructure.

"Opening up a server over there at a garrison base where it had been running a couple of months, the dust was an eighth of an inch thick, at least," says Lantzy. "It looked like somebody took the cover off and just poured it in there."

Soldiers had to constantly clear out equipment with brushes and fans. In some cases, they improvised makeshift telecom facilities and data centers to protect equipment from the elements.

At first, in mid-March and early April 2003, the heat wasn't too bad in Kuwait, hovering in the 70s. Later, temperatures crept up to summer highs of 130 degrees. "You could be standing outside, and you felt that you had 2,000-watt hair dryers blowing in your face," says Dettamore. The 335th deployed air conditioning units to keep buildings, tents and shelters cool.

"You'd much rather be in the air conditioning taking care of the equipment than trying to sleep in a tent when it's 130 degrees," he laughs. "Given the two choices, it's no wonder that the equipment was clean."

Combat Conditions

Even with the occasional relief of cool air, the 335th had to keep systems up and secure under difficult conditions. Under the threat of chemical attack, Lantzy and his unit lived in their heavy protective suits for nearly two weeks. A rising and falling wail announced incoming missiles, and everyone at the base had to don a gas mask, boots and gloves. The sirens would give way to the whoosh of intercepting Patriots.

The threat of chemical-tipped missiles didn't stop the mission. IT specialists often had to work through the air raids, which presented their own challenges.

"It's hard to type," Lantzy says. "Most people use a pencil to type one letter at a time, because the gloves are so [thick] that you mash several keys at the same time. It's a very frustrating exercise." No matter the threat, the basic tasks facing corporate information security personnel were the same. IDSes and firewalls needed configuring, servers needed patching and AV needed updating. Soldiers of the 335th had to monitor attempts to breach the network. Their mission was complicated by the massive scale of their operation and the possibility that the next moment might be their last.

In one case, a server in one of the forward units hadn't installed a critical patch. When the command centre called, the unit said it would take a while to install the fix — its sysadmin had been wounded in a mortar attack.

All the work paid off, with uptimes on all equipment and systems exceeding 99 percent. Dettamore reports that not a single critical video teleconference or data link was lost during the war.

Coming Home

Things are quieter on the home front, and many of the veterans have a greater clarity of mind knowing that safety will always be more important than the latest Internet worm.

But their minds wander back to the desert. Some miss the adrenaline boost of near death and total commitment to a job. Newscasts also bring reality to their doorsteps.

"One of the guys we did some planning with was killed in November," says a subdued Lantzy. "They're your friends, your coworkers, and they're still over there, and there's still a threat."

THE MILITARY ROLE IN NATIONAL CYBERSECURITY GOVERNANCE

Cybersecurity – A New Challenge for Governments

The emergence of sophisticated information systems has transformed the world. But it has also created a major new challenge for governments. Cyber threats do not fit easily into the traditional security framework that now exists in most modern states. Under that model, law enforcement has evolved to protect us from threats within our society, while militaries have evolved primarily to protect from external threats (accepting that the extent to which the military is involved in domestic affairs varies from state to state). However, cyber threats often come from overseas, making it difficult for law enforcement to deter or punish them. Yet, as argued below, such threats rarely rise to the level that would warrant a military response. New approaches are required, and none of them are straightforward. Yet, how governments respond to those challenges will have international as well as domestic implications. The appropriate role of the military is central to this.

Use of the Military for Cybersecurity: Pros and Cons

This does not mean that cyber threats below the level of "war" should not be taken seriously. But it also raises the question of the appropriateness of using the military to address such threats as sabotage, subversion, and especially espionage and crime.

There are undoubted attractions to using the military in such a role. Most serious militaries have some cyber capability (or aspire to develop one), both to support the fighting on the battlefield and to defend their own systems during peacetime. Very often militaries provide nations' national signal intelligence, and as such, the information that underpins the most sophisticated cyber operations. More generally, militaries are mission-oriented: they are often better resourced than other arms of government; and they are structured to develop the personnel required – all exactly what you would want for an effective cyber defense force.

Nevertheless, overuse of the military presents challenges, too, for at least two reasons. The first is the practical risk of creating a "crowding-out" effect. Cyber threats are not going away. On the contrary, they are proliferating at a dramatic rate, in part because we are making more and more use of information systems. For that reason, cybersecurity will need to be a discipline that everyone in a country takes seriously, not just something that citizens and private companies can expect to outsource to the military. Any country that depends too heavily on the military for cybersecurity will likely find itself reducing the incentives for the private sector to develop longer-term solutions.

Second, but of no less concern, is the risk of militarizing a major new aspect of domestic security, which in many countries would be considered a very bad thing. In order to achieve truly effective cybersecurity it is necessary to be permanently operating on the defended systems. Few private sector companies are likely to welcome such hands-on assistance from the military, not least because they may well feel that they are better placed to defend their own networks.

Alternatives

Central to the question of the role of the military in "defending the nation" against cyber threats is what else governments can do. Traditionally, the other institution that provides security is law enforcement. Police and other law enforcement agencies are often constrained by the laws under which they operate and the challenges of developing cases that lead to successful prosecutions. However, in recent years innovative agreements such as the European Council's 2001 Convention on Cybercrime (now with 50 signatories across every continent) have made it harder for cyber criminals to avoid justice by basing themselves outside the country they are stealing from. Meanwhile, law enforcement like the U.S.'s Federal Bureau of Investigation are working with international colleagues and major companies like Microsoft to disrupt the very worst criminals (such as the takedown earlier this year of the Citadel network botnet used to steal over $500 million from bank accounts).

Another potential approach for the government is to support the private sector in providing its own security. This can be as simple as creating an appropriate incentives structure for information-sharing between companies or raising basic cybersecurity standards (sometimes through government regulation). This might also involve more practical help, like sharing secret intelligence with private sector companies, to improve their defenses and allow Internet Service Providers to screen out known malware.

It could also involve licensing the private sector to respond to intrusions themselves, so-called "hacking back." Currently the law in many countries does not permit hacking-back and for good reason, namely the risk of inadvertently putting their own countries on an unwanted and escalatory path towards conflict. But such approaches have strong advocates and may gain traction in future. More positively, government might support the establishment of additional Computer Emergency Readiness Teams (CERTs) to coordinate incident response by the private sector.

CYBER NATIONAL SECURITY THREATS SHORT OF WAR

In practice, therefore, the appropriate level of military involvement needs to be informed by both the dangers to national security and the alternatives available (including the risk of misemploying the military). Each nation will face different considerations. The result, however, might look something like this:

- The theft of information from government and defense contractors probably ranks as the most serious threats to national security, and as such, would almost certainly justify some government action. There are various possible motivations for such intrusions, including a commercial one, but they also represent a compromise of future military effectiveness (especially if the intruder is a potential adversary or is willing to give/sell their information to one).
- The potential for a devastating attack critical on national infrastructure (including the finance, energy, transportation, communications and other economic sectors vital the life of a nation) is another grave concern, although arguably less immediate a threat than the theft of national security secrets. While the military might be expected to be ready to support a response to an attack, in most countries some proportion of critical infrastructure is in private hands making military approaches less practical or acceptable. This is an area where the government's best approach might be use of economic incentives, including regulation to improve security levels.
- Commercial espionage, either of intellectual property or sensitive business information, is another area where military approaches might not be appropriate. However,

given the potential economic impact, especially when state-backed Advanced Persistent Threat techniques are used, this type of activity has the potential to significantly destablize international relationships. Governments could then resort to sanctions or, if under pressure, to licensed private responses.

- Fourth, there is the threat of cybercrime. Although not a direct threat, it could develop into one if left unchecked because of the potential for terrorists or states to leverage criminal networks. This is generally not a role for the military but rather for law enforcement. Their challenge is deciding whether to disrupt the criminal or to seek prosecutions.

IMPORTANCE OF CYBER SECURITY

Cyber space is the domain generated from the interconnection between computers and telecommunication networks in order to store, modify, and exchange data via networked systems and associated physical infrastructures without regard to physical geography. Therefore, its security largely depends on the data and the ICTs' security.

Actually, because of cyber space's great dependence on informatics and telecommunications for almost every activity and service, it's extremely dangerous to ignore the growing phenomenon of cyber crimes and the increasing number of threats to citizen lives, citizen activities, and governmental systems.

Sources of cyber threats may be unintentional accidents, or due to vulnerabilities and negligence. However, they can also be intentional, like direct attacks on systems. Objectives of systems attackers can be to shut them down, to gain access to such systems and steal crucial data, to make illegal financial transfers, to disrupt records, or to manipulate data and code in order to introduce harmful instructions. Attackers can be recreational hackers, crackers or terrorists. This is can happen for business entities and interests, as well as for the public sector and the government.

Banking institutions, energy, state agencies, hospitals, business, education, and even social affairs heavily rely on their online presence. With information flowing through boundaries of different legal systems connected to different networks around the globe, there is a growing need to protect personal information, funds and assets, as well as national security.

Thus, cyber security issues are gaining interest by both the public as well as the private sectors.

Background

Cyber security is about building confidence and security in the use of ICTs so as to ensure trust by the information society. Consequently, we can define it as all activities and operations aiming at the reduction and prevention of threat and vulnerabilities, and having in place policies for protection; incident response; recovery, data assurance, law enforcement, and military and intelligence operations relating to cyber space security.

Thus cyber security touches practically all activities and all citizens around the globe; it provides tremendous opportunities for enhancing human development as well as achieving better integration in the information society. It also supports wider access to knowledge and education, as well as to the development of policies and strategies.

Moreover, it imposes new types of commercial, professional and social paradigms, giving rise to a number of legal and technical problems that must be addressed on the basis of respecting its special nature and needs. Hence, a different approach and different methodologies than what has been adopted before the age of information and communication technology are needed.

Nevertheless, many governments and societies fear the negative impact ICTs can have on their own citizens because of the potential dangers it carries, and because of the economic, social, and security challenges it poses.

Accordingly, lack of security in cyber space undermines confidence in the information society. This is especially the case with many intrusions around the globe resulting in the stealing of money, assets, and sensitive military, commercial and economic information.

In legal and regulatory institutions that lack cyber space

security undermines the realization of the full potential of the information technology revolution.

Consequently, special attention is needed to prevent cyberspace from turning into a source of danger for states and citizens, and to prevent the appearance of a cyber crime haven.

The authorities in charge are trying to find a way to prevent and punish new forms of criminal activity such as ICT crimes involving computer-based assaults. Many governments have already adopted particular regulations and legislations as an answer to the need of ensuring the adoption of security measures.

Cooperation between countries

In the same context, scholars, experts and policy makers are highlighting the importance of cooperation between nations and governments to answer challenges imposed by cyberspace's particular nature and to achieve cyber security. As a matter of fact, without cooperation between nations and countries, it is doubtful that any country can protect itself.

In many Arab countries where there is a shortage of legislation and regulatory texts, responsibilities for cyber security are not defined or well established across the departments and the authorities in charge of law enforcement. This situation certainly hinders dealing with cyber crime issues in a consistent way.

Hence, the Arab world is not yet organized enough to address the growing threat of cyber crime and organized crime intrusions, let alone state-sponsored attacks and operations or organized crime networks.

The Arab world must be serious about addressing cyber security challenges with strong leadership and vision. Leadership should be lifted up and strongly anchored within competent official authorities capable of coordinating action and of achieving results. And while providing policy, strategy, legal structures, and coordination to empower concerned authorities to perform their missions, special attention should be paid to strengthen accountability for cyber security at all levels.

CYBER SECURITY FOR THE MILITARY AND DEFENCE SECTOR

With a greater dependence on computer systems and a reliance on integrated networking, today's armed forces are faced with an ever changing set of challenges in maintaining cyber security from the threat of attack. Rapid evolution in technology has forced governments and industry alike to continually develop secure systems that remain one step ahead of the enemy. As cyber systems become increasingly integrated the requirement for a multi-layered, adaptive and self learning security system becomes imperative. With the prevalence of electronic communications, the growth of social media, a widespread access to mobile networked devices and the defence industry's increasing reliance on "Big Data", the cyber threat to today's defence sector has never been more apparent. The 'cyber landscape' is both dynamic and borderless and forces us to address our security in terms of technology, international cooperation as well as individual user awareness.

This year's conference will focus on the military as well as the industrial defence sector itself; establishing what the current threats are, in terms of both state-sponsored intrusion as well as independent hackers and terrorist cells, what technology is currently available and where the gaps in our protection are. Additionally, with increasingly networked systems the defence sector has been presented with a whole array of emerging challenges in cyber defence. Cyber Security for the Military and the Defence Sector 2013 will tackle this by gathering senior experts from both industry and the military to discuss and ideas share to ensure that our governments remain educated, up-to-date and secure.

8

Criminal Networks and Military Disruptions

NATIONAL SECURITY IN THE COMING DECADE

Defense technologists are most successful when they hone in on specific problems. The Pentagon's research agencies and their contractors were asked in 2003 to come up with ways to foil roadside bombs in Iraq and Afghanistan, and although they did not defeat the threat entirely, they did produce a number of useful detectors, jammers and other counter-explosive systems. More recently, military researchers received marching orders to help tackle the so-called "anti-access area-denial" threats, which is Pentagon-speak for enemy weapons that could be used to shoot down U.S. fighters and attack Navy ships.

The next wave of national security threats, however, might be more than the technology community can handle. They are complex, multidimensional problems against which no degree of U.S. technical superiority in stealth, fifth-generation air warfare or night-vision is likely to suffice.

The latest intelligence forecasts by the Obama administration and other sources point to five big challenges to U.S. and global security in the coming decades.

Biological Weapons: The White House published in 2009 a National Strategy for Countering Biological Threats with an underlying theme that biological weapons eventually will be used in a terrorist attack. To prevent deadly viruses from being turned into mass-casualty weapons, officials say, one of the most difficult challenges is obtaining timely and accurate insight on potential attacks. The Defense Threat Reduction Agency has a team of researchers working these problems. But they worry that the pace of research is too slow to keep up with would-be terrorists.

Nukes: Large stockpiles of nuclear weapons are tempting targets for nation-states or groups set on attacking the United States and its allies, officials assert. Black-market trade in sensitive nuclear materials is a particular concern for U.S. security agencies. "The prospect that al-Qaida or another terrorist organization might acquire a nuclear device represents an immediate and extreme threat to global security," says an administration report. No high-tech sensors exist to help break up black markets, detect and intercept nuclear materials in transit and there are no financial tools to disrupt this dangerous trade. A much-hyped Department of Homeland Security effort to detect radioactive materials at U.S. ports has been plagued by technical hiccups. Analysts believe that although a full-up nuclear weapon would be nearly impossible for an al-Qaida like group to build, a more likely scenario would be a low-yield "dirty bomb" that could be made with just a few grams of radioactive material.

Cyber-Attacks: The drumbeats of cyberwarfare have been sounding for years. Network intrusions are widely viewed as one of the most serious potential national security, public safety and economic challenges. Technology, in this case, becomes a double-edge sword. "The very technologies that empower us to lead and create also empower individual criminal hackers, organized criminal groups, terrorist networks and other advanced nations to disrupt the critical infrastructure that is vital to our economy, commerce, public safety, and military," the White House says.

The cybersecurity marketplace is flooded with products that promise quick fixes but it is becoming clear that the increasing persistence and sophistication of attacks will require solutions beyond the traditional.

Climate Change: The national security ramifications of climate change are severe, according to Defense Secretary Leon Panetta. While the topic of climate change has been hugely politicized,

Panetta casts the issue as a serious security crisis. "In the 21st century, we recognize that climate change can impact national security — ranging from rising sea levels, to severe droughts, to the melting of the polar caps, to more frequent and devastating natural disasters that raise demand for humanitarian assistance and disaster relief," Panetta said. The administration projects that the change wrought by a warming planet will lead to new conflicts over refugees and resources and catastrophic natural disasters, all of which would require increased U.S. military support and resources. The scientific community, in this area, cannot agree on what it will take to reverse this trend. There is agreement, though, that there is no silver bullet.

Transnational Crime: U.S. defense and law-enforcement agencies see transnational criminal networks as national security challenges. These groups cause instability and subvert government institutions through corruption, the administration says. "Transnational criminal organizations have accumulated unprecedented wealth and power through the drug trade, arms smuggling, human trafficking, and other illicit activities. ... They extend their reach by forming alliances with terrorist organizations, government officials, and some state security services." Even the United States' sophisticated surveillance technology is not nearly enough to counter this threat, officials say.

In this special report, National Defense examines the top five threats in greater detail.

Bio-Threats

The public health community's dream is to make the arrival and spread of communicable diseases as easy to predict and track as the weather.

Just as a meteorologist spots the seeds of a hurricane off the African coast, and begins to plot its possible path as it makes its way toward the Caribbean, a global bio-surveillance network would allow officials to detect a bio-weapon or the emergence of a deadly flu virus in China and track it as it spreads throughout the world. Measures could then be taken to quickly develop and distribute vaccines.

Despite the onset of the information age, where a doctor in Asia could theoretically inform a centralized information clearinghouse on the other side of the world of a new virus within seconds, realizing this dream is years away, experts at a recent National Defense Industrial Association Biosurveillance conference said.

Making diseases as predictable as the weather is a lofty goal, but the weather analogy is an imperfect one, said Steve Bennett, director of the Department of Homeland Security's National Biosurveillance Integration Centre. To start, the medical community doesn't have all the prediction models that weather watchers can use to plug data into. They just don't exist.

"Prediction is a pretty difficult thing to achieve," he said. "Real-time situational awareness, I think we can get close."

Congress established the centre in 2007 to pull together the efforts of 12 federal agencies and departments that are charged with tracking diseases. Its goal is to "rapidly identify, characterize, localize and track a biological event of national concern; integrate and analyze data relating to human health, animal, plant, food, water, and environmental domains; and to disseminate alerts and pertinent information."

The Defense Department's Defense Threat Reduction Agency, the Centers for Disease Control and Prevention, the Departments of Health and Human Services and Agriculture are all among the entities that track diseases.

"I think there was this idea in 2007 when that law was stood up ... there was this thought that there were these databases all around the federal government and the states and all we had to do was put $100 million into an IT system and hook it all together, and out comes wisdom," Bennett said.

The databases don't exist, or they exist in spreadsheets on different systems, and they are not structured at all, he said. Five years after the law was passed, Bennett still spends the bulk of his time visiting other agencies to keep tabs on what is happening.

"It is people and relationships. I wish there was a more technical solution, but that is kind of the way it is," he said.

As far as developing a real-time global picture of what diseases are spreading and where, there seem to be more questions than answers.

"Right now the sum of biosusurveillance is based on ambiguous data. And to go from ambiguous data to a decision is a very difficult thing to do," said C. Nicole Rosenzweig, a research biologist at the Army's Edgewood Chemical Biological Centre in Maryland.

How do analysts take something that is at some level, research, and assess it as though we have complete confidence in it? she asked. "A lot of research will have to go into this," she added.

Information technology systems that could collect and coordinate the data and give public health officials a picture of where diseases are emerging is only one part of the problem.

The main issue is that the policies and procedures on how to do this have yet to be worked out.

Harshini Mukundan, a scientist in the chemical division at Los Alamos National Laboratory, said diseases emerge in food, humans and animals.

"They are all interconnected and having separate agencies monitoring each [one] defeats the cause," she added.

Who owns the biosurveillance data? she asked. Is it going to be governments or the World Health Organization? "It is hard to envision what the system will look like and how exactly it will function. ... We need some direction on that from the government to start imagining how it will be implemented," Mukundan added.

Bennett said: "There are lot of systemic issues that we need to fix, process issues, authority issues, things that can make decisions faster."

Laurie Garrett, a policy analyst and senior fellow for global health at the Council on Foreign Relations, said all the technical problems could be solved in five to 10 years, "but I don't believe we have the capacity or the will to implement" them.

The political crisis in the United States today means it is difficult to get any kind of decision from the federal government. Many state legislatures are suffering from similar gridlock, she said. "Are the problems bureaucratic, financial or policy? The answer is 'yes,' [to] all three," she said.

Transparency has been an issue on the federal government's end. For example, it issued a gag order on federal scientists during the 2001 anthrax attacks.

"As a result, on the local level, they were operating almost blind and did not have vital information," she said.

Meanwhile, the government may be turning to the public for help.

Health and Human Services recently sponsored a grand challenge asking competitors to use Twitter to create a web-based application that would compile the top five trending illnesses in a geographic area and distribute the findings to state and local public health officials.

Bennett said there is valuable data contained in insurance claims. Such forms have geo-location tags and could help public health officials to see where diseases are cropping up. But then there are privacy issues.

"I don't need to know specific patient information....I need to know general trends."

The national security community may not need to know the kinds of data that would intrude on personal privacy, he added.

Jason Pargas, special assistant to the director at the Defense Threat Reduction Agency's chemical and biological technologies directorate, said he believes that these issues will all be worked out in five to 10 years. He is in the research-and-development community, so he has to be an optimist, he said. Prediction models, applied math and computing may converge to where disease forecasts could become possible, he said.

But governments need to see the public as a partner.

"If you engage the public, you will have a much more redundant, highly, highly effective system," he said.

Nuclear Weapons

Still at the top of the list of the most terrifying threats to the United States are nuclear weapons. The nation has spent an almost incalculable amount of money over the past six decades to find them, monitor them, and destroy the means by which they are delivered. Open source information suggests there is still a lot of work to be done.

Research into hitting an intercontinental ballistic missile bearing a nuclear warhead with another missile began in the Eisenhower administration 50 years ago. Yet today, this can still only be accomplished under the most controlled circumstances with questions remaining on whether decoys could easily defeat the "hitting a bullet with a bullet" scenario.

President Reagan's dead-end effort to shoot down missiles from space, better known as Star Wars, came to naught. The Airborne Laser program, which envisioned destroying missiles on the launch pad by using directed energy shot from an aircraft, also came to a halt.

The mutually assured destruction doctrine offset these defensive shortcomings. But as many analysts have noted, non-state actors such as terrorist groups, if they were to get their hands on a nuke, don't play by those rules.

More recently, the Department of Homeland Security abandoned a program to develop Advanced Spectroscopic Portals that could detect a smuggled warhead inside a shipping container. The congressional mandate to scan every container entering the United States means that this effort will continue, although on a smaller scale.

Less overt is the detection problem. Who has nukes? And where are they?

The answer is: underground.

North Korea's nuclear weapons program is hidden deep in its mountains, as are Iran's alleged efforts.

Army Lt. Gen. Ronald L. Burgess Jr., director of the Defense Intelligence Agency in his annual threat assessment released in February before his retirement, said underground facilities that may hide missiles and weapons of mass destruction are "spreading."

Finding, assessing, mapping and ultimately destroying a hard and deep buried target — HDBT in military lingo — has become an increasingly difficult challenge for the military and spy communities, Air Force Lt. Col. Craig Baker, wrote in an Army War College paper, "The Strategic Importance of Defeating Underground Facilities." The two communities have placed a great deal of emphasis on tackling this problem during the last decade, he wrote. Most of it has been carried out with little attention. Despite the low profile, the military has been taking the problem seriously.

"America's potential adversaries have realized that current non-nuclear penetrating weapons are relatively ineffective in destroying underground facilities," Baker wrote. Weapons of mass destruction programs are now underground in an effort to remain out of reach. New commercial tunneling technologies have also made underground bunkers less expensive to build, he noted.

The National Reconnaissance Office, National Geo-Spatial Intelligence Agency and the Air Force all need sensors to detect nuclear weapons, as well as the underground bunkers where they are hiding. The Air Force's Technical Applications Centre, based at Patrick Air Force Base, Fla., has been tasked with searching for nuclear weapons and verifying treaties.

Much of its work is classified. If the U.S. is to preemptively destroy a nuclear weapons program, it will require intelligence on where these weapons are located and how deep underground they are stored.

An effort to destroy an underground complex may require repeated bombings by massive ordnance penetrator. These can only be carried by B-2 bombers, and only one at a time.

Jeffrey Richelson, senior fellow at the National Security Archives, a research institute that pries secret documents out of the government through Freedom of Information Act requests, said, "We obviously need weapons that can penetrate through certain depths, through certain hardness. But whether they can even build them to attain certain levels of destruction, I just don't know ... I'm not even sure the people in the Defense Department know. They are guessing, trying to figure it out using various models." Then comes the difficult question of battlefield damage assessment. Some things could be determined from outside, such as whether a bombing campaign collapsed an entrance. But since there may be an incomplete picture of what was inside a deeply buried bunker in the first place, it would be hard to know if a strike was successful, he said.

Documents show that the Defense Department and intelligence community over the past decade have been taking this problem seriously. "It has become more prominent and more important in recent years," Richelson said.

Baker's paper identified more than $1 billion being spent tackling underground facility defeat issues during fiscal years 2009 and 2010.

There is some good news. The Comprehensive Nuclear Test Ban Treaty, signed by most countries, has yet to be ratified. But it has helped create a robust global network that can monitor clandestine underground nuclear weapon detonations. A National Academies report released in 2000 spelled out the shortcomings signees would have in attempting to detect tests. On a typical day, the Earth experiences hundreds of earthquakes and large mine blasts. The seismic clutter made it difficult to detect underground nuclear explosions, said Paul Richards, a Colombia University emeritus professor of geophysics and seismology at a Centre for Science, Technology and Security Policy briefing on Capitol Hill.

A follow-up report released this year showed remarkable progress over the last decade. Hundreds of seismic and air-sniffing sensors have been placed all over the world, and countries have done a better job of sharing their legacy seismic sensor data with those who monitor the treaty, he said.

The radioactive particles released by the Fukushima Daiichi Nuclear Plant accident last year were detected all over the globe and as far as South America, said Robert Werzi, who maintains the Comprehensive Test Ban Treaty Organization's 80 radionuclide air monitors. If a sensor detects a manmade radioactive particle, analysts can then determine how many days old it is, backtrack the weather patterns, and pinpoint its origins, he said.

Officials believe the network of seismic sensors is good enough to detect 90 percent of any clandestine attempt to test a nuclear weapon that is over 1 kiloton. The lower the yield is on a test, the less effective it is. Richards said it is necessary "to consider how well nuclear tests can be carried out evasively."

There is a need for a continuing research-and-development program to improve the network of sensors, he added.

"The goal of the monitoring effort is to drive ever downwards the yield of anything that might go undetected or identified," he said.

The Future of Cyber-Wars

Army Gen. Keith Alexander, commander of U.S. Cyber Command, sees a day in the not too distant future when attacks on computer networks cross the line from theft and disruption to "destruction."

And this chaos will not all take place in the digital world of ones and zeroes. He is referring to remote adversaries taking down infrastructure such as power grids, dams, transportation systems and other sectors that use computer-based industrial controls.

The last decade has seen mostly exploitation by adversaries, or the theft of money and intellectual property. Next came distributed denial of service attacks when hackers overwhelm networks and disrupt operations of businesses or other organizations, Alexander said at a recent Woodrow Wilson Centre panel discussion on cybersecurity.

Other than intercontinental ballistic missiles and acts of terrorism, an adversary seeking to reach out and harm the United States has only one other option: destructive cyber-attacks, Alexander said.

This could result in loss of life and damage to the economy on par with what occurred after 9/11.

"All of that is within the realm of the possible," he said. "I believe that is coming our way. We have to be out in front of this," Alexander said.

How to thwart such attacks is the problem the nation is facing.

Most of the Internet's infrastructure through which malware is delivered is in the private sector's hands. So too are the banking, energy, transportation and other institutions that are vulnerable to the attacks. During the past year, there have been 200 attacks on core critical infrastructures in the transportation, energy, and communication industries reported to the Department of Homeland Security, said Sen. Susan Collins, R-Maine, and ranking member of the Senate Homeland Security and Governmental Affairs Committee.

"And that is only the tip of the iceberg. Undoubtedly there are more that have not been reported," she said during the panel.

"In this case, the dots have already been connected. The alarm has already been sounded, and we know it is only a matter of when, not whether we have a catastrophic attack," she said.

Alexander, Collins and others are advocating for a more coordinated national effort to share information on cyberthreats. Cyber Command and the National Security Agency have loads of expertise, but can't always share classified information, or cross lines when it comes to the privacy of U.S. citizens. The rest of the federal government has bits and pieces of information, and different responsibilities. Private sector companies are sometimes reluctant to disclose attacks for fear of upsetting shareholders or opening themselves up to lawsuits. Legislation co-sponsored by Collins to help pave the way for better information sharing died in Congress last summer.

Despite having poured countless amounts of money into cybersecurity on both the federal and private levels, there is still a lot to be learned about the threat, said one analyst.

"Why do we have a cyberwar community? Because we haven't mastered cyber," said Martin Libicki, senior management scientist at Rand Corp. The main problem is that computers were originally seen as something to be "tinkered" with, Libicki said.

"We've built the most important infrastructure on things that were made to be toys," said Libicki. Being toys, computer systems from the start have gaps and vulnerabilities needing to be patched.

"Every cyber-attack is a reflection of some vulnerability in the system," said Libicki.

Greg Giaqunito, an analyst at Forecast International, said it's not enough to defend the nation from attacks, offensive capabilities are required.

Increasingly, the United States is taking more proactive measures against adversaries and initiating activity, Giaqunito said.

"We are actually taking proactive action against other adversaries, so it's not only protecting ourselves, but the U.S. taking more proactive stances and actually initiating some activity against U.S. adversaries," he said.

Over the next few years, the hackers will become more sophisticated, said Charles Croom, vice president of cyber security solutions at Lockheed Martin Information Systems & Global Solutions. This doesn't necessarily mean that the technologies are becoming more advanced — even the most sophisticated threats often use known vulnerabilities and malware, Croom said — but the adversaries have become more effective.

Lockheed Martin's Security Intelligence Centre has over the last 10 years compiled a database of patterns and hacking groups. This information can help analysts as they work to stop threats.

While innovation in technology is important, Croom said the backbone of its security system is its analysts.

A shortage of network security experts continues to be a problem in both government and the private sector. Alexander said because of the poor economy, he isn't having a problem attracting and retaining service personnel and civilian employees to Cyber Command now, but that won't always be the case. Incentives and bonuses may be needed to retain experts, he said.

Duke Ayers, program manager of SAIC's CyberNEXS initiative, a live-training program that focuses on cyber education, said, "We know that we're not developing people fast enough in cyber or the technical skills." SAIC, along with other partners such as the University of Texas at San Antonio, developed the CyberNEXS program that gives immediate feedback to participants as they pursue cyber-education.

Industry, the Defense Department and the Air Force Association have also teamed up to work on the CyberPatriot program, a nationwide high school-level competition intended to motivate high school students to get involved in the cybersecurity sector early and to cultivate talent.

Industry has also formed partnerships with academia to help stop attacks. In 2009, Northrop Grumman started its Cybersecurity Research Consortium, which includes Carnegie Mellon, MIT and Purdue University. There they investigate the various security threats that face the economy and national security and work on solutions that can help stop them, said Mike Papay, vice president of Cyber Initiatives at Northrop Grumman Information Systems.

With cybersecurity, Papay said, government and industry need to work together from the beginning during the procurement process. This, he said, is one way to reduce costs and achieve better cybersecurity.

"It's not just about acquiring pure cybersystems anymore; it's about acquiring UAV's, radars, ships, etc., where cyber needs to be embedded to ensure mission success. Government and industry need to consider cyber in almost everything they do," said Papay.

Despite all these initiatives, Collins struck a pessimistic tone, especially when it comes to the federal government's response.

"In all the years that I have been working on homeland security issues, I can't think of another area where the threat is greater, and we have done less," she said.

Climate Change

For the U.S. military, climate change is a "ring-road" issue that surrounds its future strategic planning.

No matter which way the Defense Department turns, U.S. global interests will eventually intersect with the effects of a warming planet, analysts said.

While politicians debate the legitimacy of climate science, the Defense Department has recognized it has a practical, hard-security interest in tackling issues like its energy footprint, said David Michel, director of environmental security at the Stimson Centre.

"There's no tree-hugging, sandal-wearing, granola eating aspects to the military's approach," Michel told National Defense. "The water-food-energy nexus of issues caused by climate change is going to be a rising challenge for the military and the national security strategy reflects that." The military will have an ever-increasing need for sensors and observation platforms to keep constant watch on how climate change manifests itself through weather and ecological phenomena, said Michel.

"These technologies are increasingly particularized and specialized," he said. "We need to make sure that all of our eyes in the sky are not only looking at North Korea, for instance, but gathering a wealth of data from many areas. We need an inclusive data network to which many different observation technologies contribute."

At the ends of the Earth, where climate change is already noticeable in receding ice caps, the same technologies are needed to monitor the melt, said Heather Conley, director of the Europe Program at the Centre for Strategic and International Studies. The Coast Guard will also need new ships that can patrol the cold waters of the Arctic, to provide a constant presence in what could become the world's newest contested open ocean, she said.

The 2010 Quadrennial Defense Review lists resource scarcity, climate change, disease, and demographics as "enduring trends" that threaten national security.

The challenge for the U.S. military, as it shifts its primary focus to the Pacific Ocean, will be balancing its response to acute events with a chronic, sustained preparedness for the long-term effects of climate change, Michel said. The Pacific already averages 70,000 annual deaths to natural disasters ranging from floods to typhoons and earthquakes.

"We're likely to see more of those sorts of acute events," Michel said. "But even at the same frequency and strength as we see them today ... as populations continue to grow, as urbanization along coastlines continues, more people will be exposed."

The U.S. military has a unique ability to provide infrastructure at nearly a moment's notice when disaster strikes. A single carrier strike group can provide medical supplies, lift capabilities and communications to a country devastated by a catastrophic event, as it did after a massive earthquake ravaged Haiti in 2010. The Marine Corps, along with the Navy, has pledged that disaster relief and humanitarian aid will be two of their main duties within a Pacific-centered security strategy.

The chronic results of climate change are more challenging. Funneling resources to combat a problem that might not manifest for decades is a hard sell, especially with constrained budgets, Conley said. But phenomena associated with climate change like persistent drought, violent flooding and agricultural disruption are real and immediate concerns for many of the nations the United States partners with around the world, Michel said. The effects are also causing the most disruption in some of the world's most politically unstable regions — Southern Asia, Sub-Saharan Africa, South America.

"To the extent that climate change is an issue for our partners ... it is going to become an issue for us," Michel said. "The military is also aware that ... climate impacts could be accelerants of instability in the countries where we have political interests or strategic concerns."

There are opportunities also associated with a warming planet. Some effects like the melting polar ice caps are regrettable ecologically but potentially a windfall for global commerce, said Conley. A receding Arctic icecap could mean the Northwest and Northeast passages and Russia's Northern Sea Route could remain open longer in summer. Eventually they could remain navigable to commercial shipping year-round.

The National Snow and Ice Data Centre in September announced that the polar ice cap shrank over the summer months to the smallest area in the 33 years that records have been kept — just 1.5 million square miles at its nadir.

"We're really seeing a dramatic acceleration of Arctic ice melt," Conley said. "As the ice recedes, there are increases in commercial and other human activity. It also opens new sources of oil and gas and tourist opportunities in new waters."

The implications of the sudden availability of natural resources and shipping lanes through the Arctic have drawn much attention from nations spanning the globe. The obvious players — the eight-member Arctic Council, which includes the United States, Canada, Denmark, Finland, Norway, Russia, Sweden and Iceland — are concerned about border security where a sea of ice once did the work for them.

Other nations as far away as India and China are trying to gain admission to the council to advocate for their interests in shipping through an open Arctic, which could lessen by a third the time and cost of trans-oceanic shipping, said Conley.

For those and other reasons, the U.S. military "is just as interested in the decline of polar ice as the polar bear people," Michel said.

It is another instance where the military, by addressing a practical challenge to national security, can have a positive ecological impact, like the Navy being a champion of biofuels. Navy officials view renewable energy as a means of bringing down the cost of operations. The Marines care less about curbing global warming than they do about keeping fuel and water convoys off vulnerable roads. But the net result of sustainable resource programs is a significant reduction in the military's carbon footprint, Michel said.

In the Arctic, however, the United States is woefully unprepared for the challenge. The Coast Guard has a single operational icebreaker and the military hasn't built one for more than 30 years.

"This summer, when Shell Oil attempted to drill offshore in the Arctic, they were able to bring more assets to bear than the U.S. Coast Guard could ever hope to muster," Conley said. "When we need resources, we borrow them from other countries. By the time there is a crisis there, we won't have the ability to address it."

There are other strikes against U.S. polar preparedness. Because the disappearance of the ice cap is a long-term issue that may not have consequences for decades, it is difficult to interest policymakers and even more difficult to pin down funding for infrastructure and ships, Conley said.

The Arctic is also an area where 20 federal agencies have some role, creating headaches for strategists and diplomatic efforts to manage competition there. "Coordination of Arctic policy is a nightmare on a good day," she said. In the Arctic, as in Asia and the Pacific, the United States will be forced to acknowledge and address climate change, if it is to uphold its professed role as a global power to secure and maintain the free-flow of public goods,

Michel said. "If we say climate change is one of our major concerns that is going to shape the 21st century and then we ignore it, the international community will notice," he said.

Transnational Crime/Terror

Well before the May killing of Osama bin Laden at the hands of U.S. Navy SEALs, the terrorist organization he headed had become a dispersed, loosely linked network of international terror and criminal groups. Add to that the existing transnational trafficking in narcotics, weapons and people, and the recipe yields a complicated problem for U.S. military and law enforcement agencies at home and abroad.

"We're going to continue to have this transnational, non-standard set of threats and everything that goes with that," said Garry Reid, principal deputy assistant secretary of defense for special operations, during a discussion of future SOF operations at the annual Air and Space conference in September. "Those threats are going to persist in multiple environments over the next 10-plus years." Countering those threats is made all the more difficult given that the U.S. military can't take its eye off state-level actors to fight non-state, non-standard actors.

"Our national defense focus and clearly the focus of our Special Operations Command has got to equally be on … high-end threats and state competitors of the future," Reid said. Events like the Arab Spring have created power vacuums and ungoverned lands where criminals and terrorist groups are able to operate with impunity.

While much of the U.S. military's attention has been on the Middle East, anti-U.S. terror groups and al-Qaida sympathizers have spread elsewhere. Today, the arc of instability, from West to East Africa to Pakistan to Bangladesh has any number of al-Qaida copycat sympathizers, Arnaud de Borchgrave, senior adviser and director of the Transnational Threats Project at the Centre for Strategic and International Studies, wrote in January.

Illegal trade is "increasingly converging with ideologically-motivated networks, fostering a new generation of hybrid threats," according to information from the project's website. Mali and

Libya were two examples given by Reid of places where those two forces are converging. A coup last year in Mali left the country's inhospitable north largely ungoverned. "Bandits and kidnappers" have since set up shop.

Al-Qaida in the Islamic Maghreb has reared its head in Mali, operating without constraint in the arid north, some of the most inhospitable terrain on earth. "Al-Qaida branched into there a few years ago and showed mixed results with proselytizing their ideology," Reid said. "They have not posed a transnational threat per se to attack the United States homeland, but they are of growing concern to our interests in the region."

The group draws its origins from desert bandits and smugglers taking advantage of a power vacuum to advance their and al-Qaida's interests. The instability in Libya has afforded them an opportunity to spread their beliefs there also, Reid said. They gain a significant amount of resources from kidnapping for ransom — tens of millions of dollars go into their treasure chests. For al-Qaida, kidnapping to fund terrorist activities is a relatively new brand of criminality, he said.

These are small-scale crimes with regional implications for which military intervention is not well suited. They call instead for foreign military engagement by special operations forces, which have been overstretched this last decade, and for which no respite is in sight, Reid said. "We see ourselves being pretty busy in the future," he said. The situation calls, as many others do, for technologies that are force multipliers, like intelligence, surveillance and reconnaissance platforms that are easily deployed and operated by militaries short on resources.

There are "issues of partner-nation absorption," of what portion of the enforcement burden native societies and militaries can take on, Reid said. Technologies like unmanned aerial vehicles and persistent border surveillance can enhance that absorption, he said. But it is "not as simple as providing a piece of kit and waving goodbye," he said. "How do we allow a small nation to have the advantage of these capabilities? These technologies will have to be scalable."

Simply handing over or lending the U.S. military's large and complicated unmanned aerial vehicles and surveillance systems won't do. Once criminal activity is detected, the host nation must be have the will and training to curtail it. That will require a steady presence of SOF personnel in remote parts of the world. Distributed operations of that nature and scope call for a secure communications network the United States doesn't currently have, Reid said.

The transnational threat also hits close to home. The United States is the world's primary market for illicit drugs. They flow over the nation's land and maritime borders by the ton and government agencies catch only about a third of what's smuggled, Gen. Douglas Fraser, then the commander of U.S. Southern Command, told defense reporters in March. An estimated 1,200 to 1,500 metric tons of illegal drugs are produced in South and Central America each year, Fraser said. Of that, about 60 percent eventually makes it to the United States, he said.

Here again, intelligence, surveillance and reconnaissance technologies can help.

But eyes in the sky can only spy, and in South America are often hampered by rain forests. In countries like Colombia and Honduras, criminals hide beneath a triple-canopy rain forest through which current sensors cannot penetrate, Fraser said. "That's really a [research-and-development] effort right now.... We have not gotten to a penetrative capability yet."

UAVs, however, cannot interdict drugs or smugglers once they are found. The Coast Guard and Navy need more ships for that task, or other weapon systems that both spot and stop illegal drug and gun trafficking, he said. But technology is not always the silver bullet, Fraser said. Just as in North Africa, countering transnational threats in South America is accomplished by using some technologies like maritime radar but is best done through direct cooperation with regional allies and old-fashioned word-of-mouth intelligence gathering, he said.

While UAVs have developed rapidly because of successes in Iraq and Afghanistan — Reid credits many of SOF's "most public successes" on their spying abilities — they aren't necessarily the best platform for every job, Fraser said.

CYBER COMBAT: ACT OF WAR

The Pentagon has concluded that computer sabotage coming from another country can constitute an act of war, a finding that for the first time opens the door for the U.S. to respond using traditional military force. The Pentagon's first formal cyber strategy, unclassified portions of which are expected to become public next month, represents an early attempt to grapple with a changing world in which a hacker could pose as significant a threat to U.S. nuclear reactors, subways or pipelines as a hostile country's military.

The Pentagon intends its plan as a warning to potential adversaries of the consequences of attacking the U.S. in this way. "If you shut down our power grid, maybe we will put a missile down one of your smokestacks," said a military official.

Recent attacks on the Pentagon's own systems—as well as the sabotaging of Iran's nuclear program via the Stuxnet computer worm—have given new urgency to U.S. efforts to develop a more formalized approach to cyber attacks. A key moment occurred in 2008, when at least one U.S. military computer system was penetrated. This weekend Lockheed Martin, a major military contractor, acknowledged that it had been the victim of an infiltration, while playing down its impact. The report will also spark a debate over a range of sensitive issues the Pentagon left unaddressed, including whether the U.S. can ever be certain about an attack's origin, and how to define when computer sabotage is serious enough to constitute an act of war. These questions have already been a topic of dispute within the military.

One idea gaining momentum at the Pentagon is the notion of "equivalence." If a cyber attack produces the death, damage, destruction or high-level disruption that a traditional military attack would cause, then it would be a candidate for a "use of force" consideration, which could merit retaliation.

The War On Cyber Attacks

Attacks of varying severity have rattled nations in recent years.

June 2009: First version of Stuxnet virus starts spreading, eventually sabotaging Iran's nuclear program. Some experts suspect it was an Israeli attempt, possibly with American help.

November 2008: A computer virus believed to have originated in Russia succeeds in penetrating at least one classified U.S. military computer network.

August 2008: Online attack on websites of Georgian government agencies and financial institutions at start of brief war between Russia and Georgia.

May 2007: Attack on Estonian banking and government websites occurs that is similar to the later one in Georgia but has greater impact because Estonia is more dependent on online banking.

The Pentagon's document runs about 30 pages in its classified version and 12 pages in the unclassified one. It concludes that the Laws of Armed Conflict—derived from various treaties and customs that, over the years, have come to guide the conduct of war and proportionality of response—apply in cyberspace as in traditional warfare, according to three defense officials who have read the document. The document goes on to describe the Defense Department's dependence on information technology and why it must forge partnerships with other nations and private industry to protect infrastructure.

The strategy will also state the importance of synchronizing U.S. cyber-war doctrine with that of its allies, and will set out principles for new security policies. The North Atlantic Treaty Organization took an initial step last year when it decided that, in the event of a cyber attack on an ally, it would convene a group to "consult together" on the attacks, but they wouldn't be required to help each other respond. The group hasn't yet met to confer on a cyber incident.

Pentagon officials believe the most-sophisticated computer attacks require the resources of a government. For instance, the weapons used in a major technological assault, such as taking down a power grid, would likely have been developed with state support, Pentagon officials say.

The move to formalize the Pentagon's thinking was borne of the military's realization the U.S. has been slow to build up defenses against these kinds of attacks, even as civilian and military infrastructure has grown more dependent on the Internet. The military established a new command last year, headed by the director of the National Security Agency, to consolidate military network security and attack efforts.

The Pentagon itself was rattled by the 2008 attack, a breach significant enough that the Chairman of the Joint Chiefs briefed then-President George W. Bush. At the time, Pentagon officials said they believed the attack originated in Russia, although didn't say whether they believed the attacks were connected to the government. Russia has denied involvement.

The Rules of Armed Conflict that guide traditional wars are derived from a series of international treaties, such as the Geneva Conventions, as well as practices that the U.S. and other nations consider customary international law. But cyber warfare isn't covered by existing treaties. So military officials say they want to seek a consensus among allies about how to proceed.

"Act of war" is a political phrase, not a legal term, said Charles Dunlap, a retired Air Force Major General and professor at Duke University law school. Gen. Dunlap argues cyber attacks that have a violent effect are the legal equivalent of armed attacks, or what the military calls a "use of force."

"A cyber attack is governed by basically the same rules as any other kind of attack if the effects of it are essentially the same," Gen. Dunlap said Monday. The U.S. would need to show that the cyber weapon used had an effect that was the equivalent of a conventional attack.

James Lewis, a computer-security specialist at the Centre for Strategic and International Studies who has advised the Obama administration, said Pentagon officials are currently figuring out what kind of cyber attack would constitute a use of force. Many military planners believe the trigger for retaliation should be the amount of damage—actual or attempted—caused by the attack.

For instance, if computer sabotage shut down as much commerce as would a naval blockade, it could be considered an act of war that justifies retaliation, Mr. Lewis said. Gauges would include "death, damage, destruction or a high level of disruption" he said.

Culpability, military planners argue in internal Pentagon debates, depends on the degree to which the attack, or the weapons themselves, can be linked to a foreign government. That's a tricky prospect at the best of times.

The brief 2008 war between Russia and Georgia included a cyber attack that disrupted the websites of Georgian government agencies and financial institutions. The damage wasn't permanent but did disrupt communication early in the war.

A subsequent NATO study said it was too hard to apply the laws of armed conflict to that cyber attack because both the perpetrator and impact were unclear. At the time, Georgia blamed its neighbor, Russia, which denied any involvement.

Much also remains unknown about one of the best-known cyber weapons, the Stuxnet computer virus that sabotaged some of Iran's nuclear centrifuges. While some experts suspect it was an Israeli attack, because of coding characteristics, possibly with American assistance, that hasn't been proven. Iran was the location of only 60% of the infections, according to a study by the computer security firm Symantec. Other locations included Indonesia, India, Pakistan and the U.S.

Officials from Israel and the U.S. have declined to comment on the allegations.

Defense officials refuse to discuss potential cyber adversaries, although military and intelligence officials say they have identified previous attacks originating in Russia and China. A 2009 government-sponsored report from the U.S.-China Economic and Security Review Commission said that China's People's Liberation Army has its own computer warriors, the equivalent of the American National Security Agency.

That's why military planners believe the best way to deter major attacks is to hold countries that build cyber weapons responsible for their use. A parallel, outside experts say, is the George W. Bush administration's policy of holding foreign governments accountable for harboring terrorist organizations, a policy that led to the U.S. military campaign to oust the Taliban from power in Afghanistan.

STRATEGIC CHALLENGE FOR THE PERMANENTLY DISRUPTED HIGH-TECH HOMELAND SECURITY ENVIRONMENT

The task of defining a homeland security environment is tricky. Framing it seems like an invitation to oversimplify its nature as a series of elements that can be fitted into a tightly packaged description that might look elegant, but also provides us with a false sense of linear order and predictability for what it is in reality an interactive, complex, and evolving web of forces, constraints, incentives, and conditions.

The chaotic nature of the homeland security environment and maintains it in a permanent state of disruption. This has given birth to a new phenomenon that I call "the power of the few," where technology has lowered the barriers to entry for disruption, both positive and negative, thus creating the need for a new kind of security strategy to prevent innovation and freedom being turned against the legitimate users of social and physical infrastructure. I conclude with an exploration of the limits of the current homeland security institutional framework to adapt to this rapidly evolving and unpredictable environment, and propose a new strategic approach to homeland security, based on the different natures of incremental and disruptive threats, to counter more effectively the negative effect of the power of the few.

Whereas the normal approach to describing an environment for strategic purposes is to think of it as a static abstraction of reality, akin to the chessboard where players distribute their pieces and make their moves (think of a battle map, as shown in Figure 1), a social environment for public policy is not a snapshot frozen in time, but a mutating context in which people operate and interact with each other and with the natural and man-made structures that surround them, and each interaction morphs a little bit the state of the system. It is more an ecosystem than a photograph.

As such, the homeland security environment should be understood as a chaotic system where long term planning is very difficult and forecasting is in reality impossible. As Levy explains it, "chaos systems do not reach a stable equilibrium; indeed, they can never pass through the same exact state more than once." Therefore, "we cannot learn too much about the future by studying the past: if history is the sum of complex and nonlinear interactions among people and nations, then history does not repeat itself." Trend analysis, the basis of most forecasting based planning, is not a useful tool to plan and prepare against future disruptive threats because that previously mentioned metaphorical chessboard will not have the same number of squares twice, and the pieces constantly change the way they move.

Secretary of Defense Robert Gates described the limitations of forecasting for defense, strategy, and war:

We can't know with absolute certainty what the future of warfare will hold but we do know it will be exceedingly complex, unpredictable, and — as they say in the staff colleges — "-." ... And I must tell you, when it comes to predicting the nature and location of our next military engagements, since Vietnam, our record has been perfect. We have never once gotten it right.

Heraclitus and Asimov Were Right

In Cratylus, Plato imagines a dialogue where Heraclitus expresses: "all things are in motion and nothing at rest...[it is] like the stream of a river ... that you cannot go into the same water twice. Isaac Asimov, the science fiction writer, updated the quote: "It is change, continuing change, inevitable change, that is the dominant factor in society today. No sensible decision can be made any longer without taking into account not only the world as it is, but the world as it will be."

That is why trying to describe the current state of the homeland security environment is a flawed approach to developing a strategy, mainly because the current state is just an instant in the evolution of this complex and randomized system. Instead, I will focus on demonstrating how scientific and technological progress (two of the main motivational forces for societal transformations) have accelerated the pace of this evolution, reducing in the process the "shelf life" of some of the security paradigms and doctrines that condition the reactions of our institutions in the homeland security environment. This accelerated pace implies a change of scale that empowers small groups.

Over the last century, radical technological changes have disrupted the human environment in profound and permanent ways. In this very short amount of time, a 100-year-old person alive in 2011 would have witnessed the arrival of the power grid, the telephone grid, the mass produced automobile and the interstate highway system, radio broadcasting, television, the cell phone network (first transmitting only voice and then voice and data), the computer and, of course, the Internet. None of these technologies that shape and sustain the human ecosystem today were generally available the day he was born.

In those same 100 years, new techniques and construction materials have reshaped our urban environment. Reinforced concrete and the steel frame allowed us to build higher, giving birth to the modern skyscraper and opening the door to a new level of urban concentration. Paradoxically, stronger and more flexible infrastructures (dams, pipelines, power plants, the grid, tunnels, bridges, highways, and airports) gave us the capacity to locate people and resources over much greater distances than before, enabling a technological urban sprawl.

This contemporary urban environment is dependent on technological infrastructure operating unceasingly. As Weisman's provocative narrative describes, it would take less than a week without functioning infrastructure for places like New York City to start a process of rapid decay.

Because of innovations in transportation and information technologies, the rapport of the individual with space also suffered multiple disruptions and our environment has "shrunk." Low transportation costs made possible unrestricted and rapid travel to almost anywhere in the world for less than one thousand dollars using the global civilian aviation network, and provided the ability to ship any product anywhere for just a few hundred dollars. This modified our relation with time, as spatial processes that used to take months — like sending a shipment across the world, traveling, or sending a letter — can now be accomplished in days for what used to take months, and instantly for what it used to take days. The grace period that societies used to enjoy to prepare for a disruption coming from overseas no longer exists, or at least it has been greatly reduced. Disruptions not only can travel far and cheap, they can also travel fast.

Lastly, our relationship with the working and productive environment also endured important changes that affect the way we deal with technological innovation. In the last 100 years high tech societies have become postindustrial, and knowledge creation has replaced manufacturing as the main added value for economic growth, with consequences for every production sector.

The food industry operates today in an environment where, thanks to agrotechnology, produce is abundant and easily transported from its source to the consumer. In this high-tech environment, less than 4 percent of the population of any given developed country can grow enough food to feed all its inhabitants and still sell an "exportable surplus." Furthermore, the primary sector is being disrupted by the recently gained knowledge of how genetics work and how genes can be converted into information and manipulated digitally, freeing genetic scientists from the physical limits of Mendelian inheritance.

Regarding the secondary sector, affordable energy, robotics, and outsourced cheap labor made possible by communication and transportation technologies have made dull and repetitive manufacturing tasks unprofitable and undesirable inside the labor environments of most high-income nations, forcing their citizens into more information driven endeavors. In fact, this labor environment has seen "a huge increase in the number of people paid to think or talk, rather than produce or transport objects." That is, people are being paid for their capacity to produce and manage information (granted, not all of it creative) and not for their muscles, thus multiplying as a result the amount of knowledge that can be recombined and therefore the potential for disruption (voluntary or involuntary) of the environment in cumulative way.

This takes us to the two main patterns that govern our innovation and security environment and are to blame for the emergence of the phenomenon of the "power of the few."

The first one has to do with the cumulative, combinatorial, evolving and unpredictable behavior of the system: waves of new technologies lay the foundations for the next technologies with cross-pollination during the same wave. Some new technologies, like the printing press and the combustion engine, have ripple disruptive effects across many domains, and affect security in many ways. Others are just incremental upgrades from previous technologies and security strategies do not need to be altered. Nonetheless, all new technologies inherit some elements from previous generations of scientific discovery and technological advances. While this process can be traced back in time, in what Bryan Arthur denominated "Combinatorial evolution," he also concluded:

So, the first pattern exhibited by the system is that technological environments evolve in a combinatorial way, and modern technology has made recombination, including convergence, simpler. For example, when material products are transformed into binary data, they can be manipulated with little to no associated manufacturing cost. As Chris Anderson points out, "once something becomes software, it inevitably becomes free — in cost, certainly, and often in price." Products that used to be "things" are today binary code: music CDs or LPs, VHS tapes or DVDs, typewriters, solitaire decks, blueprints, calculators, libraries full of books, office files, medical test results, genetic strings, to cite just a few. While this convergence might seem today logical and understandable, just a few years ago (before the computer era) it would have been difficult to find something linking medical research and film distribution.

The second key pattern derivates from the first one. As part of this evolution and the iterative learning process that comes with it, technology gets cheaper and better with time incrementally. Any early adopter of technology has witnessed this phenomenon when, after a few generations, his or her first generation model has become an obsolete object that cost twice as much as the new model. This kind of innovation was baptized "sustaining" by Clayton Christensen. In his words, sustaining technologies "improve the performance of established products." But he also recognized that sometimes "disruptive" technologies emerge. They bring to "a market [I would say to the security environment] a very different value proposition than had been available previously."

So, for the purposes of this chapter, the second important environmental pattern is that innovation brings change to the system either incrementally or disruptively. Incremental improvements of existing mainstream technologies makes them better and cheaper, but disruptive innovation can and often does change the environment in unexpected ways, disrupting (hence the name) the rules that governed what seemed, for a while, a stable ecosystem.

Disruptive technologies are the ones that normally modify the physical qualities of our environment and more importantly, the fabric of our technologically dependent civilization. For example, the combustion engine not only replaced the horse as the main human means of transportation, it also completely disrupted the way humans interact with their urban space, making modern cities and suburban sprawl possible; this created new conditions and constraints for spatial planning. It also created new social vulnerabilities and risks, as the thousands of road fatalities per year demonstrate, catapulting accidents — in less than a century — to the fifth leading cause of death in the United States and creating the need for a highway safety and security strategy.

Technological innovation is a natural consequence of scientific progress. Every time a new phenomenon is understood or, to use Brian Arthur's words, every time a phenomenon or effect is "harnessed" by science, it can be exploited by technology. Then, market forces and human behavior normally determine how and if these new technologies will be assimilated and become a permanent part of the environment.

Each new technology that we adopt creates new structural vulnerabilities. As Ted Lewis points out "highly technological societies are vulnerable because they depend heavily on technology." The more technology we use, the more potential vulnerabilities there are. Because technology now has such a high level of combinatorial complexity, it can safely be said that the environment has reached a state where the periods of stability between disruptions are short lived (certainly shorter than before), and we should assume that disruption is the permanent default state.

You cannot go to the same water twice, and when the water reaches the ocean, the shape of its breaking waves cannot be predicted. Change is indeed the main factor of society today. Therefore, the current mutating environment encourages disruptive participation of small groups of new actors that, until recently, had not enough resources to achieve disruption on a global scale. Because of the two previously described environmental patterns (the combinatorial evolution of the technological environment and the intrinsic characteristics of "sustaining" and "disruptive" technologies), the scale has been altered to favor the small groups I refer to as "the few," and away from big organizations or governments that used to hold a monopoly on system based disruption.

The Power of the Few:

On September 11, 2001, "a few" hijackers were able to bring to a halt the entire nation, cripple the economy, place continuity of government at risk and inflict more than 3000 casualties. The only other occasion when the United States suffered comparable loses from a single attack was during Pearl Harbor, when the combined fleet of six carrier battle groups (the Kido Butai) backed by the full power of the Japanese Empire was deployed to accomplish a similar result.

In 2001, a cell of nineteen hijackers did what only a powerful empire could do in 1941.

How is it possible that a twenty-first century cell has been empowered to provoke the same kind of damage as a twentieth century empire?

The more technologies we integrate incrementally into our society's environment, the more options or choices for recombination are created, and the more unforeseeable vulnerabilities appear. New technologies have commoditized certain key resources needed to affect the environment on a global scale. In addition, the expensive physical infrastructure that was formerly required to do this has often been replaced by technologies that can be modified and recombined without heavy machinery and big factories.

The Quadrennial Defense Review of 2010 explicitly recognized this as one of the key sources for uncertainty in the current security ecosystem:

It is no longer true that technological innovation requires a heavy investment to manipulate nature and produce a result capable of having an impact in the real world, as when most technology represented a tangible single-purpose achievement, designed to obtain a specific desired effect. In the past, the pace of disruption was limited by the constraints of the physical world and as such, disruption moved more slowly and was more expensive than it is now. Today, technology is cheaper to create, easier to recombine, and more integrated in our social environment; because of this, the barriers to entry for achieving world wide disruption have been reduced.

The price of the transistor, backbone of the current computing paradigm and essential to recombining technology, has shrunk exponentially since the 1960s, and computing power has become accessible to everybody for many purposes. As a consequence, digital technology has invaded our environment, replacing in many instances the single purpose "moving parts" that existed before. The digital world serves as a common denominator for an enormous number of social and natural phenomena and directly affects the analog (i.e. the "real") world: anything that can be transformed into binary data can be processed digitally and recombined with other seemingly unrelated phenomena, all for a marginal cost that quickly approaches zero.

We have assimilated into our innovation landscape some of the positive consequences of this new phenomenon. Nowadays, some independent blogs have a readership as large (or larger) than established newspapers with more editorial influence and without the need for expensive presses or distribution channels. Small groups of entrepreneurs were capable of creating "garage startups" that became big multibillion household names like Apple, Microsoft or Google, mainly selling a programmable idea without the initial requirement of large industrial capacity. The original capital needed to jumpstart these companies was in the hundreds of thousands rather than millions of dollars.

Grassroots movements of loosely interconnected individuals (at the left and right of the political spectrum) have been emerging around the world, using Web 2.0 tools to transform political landscapes without the need for cumbersome party bureaucracies, but also with new vulnerabilities hardwired into their structure because of their need to communicate online.

Aggregators like Wikipedia have started to take advantage of the fragmented knowledge and the free unstructured time of millions of individuals, who are willing to donate this time "just for fun," capitalizing on what Clay Shirky calls an enormous and yet unexploited cognitive surplus. This effort has created a source of information many times bigger than any physical library, accessible from anywhere where there is an Internet connection. This dematerialized knowledge distribution is leveling the information field, independently of how far people are from the cultural centers. It might be true that Wikipedia is the result of the work of many thousands of volunteers working together, but thanks to aggregation and crowd sourcing technology, this is done at the individual level (the scale of the few) replacing big centralized teams.

As all the previous examples demonstrate, global consequences for the actions of small groups of individuals have been commoditized to the extreme. There is one last example that is more dramatic than any other: Thanks to computer modeling, geo-engineering projects to alter weather patterns are now within reach of wealthy individuals like former Microsoft CEO William Gates. In 2008 (well before Gates announced that he had any interest in funding this kind of projects) David Victor wrote "a lone Greenfinger, self-appointed protector of the planet and working with a small fraction of Gates bank account, could force a lot of geo-engineering on his own. Bond films of the future might struggle with the dilemma of unilateral planetary engineering."

Current technologies make it possible for small groups of individuals ("the few" or "the one") to alter Earth's weather patterns. This is the degree of change in the scale for disruption: one person, financing a "few", can change the planet, and not only in a metaphorical way. In less than fifty years, individual disruption potential has reached a global scale. In the 1970s, Alvin Toffler coined the term "future shock" to describe the effects of rapid and accelerating changes in society. In his words, The rate of change has implications quite apart from, and sometimes more important than, the directions of change. No attempt to understand adaptivity can succeed until this fact is grasped. Any attempt to define the "content" of change must include the consequences of pace itself as part of that content.

In this rapidly changing environment, where consecutive waves of disruptive technologies are reshaping society faster than it can adapt to the last wave, the small and unstructured "few" are capable of adapting to the pace of change faster than vertical organizations or big governments. As this is a tool-based phenomenon, and tools have no morals or ethics, the "power of the few" can be moral or immoral, legal or illegal.

Without the proper countermeasures, small groups (i.e., terrorist cells, gangs or cartels) or even just lone individuals (e.g., skilled hackers), have a new capacity to inflict damage, fear, and death due to potential access to the same tools that also empower positive behavior and sustain our technologically dependent environment.

The implications of this are fundamental for homeland security's strategic culture. New technologies, especially disruptive technologies, come with new recombining potential. Because "the few" have better adaptivity than "the many," small groups can take advantage of unforeseen consequences of the new altered environment more rapidly than authorities can identify a new potential threat and react to it. Convergence of different technologies makes this a multi-layered vulnerability, beyond just information technology risks. For example: human beings outfitted with Life Critical Implantable Medical Devices, (e.g., pacemakers, defibrillators or neurostimulators) have potentially become "hackable" targets. Most of the new versions of these lifesaving devices are activated and deactivated via wireless protocols and "the lack of authentication and integrity mechanisms put patients at risk from attack by anyone with a transmitter." Without the proper countermeasure, "the few" might conceivably be empowered to literally stop a heart or a mind by just thinking about it (and programming the proper code).

The permanently disrupted environment cannot and should not be reversed, as its positive effects far outweigh its negative implications. In those places where, in the last 200 years, science and technology have become permanent fixtures of the social landscape, quality of life and security are greater than ever. As Indur Goklany explains in his thoroughly researched book, meaningful indicators like hunger, infant mortality, life expectancy, education, political rights and the UN "human development index" are all positively affected by the presence of "unparalleled technological change, which has transformed the world more in the past two centuries than all the other events put together since the beginning of agriculture 10 millennia ago." He then points out: "Economic growth and technological change have redefined the role of women and children, restructured the workplace, undermined age-old arrangements of caste and class, expanded the middle class, and developed new institutions and organizations."

A policy that would try to stop innovation and progress in the name of security would also be immoral, as it would do more harm than good by denying solutions to some of our most pressing problems. It would also would be Orwellian, as it would transform the creativity and imagination of innovators into "thoughtcrimes" punishable by law. The suppression of technology has rarely if ever been proved to be an effective strategy. Instead, we need a security strategy designed to protect the safety of "the many" from this recently acquired power of "the few," while at the same time preserving the technological tools needed to unleash innovation and entrepreneurial creativity.

A high-tech environment is also a target-rich environment, where society's infrastructure is not only vulnerable to sabotage — it can even be "illicitly appropriated," by clandestine actors, and turned against its legitimate users. Even the consequences of natural disasters are worse today because of our social dependency on technological infrastructure in dense population centers. As Mitchell and Townsend observe:

By bringing down the networks it depends upon, a city can be killed. Those networks can also be hijacked and turned against their creators delivering destruction by appropriating the very transfer and distribution capability that motivated their construction ... for an attacker it can be a better strategy to exploit, rather than destroy, an enemy's networks. If access to large-scale network can be gained, it eliminates the need to expend a lot of effort and energy to get to them. It isn't even necessary to possess comparable forces. Violence and destruction can be delivered with modest means but pinpoint accuracy, by infiltrating or hijacking those networks.

Furthermore, complex networked environments like the ones previously described tend to self-organize critically, injecting a degree of randomness into the security landscape in which, as Lewis points out, catastrophe is hard to avoid: "A small (random) perturbation in these systems can trip a major collapse, unexpectedly, dramatically, and resoundingly. Because the cause is not obvious (until after the fact), and it is often a very minor perturbation, the collapse comes as a shock."

On 9/11, the illicit appropriation of the civilian aviation network was catastrophically recombined with the steel frame of the skyscrapers in a very disruptive way, to circumvent the security systems of the continental United States. Basically, on that day, the United States of America was hacked by a terrorist cell.

While homeland security has been redefining the role of the state in the fight against asymmetrical attacks, the current strategy has structural limitations in its capacity to deal with "out of the box" vulnerabilities created by our dependence on new technologies and the accelerated pace of technological change. A new strategy capable of taking advantage of this disrupted environment is urgently needed for our era, as the acceleration changes in new technologies — like bio or nanotechnology, robotics and geo-engineering — means the clandestine "few" can find new possibilities every day to appropriate more systems, recombining them in unforeseeable ways.

No traditional, slow reacting bureaucracy is agile enough to respond to this challenge, and the current homeland security institutional model is no exception. Therefore, I argue here that a new organizational change to America's homeland security institutions is needed to prepare them to be proactive actors in this disrupted high-tech environment.

The Limits of Current Homeland Security's Adaptability to Disruption

How can a traditional security bureaucracy react to this permanently disrupted environment of innovation and fast paced technological evolution? How can a big enterprise made of bureaucratic institutions composed in their turn of hundreds of thousands of individuals, respond to the new vulnerabilities and threats posed by disruptive multipurpose technologies that raise, recombine and fall in cycles measured in months and not years, empowering the adaptable few in unexpected ways?

The answer is that it simply cannot. To understand why and what choices are available to defend society's freedoms in this innovative but unstable landscape, it is essential to consider two key determinants regarding the current nature of the threat and how homeland security institutions are expected to confront this threat with a two-pronged approach.

The first essential determinant is that while terrorism should be a big part of any current asymmetrical threat assessment — if only because it is the tactic of choice not just of the weak, but also of the clandestine few (while they are more adaptable than the many, they are not always weaker) — the narrow framework of terrorist conduct does not suffice to describe the homeland security threat posed by the few. Most institutional definitions of terrorism concur that one of the main elements of any terrorist's conduct is the motivation behind the calculated use of violence. Whether this motivation is political, religious, or ideological, the terrorist act has to be oriented to modify the conduct or policy of a government. Yet, in a permanently disrupted environment, what defines the threat posed by the few has less to do with the motivation than with the employed means.

The new vulnerabilities of this high tech society make motivation irrelevant. Whether a critical infrastructure is sabotaged or illicitly appropriated to pursue a political or religious agenda, to look for personal gain, to just prove that it can be hacked, or even by accident, the catastrophic consequences for "the many" are the same.

In that sense, homeland security's response to the power of "the few" has to shift its focus beyond motivation to the means. To phrase it differently, not all homeland security threats will be terrorist attacks per se (i.e. politically, religiously or ideologically motivated acts designed to affect the government's policies), nor will all homeland security adversaries will be traditional terrorists. Nevertheless, understanding how a technology can be sabotaged, penetrated, or illicitly appropriated to harm society's interests can be achieved independently of the motivations of the adversarial actor, and a "homeland security response" can be preemptively deployed to address this technological risk.

Without question, confronting the underlying causes which incite a particular group of "the few" to try to do harm to "the many" must be an important and permanent objective of the entire nation and not just of the homeland security enterprise. These causes can be diverse and are often beyond the reach of any security policy. Issues like international Islamist radicalization, domestic racism and xenophobia, organized crime, radical rejection of the federal authority, bullying and social rejection in American schools and colleges, to name just a few, are all social problems for which a solution has to be actively pursued. However, a security and defense policy that would try to address all underlying causes would be diluted in its diversity and faulty in its means, since these and other asymmetrical sources of conflict, almost with the only exception of international state sponsored terrorism, are not at the outset a security or defense problem, but a social one. Consequently, responding to these sources of conflict is a mission for a nation, not for a security strategy.

The second determinant is that we demand from homeland security institutions (composed of more than just the Department of Homeland Security) a two-pronged approach, shaped by two seemingly opposing missions. On the one hand, these agencies are supposed to manage an organizational system of systems using standardized procedures and best practices to prevent known kinds of vulnerabilities in our high tech environment. When a traveler removes his or her shoes to be x-rayed by the Transportation Security Administration (TSA) before boarding a plane, this bureaucracy is applying a continuous security layer designed to counteract a known security vulnerability. On the other hand, homeland security institutions are supposed to "connect" the proverbial dots to anticipate all the threats and vulnerability scenarios that have not yet happened, might never happen, but are morphing rapidly because of the complex nature of the of recombining technologies (old and new), and then patch the security holes, before clandestine actors can exploit them.

Both missions are critically important, but their relation to innovation and therefore to the power of the few is very different. The difference resides in the previously explained distinction between sustaining or incremental technologies and disruptive technologies. The first mission, that I will call here the "systemic mission," deals with sustaining threats. In contrast, the second one, the "future shock mission," is supposed to neutralize disruptive — almost random — threats posed by the rapid pace of technological evolution. These differences are key to understanding homeland security's successes and "failures," and to establishing an alternative strategy to adapt to this complex ecosystem.

Contrary to what one might think, the majority of potential threats against our high tech society are incremental and not disruptive in nature. A bomb used against a soft transportation target like a subway train or a bus, for example, is a well-rehearsed and well-proven method. It has happened many times before and it will probably be tried again with just small incremental innovations to adapt it to the precise conditions of the chosen scenario (i.e., size of the bomb depending on the target, method of concealment, etc.). The same thing can be said about the suicide bomber in a highly dense urban setting, the Columbine copycats, the car bombing of public buildings, and airplane bombings (such as the Pan-Am 103 bombing of 1988, the failed attempts of the so-called shoe bomber in 2001, and the Christmas bomber in 2009).

From the point of view of technology, these are all sustaining threats made possible by the sabotage or destruction of critical infrastructure, exploiting known security holes that are difficult to close in open and technologically dependent societies. It is for these kinds of hazards that a bureaucracy is needed to manage, maintain, and ameliorate a system designed to neutralize incremental, known threats. An organizational approach is essential for this systemic mission, as most of the known security deficiencies can be corrected through standardized measures and "best practices," which create a more secure process for the technology user and ultimately for society. While in some cases budget constraints or civil liberties issues might limit the full spectrum of choices for the policymaker, forcing him or her to imagine disruptive alternatives to solve an otherwise incremental problem, in general the mission can be handled well by an efficient security bureaucracy.

As Henry Mintzberg and others point out: "the key to strategic management, therefore, is to sustain stability or at least adaptable strategic change most of the time, but periodically to recognize the need for transformation and be able to manage that disruptive process without destroying the organization."

Bureaucracies are good organizations for managing iterative processes that are subject to continuous improvement loops and must be executed every time in the same way, independently of the specific individual who takes care of the task any given day. They are the best solution to the problem of maintaining the same level of quality in a repetitive process.

In fact, because of the iterative nature of the bureaucratic processes, this organizational model embraces sustaining change. James Wilson explains, "changes that are consistent with existing task definitions [i.e., incremental innovation] will be accepted [and] only those changes that require a redefinition of those tasks [i.e. disruptive innovation] will be resisted." Mintzberg goes one step further when he suggests:

[Traditional planning] usually institutionalized a form of incrementalism [with relation to planned change] ... because incremental change — change at the margin, with limited scope

— is consistent with the established orientation of the organization, and is planning itself. In contrast, quantum change — which means comprehensive reorientation ... disrupts all the established categories of the organization, on which planning depends. As a result, such change tends to be resisted, or more commonly, ignored, in the planning process.

For Mintzberg, an organization pays the price of having an enunciated strategy with their "ability to change when it must."

The "systemic" homeland security mission appears to be executed in an acceptable way. Most of the time there are no casualties linked to acts of sabotage against or appropriation of the critical infrastructure of the United States; since the establishment of the homeland security policy, only one plane has been used to perpetrate an attack. In 2010, a single-engine plane was deliberately directed against a government building in Austin, Texas, killing one person besides the pilot and prompting a vivid debate about as to whether or not this incident qualified as an act of terrorism, given the sui generis motivations of the perpetrator (an IRS audit).

If I suggest that the systemic mission appears to be well executed, it is because measuring the success of the homeland security deterrence strategy takes us into the difficult realm of measuring the success of a negative. How do we "tally the score" of events that did not happen because they were deterred by a systemic approach? What statistical indicators are available to determine if the homeland security institutions are doing a better job today than yesterday and a worse one than tomorrow (the basis of continuous improvement)? And, what is more important, how do we know that we are safer and more secure today — because of all this organizational effort — than before 9/11, our baseline?

Answering these questions is essential for both, the "incremental" and the "future shock" missions, albeit even more complicated for the second, as I will later demonstrate.

There is, of course, a simple methodology to prove the effectiveness of most homeland security measures to protect our security environment. A controlled experiment could, for example, shut down all iterative security measures at the airports of one state, while maintaining them at all the other airports in the United States. Once all the protections and security protocols in that state were removed, we would just have to measure the difference between the amount of security incidents originating from those airports (even when flights crossed state lines), and compare them with the control group (the rest of the US) to see if there was a positive difference (i.e., the airports of that state were more secure) or a negative difference (i.e., the airports of that state where less secure).

This is the underlying logic of the tests used by the pharmaceutical industry and the FDA to determine the safety of a drug, or by the computing industry to test the effectiveness of the security architecture of their networks.

A homemade version of this test can be tried by anyone: it would just be necessary to take a personal computer and install a version of Windows XP without Service Pack 1 and 2, no firewall and no antivirus program, and then start using the web with Explorer 6. Then, the experimenter will have to wait and see how long it takes for the computer to get hacked or infected by a virus. After this test, he or she will now know with certainty how effective the previous security measures were. (For my computer, it never took more than three minutes for the OS kernel to be corrupted).

The moral, legal, and political implications of such an experimental and controlled approach to measure the effectiveness of a deterrence strategy for homeland security are evident. A seemingly less effective, but certainly more humane alternative to address the task of assessing effectiveness has been developed in the form of vulnerability analysis methodology for critical infrastructure protection, designed to study and determine the best way to "allocate limited funding in such a way as to minimize overall risk." While this methodology creates a more efficient resource allocation system for homeland security funding, the nature of the bureaucratic culture signifies that risk reduction will be perceived through the lens of the continuous improvement process and hence always as an incremental movement. As Christensen points out:

One of the dilemmas of management is that, by their very nature, processes are established so that employees perform recurrent tasks in a consistent way, time after time. To ensure consistency, they are meant not to change or if they must change, to change through tightly controlled procedures. This means that the very mechanisms through which organizations create value are intrinsically inimical to change.

Therefore, homeland security organizations will tend to evaluate critical infrastructure protection countermeasures, even the disruptive ones, within the current continuous improvement paradigm. This is fine for the systemic mission, but everything related to the second mission, the "future shock mission," will most probably be discarded, because disruptive and unpredictable threats posed by the recombining nature of new technologies cannot be confronted by incremental methodologies. They are by definition outside of the feedback loop.

In other words, for the yet to be planned homeland security incident that will use a new combination of technologies never tried before, the current homeland security institutional framework cannot connect the dots, because there are no dots to be connected. What makes Christensen's concept of disruptive technology so troubling for administrators all over the world is that he clearly demonstrated that good planning, and not the opposite, was in fact one of the main reasons why big companies failed and were crushed by new disruptive technologies. In the context of homeland security policy, this means that with the current organizational model, the bureaucracy might get as good as it can possibly be and still miss the next threat precisely because it has learned to be very efficient in its normal operation, thus resisting any change outside its sustaining processes. Hierarchical iterative bureaucracies are precisely the worst kind of organizations to confront "out-of-the-process" threats.

This is why we stated earlier that a traditional bureaucracy cannot be the one reacting to disruptive threats. Instead, to fight this bureaucratic hysteresis the current homeland security institutional design (indispensable for the "systemic mission") has to be complemented with another very different approach to security to confront the recombining threats of the permanently disrupted environment. A new ad-hocratic organization, with no direct involvement in the fight against incremental threats or the day-to-day operation of homeland security institutions, should concentrate its efforts on producing positive homeland security disruption to counteract the negative effects of the power of "the few."

Pushing the Borders of the Impossible:

While the first homeland security "systemic mission" of neutralizing incremental threats seems to be fulfilled in an acceptable way by the current homeland security institutional model, the second "future shock mission" focusing on counteracting the threat posed by the recombining of disruptive technologies is almost nonexistent. In fact, the relative success of the first mission is one of the biggest obstacles to accomplishing effectively the second one. As the homeland security bureaucracy becomes more effective in limiting the success ratio of incremental threats, it creates a political environment where it is very difficult for the policymaker not to keep allocating more resources to the same programs that appear to be working, therefore sustaining the investment cycle. This makes it very challenging for the few to repeat the last attack, but it also focuses the limited organizational resources and attention span on the last incremental scenario and away from the next (unforeseeable) disruptive attack. Hence, the strategic truism, which states that successful armies and navies are always preparing to fight the last war, has, in this case, metaphorical and literal significance.

In this security ecosystem defined by the accelerated pace of disruptive technological recombination, "connecting the dots" is not an acceptable strategy to avoid the next threat. Intelligence gathering is not possible for attacks that have not yet been planned or even conceived, combining technologies that are or will be available, but were conceived for other purposes. Also, while focused intelligence plays a central role for avoiding specific threat scenarios, once these scenarios are identified and hopefully neutralized they become, by definition, part of the systemic mission and an incremental threat.

Instead, homeland security institutions addressing the "future shock mission" have to be able to be proactive and become disruptive agents themselves. In this way, the state would reclaim the initiative with innovation (instead of fighting against it), provoking positive environmental changes through a sustained research and development effort. Doing this requires an organization shielded from the "systemic mission," designed to avoid the same things that make other bureaucracies so successful: iteration and incremental processes.

Administrative reforms have a bad name in homeland security, probably because there have been so many of them in a very short amount of time. Wood and Waterman established that political reorganizations might not be enough to break bureaucratic resistance to change when more than one organizational culture exists inside the bureaucratic bodies. That is the case of the Department of Homeland Security, where the so-called department components (TSA, CBP, the Coast Guard, FEMA, Secret Service, etc.) have strong organizational cultures that precede the merger that created the department in 2002.

It is precisely for this reason that a new partial reorganization is necessary, addressing the limitations of the current structure to confront the "future shock mission." The current competing organizational cultures of the homeland security bureaucracy are oriented to accomplish the old missions of the department's individual components, fighting threats in an incremental way. Any new task given to this existing structure will be watered down by an older, more successful, more proven and more consolidated organizational ethos. Wilson explains it:

Tasks that are not part of the culture will not be attended to with the same energy and resources as are devoted to tasks that are part of it. Second, organizations in which two or more cultures struggle for supremacy will experience serious conflict as defenders of one seek to dominate representatives of the others. Third, organizations will resist taking on new tasks that seem incompatible with its dominant culture. The stronger and more uniform the culture — that is, the more the culture approximates a sense of mission — the more obvious these consequences.

In the current homeland security administration model, research and development efforts are embedded in the "systemic mission" and most if not all of its current results are incremental and not disruptive in nature. Therefore, there is no incentive to look for solutions to problems that are not considered part of the operational objectives of the current homeland security environment. That is why there is so much interest and debate regarding, for example, the development and implementation of the controversial full body scanners (an incremental innovation useful to the current operational mission of DHS), and so little interest in countermeasures for security risks that have never been exploited.

In fact, Michael Greenberger demonstrated that under the current organizational model, homeland security's institutions are unresponsive even to technology solutions that are widely available. He found that because of organizational limits, the Department of Homeland Security was incapable of recognizing widely available technology solutions to security threats in at least two cases: efficient "see through" technology to screen cargo, and liquid explosive detection for airplane passengers. To combat this resistance, he proposed an institutional reform to create inside DHS a "Department of Homeland Security Technology Mobilization Board" based on the successful mobilizations boards used during World War II to "review and search out antiterrorism technology and quickly decide whether the new technology should be used and promoted in the homeland security effort." I would like to take this good proactive approach a step further, using as a model the most disruptive institution for military research and development in the history of mankind: the Defense Advanced Research Projects Agency (DARPA).

Created in 1958 after the so-called "Sputnik Crisis," when the American government was taken by surprise by the successful launching of the Soviet satellite Sputnik, DARPA's mission is "to maintain the technological superiority of the U.S. military and prevent technological surprise from harming our national security by sponsoring revolutionary, high-payoff research." It is a highly disruptive organization "with no operational mission, no service requirements and designed to protect fragile ephemeral projects." It doesn't avoid future shocks surprises in itself, but tries to create its own surprises faster than its adversaries, thus controlling the pace of military innovation.

An organization like DARPA succeeds in managing a disrupted environment because it does not negate its disrupted or disruptive-prone nature, but instead uses it to its advantage. This means that it fights surprise by creating surprise, consciously producing as many environmental disruptions as it can. When DARPA succeeds, it forces American adversaries into the uncomfortable position of being the ones reacting to American military disruption and trying to guess the next move, robbing those adversaries of the initiative that the few naturally tend to enjoy. By doing this, DARPA does not counter specific future shock surprises, but it creates a security environment where US Armed Forces have the upper hand.

As any investor knows, high return and high risk are directly correlated. Therefore, high payoff research and development need a higher institutional tolerance for risk and failure. Christensen points out that because "the ultimate uses or applications for disruptive technologies are unknowable in advance ... Failure is an intrinsic step toward success." DARPA's creative process aims to "find an area of technology that could go a long way toward serving the needs of the country if improved but that wasn't getting much attention in the private sector, put some well-considered research and development money into it to get it on its feet, and then cut it loose." Because of this high-risk approach, some of its projects fail in a way that would put in danger the career of the project manager in any other organization, while others, like the Advanced Research Projects Agency Network (ARPANET), succeed in forever transforming the human environment.

For this approach to work in the context of homeland security, it is essential to create an agency isolated from the core requirements of the "systemic mission." It would have to be a task oriented research and development organization designed to positively disrupt the security environment with technology solutions for problems not yet identified by "the few."

Some, like Joshua Cooper, have used the metaphor of an institutional immune system to describe such an approach to defend society against the negative effect of the accelerating pace of change. For him, "this constant surprise, and the demand it makes for an 'always-on' defense, is one of the reasons we need a deep-security immune system instead of an old-style Grand Strategy." An evolving homeland security immune system requires a risk management approach to identify vulnerabilities with low investment-high rewards opportunities to close a technological security hole while at the same time the usability of the concerned technology is preserved and, if possible, enhanced.

DARPA's success as the proactive component of the Department of Defense immune system is due to the fact that it is structured as an adhocracy, a term coined by Toffler to describe an organizational model where organic temporary relations are established (hence the ad hoc part of the name) to respond to a particular task (or threat) with very little or no formal hierarchy or standardized behavior. An adhocracy is a "fast-moving, information-rich, kinetic organization of the future, filled with transient cells and extremely mobile individuals." Such a model for homeland security would create ephemeral teams of experts used to close high risk security holes that would then be disbanded to make place to another team formed to tackle another disruptive challenge.

In fact, as Christopher Ford identified, some of DARPA's most recent projects have already some unambiguous homeland security implications. The "DARPA network challenge," for example, showed how social networking web tools and aggregators can be engaged to gather data, mobilize participants, foster collaboration, and build trust, in the context of multiple homeland security missions.

For the homeland security "future shock" mission, the challenge is not only to pair a disruptive solution with a disruptive problem; even the problem definitions themselves should be disruptive in nature: How to neutralize a threat that no one has yet identified as a threat? Thus, the "future shock" prevention effort must identify proactively security threats to the human environment provoked by the recombining of technology and human social and cultural behavior.

Consequently, this new homeland security institution would have to invest an important part of its resources probing disruptive security scenarios, using a "red team" methodology to identify security shortcomings. These "white hat" hackers would try to hack the whole United States of America technology environment, establishing the mission requirements for the new agency. Only then, after a critical technology has failed this highly classified penetration test or a scenario that recombines multiple technologies in a novel way has been identified, research and development could begin to find a minimum sufficient response that permits the technology to operate as efficiently as before but closes preventively the security hole. While this proactive approach will not identify every recombining threat, it will add a new layer of disruption and innovation to the human ecosystem on top of the ones that are already in place, but this time under the direct control of the homeland security institutions.

Because there is no bigger threat to America's interests than the loss of competitiveness caused by crippling its critical sectors in the name of pointless security measures — something akin to an autoimmune disease if we extend the metaphor a little bit more — the concept of a "Minimum Sufficient Response" is essential. In fact, for the effort to be successful and sustainable, most of the tasks should be dual-purpose, enhancing (rather than the opposite) the usability of the concerned technology. This would also have a protective effect on American civil liberties and human rights, by limiting the scope of the security procedures. If done properly, this new actor in the homeland security environment would identify unproductive and bloated security solutions where a risk management approach is absent (i.e. a layer of security that does nothing to enhance the resilience of a technology), and could propose the necessary changes to improve the usability of the system.

While incremental research and development is an essential part of the "systemic mission," this new organization should be isolated from them. If an attack by the few does occur, the technological solution needed to avoid such an event in the future should not be the responsibility of this new institution. Once a real "red team" has made explicit the exploitable vulnerability, fixing it has become an incremental and not a disruptive challenge.

Proving the effectiveness of this new institutional approach will be difficult and will require "out of the box" managerial and political skills. To demonstrate this, we offer to the reader a thought experiment: Imagine that an organization like the one we are describing existed in 1997.

In 1998, the organization's red teams identified the cockpit doors of commercial airplanes as weak links in the security environment of the transportation sector for many scenarios, none of which looked like the 9/11 terrorist attacks. Then, multidisciplinary research and development teams identified a Minimum Sufficient Response technology solution: by armoring the cockpit doors and making it impossible for the pilot to open them while airborne — even if he or she wants to (in case the criminal actors try to blackmail him or her by holding hostage a passenger or a flight attendant) — no asymmetrical actor would be able to gain control of the airliner, closing the security hole.

If such a process would have taken place, we would never know that something as costly as 9/11 was deterred, but we would have taken advantage of a low investment-high reward opportunity to "upgrade" the United States security ecosystem in a disruptive way, leaving mostly unaffected the usability of the technology. I use the 9/11 example because it is a disruptive threat that has already been identified and mostly neutralized by precisely this kind of solution (the most cost effective measure of all the preventive solutions identified by the 9/11 commission report). It also shows how hard it would it be to measure the effectiveness of a procedure that might deter a catastrophic event if that event never takes place because of our actions.

Finally, because what I am proposing here is a DARPA inspired model for the problem of adapting the homeland security organizational framework to respond to the power of "the few," it is necessary to explain why I do not consider the existing HSARPA a sufficient solution. First, HSARPA lacks the proper funding needed to have the same positive effect that DARPA has had for research and development. Second, HSARPA is devoting most of those resources to research incremental solutions to incremental problems.

The HSARPA mission specifically states that it was created to "enhance departmental operations." Because of this, HSARPA is not capable of addressing the "future shock mission." One employee of the science and technology directorate at DHS described HSARPA to me as an agency "suffocating" inside of the Department of Homeland Security bureaucratic structure. For an organization to be successful at confronting disruptive technologies, strong evidence suggests that an independent small organization is needed to escape the gravitational field of the incremental mission of the bigger institution and its organizational culture. Currently, most if not all of the HSARPA projects are sustaining research and development programs pivoting around the operational missions of the Department of Homeland Security.

9

Cyber Terrorism and American's Planning

TRANSFORMING NATIONAL PREPAREDNESS

Hurricane Katrina was an extraordinary storm that caused destruction on a scale never before seen from a natural disaster in the United States. The continuing Federal response—the largest disaster relief and recovery effort in our Nation's history—likewise has been unprecedented and extraordinary. But what we owe the people of the Gulf Coast, and all Americans, is the best possible response.

We must expect more catastrophes like Hurricane Katrina—and possibly even worse. In fact, we will have compounded the tragedy if we fail to learn the lessons—good and bad—it has taught us and strengthen our system of preparedness and response. We cannot undo the mistakes of the past, but there is much we can do to learn from them and to be better prepared for the future. This is our duty.

The Federal government has learned from our response to Hurricane Katrina; the remaining three will be discussed more fully here.

These seventeen lessons, and the 125 recommendations that flow from them, represent specific challenges for corrective action. But we also recognize that to overcome these challenges and fully accomplish the intent of the attendant recommendations, we require a *transformation* of our homeland security architecture.

In the aftermath of another American catastrophe—the terrorist attacks of September 11—we transformed our government architecture, policies, and strategies in a comprehensive effort to defeat terrorism and better protect and defend the homeland. With the creation of the Department of Homeland Security, the post of Director of National Intelligence, the passage of the USA PATRIOT Act, and the codification of both the National Counterterrorism Centre and the National Counterproliferation Centre, we have undertaken the most extensive reorganization of the Federal government since 1947. We have created top-level policy guidance through the*National Security Strategy, the National Strategy for Homeland Security* and the *National Strategy for Combating Terrorism,* all of which identify strategic objectives to secure the United States, its citizens and interests from terrorist attacks. Most important, we have pursued our policies and objectives through concrete action. In concert with our coalition partners, we have been on the offense, waging an unremitting campaign of direct and continuous action against our terrorist enemies and the deadly scourge of terror and intimidation more broadly. These actions, combined with an array of defensive measures at home and abroad, have enhanced the safety and security of the American people.

Preparedness is inextricably intertwined with our national security, counterterrorism, and homeland security strategies. As discussed throughout this report, we have taken essential steps over the past five years—through plans, policies, and guidelines such as the *National Response Plan,* the *National Incident Management System,*the *Interim National Infrastructure Protection Plan,* and the *Interim National Preparedness Goal*—to strengthen our ability to prepare for, protect against, respond to, and recover from the natural and man-made disasters that will occur.

But we must go further. We must continue to build upon the foundation of national and homeland security we have established since 9/11 to improve our preparedness capabilities. Our response to Hurricane Katrina demonstrated the imperative to integrate and synchronize our policies, strategies, and plans—among all Federal, State, local, private sector, and community efforts and across all partners in the professions of prevention, protection, response, and recovery—into a unified system for homeland security. This unifying system will ensure *National Preparedness.* Today there is a national consensus that we must be better prepared to respond to events like Hurricane Katrina. While we have constructed a system that effectively handles the demands of routine, limited natural and man-made disasters, our system clearly has structural flaws for addressing catastrophic incidents. But we as a Nation—Federal, State, and local governments; the private sector; as well as communities and individual citizens—have not developed a shared vision of or commitment to *preparedness:* what we must do to prevent (when possible), protect against, respond to, and recover from the next catastrophe. Without a shared vision that is acted upon by all levels of our Nation and encompasses the full range of our preparedness and response capabilities, we will not achieve a truly transformational *national* state of preparedness.

There are two immediate priorities for this transformation:

1. Define and implement a comprehensive National Preparedness System; and
2. Foster a new, robust Culture of Preparedness.

A National Preparedness System

Shortfalls in the Federal response to Hurricane Katrina highlight that our current homeland security architecture—to include policies, authorities, plans, doctrine, operational concepts, and resources at the Federal, State, local, private sector, and community levels—must be strengthened and transformed. At the most fundamental level, the current system fails to define Federal responsibility for national preparedness in catastrophic events. Nor does it establish clear, comprehensive goals along with an integrated means to measure their progress and achievement. Instead, the United States currently has guidelines and individual plans, across multiple agencies and levels of government that do not yet constitute an *integrated* national system that ensures unity of effort.

In addition, as described in the narrative section of this report, the response to Hurricane Katrina demonstrated that our current system is too reactive in orientation. Our decades-old system, built on the precepts of federalism, has been based on a model whereby local and State governments wait to reach their limits and exhaust their resources before requesting Federal assistance. Federal agencies could and did take steps to prepare to extend support and assistance, but tended to provide little without a prior and specific request. In other words, the system was biased toward requests and the concept of "pull" rather than toward anticipatory actions and the proactive "push" of Federal resources.

While this approach has worked well in the majority of disasters and emergencies, catastrophic events like Hurricane Katrina are a different matter. The current homeland security environment—with the continuing threat of mass casualty terrorism and the constant risk of natural disasters—now demands that the Federal government actively prepare and encourage the Nation as a whole to plan, equip, train, and cooperate for all types of future emergencies, including the most catastrophic.

A useful model for our approach to homeland security is the Nation's approach to *national security*. Over the past six decades, we have created a highly successful national security system. This system is built on deliberate planning that assesses threats and risks, develops policies and strategies to manage them, identifies specific missions and supporting tasks, and matches the forces or capabilities to execute them. Operationally organized, it stresses the importance of unity of command from the President down to the commander in the field.

Perhaps most important, the national security system emphasizes feedback and periodic reassessment. Programs and forces are assessed for readiness and the degree to which they support their assigned missions and strategies on a continuing basis. Top level decision-makers periodically revisit their assessments of threats and risks, review their strategies and guidance, and revise their missions, plans, and budgets accordingly.

This national security system was not created overnight. It has taken almost sixty years to build and refine. Beginning with the National Security Act of 1947-mandated creation of the Department of Defense, the Central Intelligence Agency, and the National Security Council (NSC), this system has evolved substantially through the years. It has taken time to create a strong NSC that has integrated interagency policies and efforts. Similarly, it took decades to build first the Office of the Secretary of Defense and then the Joint Staff as the central management elements for the Department of Defense. We did not accomplish the complete intent of the 1947 reforms for national security system until Congress passed the *Goldwater-Nichols* defense reorganization legislation in 1986, and the Federal government put those reforms in place in following years.

The lessons of the national security system's evolution will help us to transform our five-year old homeland security system. Of course, homeland security demands are complex. While responsibility for national security rests with the Federal government working with its international partners, the precepts of federalism make every level of government and region of the country both a contributor to, and responsible for, homeland security.

There are significant institutional and intergovernmental challenges to information and resource sharing as well as operational cooperation. These barriers stem from a multitude of factors—different cultures, lack of communication between departments and agencies, and varying procedures and working patterns among departments and agencies. Equally problematic, there is uneven coordination in pre-incident planning among State and local governments. For example, our States and territories developed fifty-six unique homeland security strategies, as have fifty high-threat, high-density urban areas. Although each State and territory certainly confronts unique challenges, without coordination this planning approach makes the identification of common or national solutions difficult. Furthermore, our current approach to response planning does not sufficiently acknowledge how adjoining communities and regions can and do support each other. For example, there is wide disparity in emergency response capabilities across the country's many local jurisdictions. Yet we currently lack the means to assess and track what these disparities are and, consequently, how we must plan to account for them in a crisis.

These include the guiding vision for preparedness as well as clarification of the Federal government's central role in organizing the national efforts of our homeland security partners. The essential importance of building operational capabilities in the Federal government by: a) Strengthening the operational management capacity of the Department of Homeland Security and strengthening its field elements; b) Reinforcing the DHS role as incident manager for the Federal response; and c) Strengthening the response capabilities of other departments and agencies in the Federal government.

A Preparedness Vision

A National Preparedness System must begin with a common vision for preparedness—what end-state are we seeking to achieve and how do we plan to get there? In Homeland Security Presidential Directive 8 (HSPD-8), the President called for the creation of a comprehensive national preparedness system, starting with a "national domestic all-hazards preparedness goal." This Goal was to outline key preparedness priorities, objectives, targets, and desired outcomes. In response to HSPD-8, DHS has developed an *Interim National Preparedness Goal* that reflects the Department's progress to date to develop each of those elements in coordination with other entities. It will remain in effect until superseded by the final National Preparedness Goal, which awaits completion.

We must now translate this Goal into a robust preparedness system that includes integrated plans, procedures, policies, training, and capabilities at all levels of government. The System must also incorporate the private sector, non-governmental organizations, faith-based groups, and communities, including individual citizens. The desired end-state of our National Preparedness System must be to achieve and sustain risk-based target levels of capability to prevent, protect against, respond to, and recover from major events in order to minimize the impact on lives, property, and the economy.

The *Homeland Security Strategy* and HSPD-8 provide the framework for the National Preparedness System. From this guidance comes the requirement for risk-based capabilities at the Federal, State and local levels that must enable the Nation to respond to a range of disasters—both man-made and natural. The required capabilities determine readiness targets for organizations at all levels. A unified effort from all homeland security stakeholders to commit the requisite resources, training, and exercising must support these targets and asset requirements.

Our National Preparedness System must also have appropriate feedback and assessment mechanisms to ensure that progress is made and that our goals are being realized. As called for in the *Interim National Preparedness Goal*, we must establish a readiness baseline for capabilities at the Federal, State, and local levels. This baseline should include an inventory of our preparedness assets as well as a metrics-based assessment of current capabilities. Thereafter, we must assess the gap between our present and target levels of capability. Over time, we must track our progress in closing these gaps.

Finally, the National Preparedness System must emphasize preparedness for *all hazards*. Most of the capabilities necessary for responding to natural disasters are also vital for responding to terrorist incidents. Yet for a variety of reasons, much of the Federal government, Congress, and the Nation at large have continued to think about terrorism and natural disasters as if they are competing priorities rather than two elements of the larger homeland security challenge. The lessons of 9/11 and Hurricane Katrina are that we cannot choose one or the other type of disaster. We must be prepared for all hazards.

The Federal Government's Role in the "National" System

Building upon the President's *Homeland Security Strategy*, Homeland Security Presidential Directives, and the *Interim National Preparedness Goal*, the Federal government must clearly articulate national preparedness goals and objectives; it must create the infrastructure—through the definition of common strategies and interoperable capabilities—for ensuring unity of effort; and it must manage the system for measuring effectiveness and assessing preparedness at all levels of government. Put another way, the Federal government must develop common doctrine and ensure alignment of preparedness plans, budgets, grants, training, exercises, and equipment.

While each State will have its own strategy and a multitude of local capabilities to meet the needs of its citizens, the Federal government—through the Department of Homeland Security—must work with State, local, and regional entities to develop strategies and plans that define how each State manages disasters within their borders as well as regionally, beginning at the local level. DHS must also identify how State, local, regional, and private-sector preparedness activities support the national strategy.

Transformation Within the Federal Government: Building Operational Capability

The creation of an effective National Preparedness System will require the Federal government to transform the way it does business. The most important objective of this Federal transformation must be to build and integrate *operational capability*. Each Federal department or agency with homeland security responsibilities needs operational capability—or the capacity to get things done—to translate executive management direction promptly into results on the ground. It includes the personnel to make and communicate decisions; organizational structures that are assigned, trained, and exercised for their missions; sufficient physical resources; and the command, control, and communication channels to make, monitor, and communicate decisions.

As described in the preceding narrative, the response to Hurricane Katrina required that the Federal government both support State and local efforts while conducting response operations in the field, in addition to making policy or implementing programs. With the exceptions of the Department of Defense and the Coast Guard—two organizations with considerable operational capabilities—the Federal government was at times slow and ineffective in responding to the massive operational demands of the catastrophe.

These shortfalls were not due to the absence of top level plans such as the *National Response Plan* and the *National Incident Management System*. Rather, the problem is that these plans lack clarity on key aspects and have operational gaps, and have not been effectively integrated and translated into action. Prior training, exercising, and equipping proved inadequate to the task of effectively responding to Hurricane Katrina. There is a difference between a plan (saying "this is what we need to do") and a trained, resourced set of defined missions (saying "this is what we are going to do, and this is how we are going to organize, train, exercise, and equip to do it"). For any plan to work, it must first be broken down into its component parts. Next, the plan's requirements should be matched to the human and physical assets of each responsible department, agency, or organization.

The imperative, therefore, is to organize coherent, proactive management of responses to catastrophic events. Virtually all elements of the Federal government must be operational—to respond to catastrophic events with unified effort. There are three principal requirements to achieve this transformational goal:

1. Strengthening DHS institutions to manage the Federal response as well as enhancing DHS regional and field elements.
2. Reinforcing the Secretary of Homeland Security's position as the President's manager of the Federal response; and
3. Strengthening the response capabilities—management and field resources—of other Federal departments and agencies.

THE DEPARTMENT OF HOMELAND SECURITY

Since the Department was created in January 2003, the management and personnel of the Department of Homeland Security have undertaken their responsibilities with energy and professionalism. Their courage and commitment to their mission have improved the security of all Americans.

But the Federal response to Hurricane Katrina demonstrated that the energy and professionalism of DHS personnel was not enough to support the Department's role as the manager of the Federal response. In particular, DHS lacked both the requisite headquarters management institutions and sufficient field capabilities to organize a fully successful Federal response effort. Within the Department, therefore, it is essential to strengthen the DHS headquarters elements to *direct* the Federal response while also providing appropriate resources to DHS field elements so that they can make an impact on the ground.

In order to strengthen DHS's operational management capabilities, we must structure the Department's headquarters elements to support the Secretary's incident management responsibilities. First and most important, Federal government response organizations must be co-located and strengthened to manage catastrophes in a new *National Operations Centre (NOC).* The mission of the NOC must be to coordinate and integrate the national response and provide a common operating picture for the entire Federal government. This interagency centre should ensure National-level coordination of Federal, State, and local response to major domestic incidents. It must combine and co-locate the situational awareness mission of the Homeland Security Operations Centre (HSOC), the operational mission of the National Response Coordination Centre (NRCC), and the strategic role currently assigned to the Interagency Incident Management Group (IIMG). During an incident, all department and agency command centers, as well as the Joint Field Office (JFO) at the disaster site, must provide information to the NOC, which develops a National common operating picture capable of being exported in real time to other Federal operations centers.

The NOC must be staffed by an experienced, well-trained, and resourced cadre of personnel who are prepared to provide expert strategic and operational management of Federal responses to catastrophic incidents. For example, these personnel must include logistical experts with the management tools to track moving resources anywhere across the Nation and ensure timely delivery of aid to affected areas. This staff must also include operations experts who understand how to combine existing resources into effective response packages for any scenario. In addition to a robust permanent staff, the NOC must include a "battle roster" of personnel who will surge to expand and sustain the NOC's capacity during a crisis.

The DHS headquarters must also possess a robust capability for deliberate operational planning. Rather than waiting for the next disaster, DHS planners must apply lessons learned as well as develop detailed operational plans that anticipate the requirements of future responses and what capabilities can be matched to them in what timeframe. Using these operational plans and capability inventories as baseline data, the Headquarters planning staff can conduct national readiness assessments, highlighting priorities for subsequent preparedness investments, training, and exercising.

Below the headquarters level within DHS, we must build up the Department's regional structures. The integration of State and local strategies and capabilities on a regional basis is a homeland security priority. Homeland security regional offices should be the means to foster State, local and private sector integration. Furthermore, DHS regional structures are ideally positioned to pre-identify, organize, train, and exercise future Principal Federal Officials and Joint Field Office staffs. Each DHS regional organization should possess the capacity to establish a self-sufficient, initial JFO on short notice anywhere in its region.

More broadly, the Department of Homeland Security must possess field personnel with the necessary resources, training, and national support. As a start, we must improve and emphasize plans that stress a proactive DHS role—in particular, the *Catastrophic Incident Annex* and *Catastrophic Incident Supplement* of the *NRP*. But DHS must also have available operational funds so that it can "lean forward" in future crises, to take anticipatory actions without budgetary concern or risk of subsequent criticism for a false alarm. In the event of a surprise contingency, battlefield commanders should not have to wait for the release of funds to execute their pre-assigned missions. The same flexibility should be afforded to our Federal homeland security responders.

MANAGING THE INTERAGENCY PROCESS IN HOMELAND SECURITY RESPONSE

In order to create robust homeland security response capabilities, we must also transform our Federal interagency processes. Most important, we must eliminate the extraordinary red tape and resulting delays in the process of requests for assistance in response efforts. Too often during the Hurricane Katrina response we found that the Federal government did not effectively use assets at the ready because the necessary requests were being "coordinated" somewhere in the bureaucracy. The solution is to enshrine in the Federal government one of the central tenets of the *National Incident Management System*—Unified Command. We must transform our approach for catastrophic incidents from one of bureaucratic *coordination* to proactive unified command that creates true unity of effort. As set forth in *NIMS,* "In a [Unified Command] structure, the individuals designated by their jurisdictional authorities... must jointly determine objectives, strategies, plans, and priorities and work together to execute integrated incident operations and maximize the use of assigned resources."

At the Federal level, the most urgent step in creating unity of effort will be to reinforce the Secretary of Homeland Security as the Federal government's preparedness and incident manager. In order to create unity of effort at the Federal level, the Department should manage and orchestrate the specialized efforts of other Federal departments and agencies within their core competencies. Although DHS by Presidential directive has this mission, its internal structures and relationships across the Federal government do not position it to fully succeed. The current arrangements are an awkward mix of the traditional, FEMA-led, approach to interagency coordination and the Homeland Security Act's creation of a powerful Department of Homeland Security.

One model for the command and control structure for the Federal response in the new National Preparedness System is our successful defense and national security statutory framework. In that framework, there is a clear line of authority that stretches from the President, through the Secretary of Defense, to the Combatant Commander in the field. When a contingency arises, the Combatant Commander in that region executes the missions assigned by the Secretary of Defense and the President. Although the Combatant Commander might not "own" or control forces on a day-to-day basis, during a military operation he controls all military forces in his theater: he exercises the command authority and has access to resources needed to affect outcomes on the ground.

The structure for command and control of defense operations. Unity of command is established in a chain of command from the

President through the Secretary of Defense to the Combatant Commander. The Combatant Commander possesses operational control over forces and resources provided by the armed services. The Intelligence Community additionally provides essential information—warning and situational awareness—to the commander in the field. The system makes a clear distinction between operations—in which the Combatant Commander is the centre of activity—and the provision of operational resources. In the latter case, the Armed Services are responsible for the training and equipping of forces.

The model somewhat parallels the original conception of the Federal homeland security response. In particular, the President directs the Secretary of Homeland Security, who coordinates interagency actions at the senior level while supervising the field commander for the Federal response—the Principal Federal Official (PFO). The PFO, in turn, is supported with resources provided by DHS and other interagency departments and agencies.

As described in HSPD-5, Cabinet members are to support the Secretary of Homeland Security as the President's incident manager directing and coordinating the Federal response. At the PFO level, this can be accomplished by ensuring that the Federal Coordinating Officer (FCO)—who possesses authority over resources—works for the PFO.

However, the comparison between the homeland security and defense operations models breaks down in two significant ways. First, the Federal commander only manages *Federal* resources in homeland security. In almost every circumstance, State and local governments maintain operational control over their own resources. Second, the Secretary of Homeland Security and the PFO must request Federal assets from other departments and agencies; they do not command the resources of other departments and agencies. HSPD-5 makes clear that one Cabinet member cannot alter or impede the ability to carry out the authorities of Federal departments and agencies to perform their responsibilities under law. Rather, HSPD-5 anticipates that future events will necessarily involve a joint approach given that several departments and agencies have distinct statutory authorities (e.g., the Attorney

General for criminal investigation of terrorist acts, the Secretary of Defense for command over our military forces, and so forth).

In this vein, we must similarly transform the existing system of Emergency Support Functions (ESFs). A vestige of the 1992 *Federal Response Plan,* the precursor to the NRP, these capability-specific coordination mechanisms, at a minimum, must be reconciled to the *NIMS* as well as responsive to the orders of the Principal Federal Official. More fundamentally, we must examine whether we should reorganize and, in some cases, redefine the ESF structures, while building DHS command and control mechanisms.

These interagency management changes recognize that Federal response to catastrophic events—potential or actual—must be both efficient and effective in meeting the needs of the victims. Without infringing upon the statutory responsibilities of the Cabinet departments and agencies, we must ensure that the President's incident manager is able to call upon the full range of the Federal government's response assets, and to aggressively orchestrate, lead, and coordinate their use in response operations.

OPERATIONAL CAPABILITIES IN OTHER FEDERAL DEPARTMENTS/AGENCIES

Beyond changes to DHS and the structure of Federal response, there is still a compelling need to strengthen operational capabilities across the Federal government. Those departments and agencies that have a responsibility to participate in a catastrophic response must build up their crisis deployable capabilities as well as their effective operational management.

To start, all Federal departments and agencies should have operational command and control structures that comply with the *National Incident Management System.* Secretaries and directors throughout the government must operate jointly, using the same systems, doctrine, and terminology. Similarly, in support of crisis operational capability, each department and agency must develop a deliberate planning capability. Planning should include not only the response plans themselves but also, both personnel and funding to train professional planners.

With these new operational planning functions, Federal departments and agencies must build the detailed supporting plans, concepts, and staffing to execute their NRP and emergency response missions. During Hurricane Katrina, it became clear that most Federal departments and agencies had not developed—much less exercised—standard operating procedures for their response.

An additional imperative is for all Federal departments and agencies to develop "battle rosters" of trained personnel who should deploy when their organization is called upon to support a Federal response to a catastrophic event. The development of these rosters must coincide with the implementation of training certification programs that ensure that personnel are trained and skilled to a high, uniform standard.

Homeland Security Training, Education, and Exercising

An effective National Preparedness System requires that management and response personnel, especially those in the field, are well versed in their missions. At all levels of government, we must build a leadership corps that is fully educated, trained, and exercised in our plans and doctrine. Training is not nearly as costly as the mistakes made in a crisis. Equally important, this corps must be populated by *leaders* who are prepared to exhibit innovation and take the initiative during extremely trying circumstances.

The narrative, the response to Hurricane Katrina revealed a lack of familiarity with incident management, the planning discipline, legal authorities, capabilities, and field-level crisis leadership. Many Federal, State, and local officials lacked a fundamental understanding of the *National Response Plan,* the *NIMS,* and State and local response plans.

The first priority for training is to ensure that our emergency managers fully understand our preparedness and response plans and doctrine. To that end, we must train all emergency managers with responsibility for the Federal response in the *National Response Plan* and the *National Incident Management System.* At the same time, the Department of Homeland Security must continue to condition its State assistance grants on all relevant State and local emergency response personnel being *NIMS* and *NRP* trained and capable. DHS and its Federal partners should develop and deploy mobile training teams to support this effort.

Beyond current plans and doctrine, we require a more systematic and institutional program for homeland security professional development and education. While such a program will centre on the Department of Homeland Security, it should extend to personnel throughout all levels of government having responsibility for preventing, preparing for, responding to, and recovering from natural and man-made disasters. For example, DHS should establish a National Homeland Security University (NHSU)—analogous to the National Defense University—for senior homeland security personnel as the capstone for homeland security training and education opportunities. The NHSU, in turn, should integrate homeland security personnel from State and local jurisdictions as well as other Federal departments and agencies.

Over the long term, our professional development and education programs must break down interagency barriers to build a unified team across the Federal government. Just as the Department of Defense succeeded in building a joint leadership cadre, so the rest of the Federal government must make familiarity with other departments and agencies a requirement for career advancement. Where practicable, interagency and intergovernmental assignments for Federal personnel must build trust and familiarity among diverse homeland security professionals. These assignments will break down organizational stovepipes, advancing the exchange of ideas and practices. At a minimum, we should build joint training and educational institutions for our senior managers in homeland security-related departments and agencies.

These Federal professional development and education programs must integrate participants from other homeland security partners—namely, State and local governments as well as the private sector, non-governmental organizations, and faith-based organizations. As in every homeland crisis, it is inevitable that Federal, State, and local homeland security officials will come together to respond, and so it is important that we recognize the value in the old military adage that we must "train as you fight; fight as you train."

Pursuant to HSPD-8, the National Preparedness System should include a robust program of homeland security exercises at all levels of government and across all disciplines. The Department of Homeland Security should serve as the President's executive agent in developing and managing a National Exercise and Evaluation Program (NEEP). The NEEP should consolidate all existing interagency homeland security-related exercise programs at the Federal level with existing DHS National Exercise Program and Homeland Security Exercise and Evaluation Program (HSEEP) through common doctrine, objectives, and management. The NEEP should sponsor an aggressive program of joint exercises that involve all levels of government, as well as problem-specific exercises at particular levels of government. NEEP planning, moreover, must be integrated with a robust national homeland security training program. Moreover, the Program must emphasize intelligence-driven, threat-based scenarios that stress the system. In particular, we should not shy away from exercising worst case scenarios that "break" our homeland security system. Arguably, those scenarios will provide us the most meaningful, if sobering, lessons.

Assessments, Lessons Learned, and Corrective Actions

The success of the National Preparedness System over time will depend upon the quality of its metrics-based assessment and feedback mechanisms. In particular, the System must possess the means to measure progress towards strategic goals and capability objectives. It must systematically identify best practices and lessons learned in order to share them with our homeland security partners throughout the Nation. It must also have an effective process for conducting corrective or remedial actions when a system challenge is identified.

With common goals and performance metrics, the new National Preparedness System must first provide us with the capacity to create a national preparedness baseline that, at a minimum, serves as an inventory of our capabilities. More importantly, the baseline will tell us how prepared we are *today* in each of our jurisdictions and nationally. Reviewed at the Federal level and compared against the National Preparedness Goal, the System must also identify gaps in our national capabilities. These gaps can then serve as the priority targets for the homeland security grant process. In turn, the grant process must be tied to performance metrics that assess progress toward meeting national objectives. The President's Management Agenda has proven an effective tool applied to Federal department and agency performance that has recently, as a result of this review, been extended to include State and local homeland security programs that are federally funded.

Furthermore, this National Preparedness System must be dynamic. Like the national security system described above, we must routinely revisit our plans and reassess our capabilities in order to account for evolving risks, improvements in technological capabilities, and preparedness innovations.

An integrated National Preparedness System must identify and share lessons learned and best practices both within departments and agencies and across jurisdictions. We understand that for many aspects of homeland security there is no single, best way of doing business. Our National Preparedness organization should systematically investigate and seek out innovative approaches being applied in the various localities, States, departments, agencies, and the private sector. The system should circulate the most promising of these practices, as well as any lessons—positive *and* negative—on a continuous basis, so that we never stop improving our security.

Finally, we must ensure that problems identified in our training, exercises, and lessons learned programs are corrected. Too often, after-action reports for exercises and real-world incidents highlight the same problems that do not get fixed—the need for interoperable communications, for example. Thus, the circle of the National Preparedness System must be closed by a Remedial Action Management Program (RAMP) that is led by DHS and coordinated by the Homeland Security Council but is resident in and executed by individual departments and agencies. Department and agency RAMPs must translate findings of homeland security gaps and vulnerabilities into concrete programs for corrective action. Then the RAMPs must track that the appropriate corrective actions are fully implemented in a timely fashion.

The Role of Congress

The challenges of transformation are not limited to the Executive Branch of government. Despite previous calls for transformation from national commissions, the U.S. Congress has not fully transformed itself for homeland security. The numerous congressional committees in both houses that authorize and appropriate funds for homeland security inevitably produce competing initiatives and requirements. For example, the Secretary of Homeland Security and his leadership team were required to testify at 166 hearings before 61 full committees and subcommittees in the Senate and House of Representatives and provided over 2,000 briefings during 2005 as of October 14, 2005. At best, the many priorities distract us from the true, *top priorities.* At worst, the many priorities and requirements can contradict each other.

Moreover, Congress has not yet embraced a purely risk-based funding approach to homeland security priorities. Although the U.S. House of Representatives and U.S. Senate have passed several forms of grant reform legislation that would permit DHS to increase the prioritization of homeland security spending on the basis of risk, the two bodies have failed to reconcile their differences. Until we as a Nation agree to a solely risk-based approach, we are in danger of allocating our limited resources in ways that do not prioritize funding to meet national homeland security goals and objectives.

Finally, our experience in building an effective national security system demonstrates that Congress will be an essential partner as we continue to transform our homeland security system. Implementing the Goldwater-Nichols defense reform, for example, required legislation, and the durability of our homeland security reforms and the new National Preparedness System will require comparable support and participation from our Congressional partners.

How Much is Enough?

An age-old question for national security and, now, homeland security planning is *how much is enough?* In particular, at what level of preparedness do we feel confident that we have adequately accounted for the threats we face, our vulnerabilities, and the means we have to manage them? Recognizing that the future is uncertain and that we cannot anticipate every threat, we as a Nation must rely on a capabilities-based planning approach to answering these questions: we must set levels of capabilities—at Federal, State, and local levels as among our other homeland security partners—that we conclude are appropriate to meet the range of risks that we may confront in the future.

In order to help identify the range of future plausible risks, the Department of Homeland Security has produced a set of fifteen *National Planning Scenarios*. The Scenarios were designed to illustrate a myriad of tasks and capabilities that are required to prepare for and respond to a range of potential terrorist attacks and natural disasters that our Nation may confront. They identify the potential scale, scope, and complexity of fifteen incidents that would severely harm our Nation's citizens, infrastructure, economy, and threaten our way of life. Examples include an outbreak of pandemic influenza on U.S. soil, a major earthquake in a U.S. city, and the detonation of a ten-kiloton nuclear device in a large U.S. metropolitan area. The Scenarios also include a Category 5 hurricane hitting a major metropolitan area.

The Scenarios, which were meant to be illustrative of a wide variety of hazards, generally do not specify a geographic location, and the impacts are meant to be scalable for a variety of population considerations. Ultimately, they give homeland security planners a tool that allows for the flexible and adaptive development of capabilities as well as the identification of needed capability levels to meet the National Preparedness Goal.

While the National Planning Scenarios have been effective tools for generating dialogue on response capabilities, they do not fully anticipate some of the worst disaster scenarios. Scenario 10, for example, depicts the effects of a Category 5 hurricane hitting a major metropolitan area in the United States. However, in the Scenario, the Category 5 hurricane actually causes fewer deaths and less destruction than did Hurricane Katrina, a Category 3, because the Scenario only characterizes the destruction caused to a metropolitan area, while a storm like Hurricane Katrina may span three or more States. Further, although the Scenario acknowledges potential delays and difficulties in evacuation, realistic circumstances such as Katrina may be worse, where more than 100,000 residents did not evacuate.

Scenario 1, the detonation of a ten-kiloton nuclear device in an American city by a terrorist group, suffers from similar limitations and fails to fully challenge our plans and preparation skills. Although devastating in terms of both death and destruction, a ten-kiloton bomb is a relatively small nuclear device. Moreover, the Scenario does not anticipate one of the most demanding characteristics of past al-Qaida operations: multiple, simultaneous attacks. How much more taxing would it be to respond to multiple and simultaneous nuclear, chemical, or biological incidents? If the purpose of the National Planning Scenarios is to provide a foundation for identifying the capabilities required to meet all hazards, the Scenarios must press us to confront the most destructive challenges.

Hurricane Katrina severely stressed our current national response capabilities. However, three other National Planning Scenarios—an act of nuclear terrorism, an outbreak of pandemic influenza, and a 7.5 magnitude earthquake striking a major city —are more daunting still. Compared with the deaths and economic chaos a nuclear detonation or influenza outbreak could unleash, Hurricane Katrina was small. But even these scenarios do not go far enough to challenge us to improve our level of preparedness. Until we can meet the standard set by the most demanding scenarios, we should not consider ourselves adequately prepared.

The most recent Top Officials ("TOPOFF") exercise in April 2005 revealed the Federal government's lack of progress in addressing a number of preparedness deficiencies, many of which had been identified in previous exercises. This lack of progress reflects, in part, the absence of a remedial action program to systematically address lessons learned from exercises. To ensure appropriate priority and accountability are being applied to address these continuing deficiencies, the Assistant to the President for Homeland Security and Counterterrorism now annually conducts four Cabinet-level exercises with catastrophic scenarios. To date, a catastrophic exercise with a pandemic scenario was conducted in December 2005; the next exercise is scheduled for this March.

While the National Planning Scenarios represent a good start for our national process of capabilities-based planning for homeland security, we must orient the National Preparedness System towards still greater challenges. We must not shy away from creating planning scenarios that stress the current system of response to the breaking point and challenge our Nation in ways that we wish we did not have to imagine. To that end, we must revise the planning scenarios to make them more challenging. Among other characteristics, they must reflect both what we know and what we can imagine about the ways our enemies think—that they will not hit us hard just once, but that they will seek to cause us damage on significant scale in multiple locations simultaneously. We must not again find ourselves vulnerable to the charge that we suffered a "'failure of imagination' and a mind-set that dismissed possibilities."

ENVISIONING A NATIONAL PREPAREDNESS SYSTEM

How our existing homeland security strategy, doctrine, and capabilities can be unified into a single National Preparedness System. The strengths of this System include first and foremost *integration*of strategy, doctrine, capabilities, response activities, and exercises, as well as assessment and evaluation. The graphic also highlights the feedback mechanisms that must be built into the System. In particular, as described above, the System must include routine reporting and assessment of program performance metrics, the readiness of particular capabilities, as well as best practices and lessons learned from exercises and activities. These assessments and findings must be reported back, as appropriate, to inform key components throughout the System.

The National Preparedness System graphic additionally highlights the constituent elements of operational capabilities: deliberate planning, resources, logistics, training, and education. Moreover, the graphic notes the importance of unity of effort in exercises and the conduct of response activities in incidents.

The National Preparedness System must be dynamic, flexible, and responsive to new developments. Like our national security system, the strategy, doctrine, and capabilities of the System should be reviewed periodically to determine their continued relevance to current challenges. Similarly, periodic reviews must assess the continued internal consistency of the System—e.g., do the doctrine and capabilities support the strategy?

Key inputs to the System include the current national vision for preparedness, laws, and policies and the use of capability-based planning that prioritizes investments to fill gaps identified by needs assessments. An equally important input is the current assessment of risks—what threats does the Nation currently confront, what are our current vulnerabilities, and what are the consequences? Against the current assessment of risks, we must continually evaluate our capability to respond effectively.

Finally, our planning and operational documents should define the critical roles played by all of our homeland security partners in the Preparedness System. Federal, State, and local governments play prominent roles throughout the System—from strategy development to assessment and lessons learned. Additionally, the private sector, NGOs, faith-based groups, communities, and individuals play important roles in operational capabilities as well as response activities.

CREATING A CULTURE OF PREPAREDNESS

The second element of our continuing transformation for homeland security perhaps will be the most profound and enduring—the creation of a Culture of Preparedness. A new preparedness culture must emphasize that the entire Nation—Federal, State, and local governments; the private sector; communities; and individual citizens—shares common goals and responsibilities for homeland security. In other words, our homeland security is built upon a foundation of partnerships. And these partnerships must include shared understanding of at least four concepts:

- The certainty of future catastrophes;
- The importance of initiative;
- The roles of citizens and other homeland security stakeholders in preparedness; and

- The roles of each level of government and the private sector in creating a prepared Nation.

Future Challenges

The first principle for a Culture of Preparedness must be a shared acknowledgement that creating a prepared Nation will be a continuing challenge. Optimism is fundamental to the American character. While it always energizes us, it also grounds us in times of tragedy and loss.

We must guard against our optimism leading us to a dangerous sense of complacency. Complacency of our citizens presents a great challenge.

We are fortunate that, because of the courage and self-sacrifice of public servants across all levels of government, we have not suffered another terrorist attack on our homeland since 2001. But we are a Nation at war, and we have a responsibility to be prepared. We must temper our optimism with sober recognition of the certainty of future catastrophes. We cannot prevent natural disasters. And though we work tirelessly against them, we cannot anticipate nor prevent every type of terrorist attack against the homeland. As the Irish Republican Army once warned British Prime Minister Margaret Thatcher after narrowly missing her in an assassination attempt: terrorists only need to be successful once; but we, their targets, must be successful everyday. We know that our enemies plot further attacks against us. We must continue to prevent them and, if necessary, respond. Regrettably, lives will be lost, citizens displaced, and property destroyed.

The certainty of future challenges should inform our national expectations. As a Nation, we will prepare ourselves in the most effective ways we know. Our Culture of Preparedness, therefore, must emphasize the importance of flexibility and readiness to cope with an uncertain future. While we cannot predict the future to our satisfaction, we can build capabilities that prepare us for a broad range of challenges. Perhaps equally important, we can ensure that our preparedness plans, thinking, and "imagination" do not become so rigid that we cannot rapidly adapt to unforeseen challenges.

Initiative

Despite reforms that encourage a proactive, anticipatory approach to the management of incidents, the culture of our response community has a fundamental bias towards *reaction* rather than *initiative*. As a result, our national efforts too often emphasize response and clean-up efforts at the expense of potentially more cost-effective anticipatory actions that might prevent or mitigate damage. The need for anticipatory response is a pillar of the National Response Plan. A list of Key Concepts in the *National Response Plan* places it second only to "systematic and coordinated incident management." Specifically, the *NRP*calls for:

Proactive notification and deployment of Federal resources in anticipation of or in response to catastrophic events in coordination and collaboration with State, local, and tribal governments and private entities when possible. Similarly, our Culture of Preparedness must stress initiative at all levels. Fundamentally, our Preparedness System and Culture must encourage and reward innovation. To do so, we must build a system and approach that better aligns authority and responsibility—those who are responsible for a mission or task must have the authority to act. In the same vein, an alignment of authority and responsibility provides us the ability to assess our performance—collectively and individually. Performance assessment and accountability, however, must not be *blame*. Our current culture of blame threatens both individual and institutional initiative, resourcefulness, and enterprise across the homeland security, law enforcement, and intelligence fields. It is time that Congress, the Executive Branch, and all of our homeland security partners develop a consensus regarding a reasonable balance of accountability, responsibility, and authority at all levels. Otherwise, the culture of blame and its related acrimony will debilitate us.

Citizen Preparedness

Our preparedness culture must also emphasize the importance of citizen and community preparedness. Citizen and community preparedness are among the most effective means of preventing terrorist attacks as well as protecting against, mitigating, responding to, and recovering from all hazards. For example, the Citizen

Corps in Harris County, Texas, brought together over 50,000 volunteers to support American Red Cross efforts and staff evacuation centers throughout Houston. As a joint team, they created an actual working city (with its own zip code) for Hurricane Katrina victims sheltering in the Astrodome.

Thus, citizens and communities can help themselves by becoming more prepared. If every family maintained the resources to live in their homes without electricity and running water for three days, we could allocate more Federal, State, and local response resources to saving lives. Similarly, if every family developed their own emergency preparedness plan, they almost certainly would reduce the demand for outside emergency resources. As the 9/11 Commission Report states, "One clear lesson of September 11 is that individual civilians need to take responsibility for maximizing the probability that they will survive, should disaster strike."

Leadership at all levels will be essential in helping to transform citizen preparedness. First, responsible public officials at the Federal, State, and local levels as well as prominent national figures should begin a public dialogue that emphasizes common themes regarding the importance of citizen preparedness. DHS should continue to build upon those programs and institutions that already work, such as Department of Education elementary and secondary school programs; Citizen Corps; State and local government training programs; and Federal cooperation with the National Governors Association. Nongovernmental organizations can also play a key role in this area. DHS has made some important progress in this area with its *Ready.gov* initiative and its public service announcements program with the Ad Council. But more needs to be done. Encouraging preparedness awareness and activity is a shared responsibility across all levels of government that we must make a priority. Preparedness today will save lives tomorrow.

In addition, DHS and other Federal agencies should identify both the individual skills and capabilities that would help citizens in a disaster as well as the types of messages from trusted leaders that would encourage citizens to be better prepared. Public awareness messaging must shift to include more substantive information, as opposed to just telling our citizens that they need to "do something." For example, the "Stop, Drop, and Roll" campaign used so successfully in fire safety as part of the "Learn Not to Burn" program provided citizens with specific steps to take. Other successful campaigns include the National Highway Traffic Safety Administration's "Buckle Up America" campaign, which prescribes proper use of seat belt and child safety seats. As with so many of these successful campaigns, the Nation's children can help lead the way.

Other Homeland Security Stakeholders and Preparedness

We must build upon our initial successful efforts to partner with other homeland security stakeholders—namely the private sector, non-governmental organizations, and faith-based groups. Each of these groups plays a critical role in preparedness. To the extent that we can incorporate them into the National effort, we will be reducing the burden on other response resources so that Federal, State, and local responders can concentrate our energies on those with the greatest need.

Private sector companies own and operate 85 percent of our Nation's critical infrastructure. Transportation, electricity, banking, telecommunications, food supply, and clean water are examples of services relying on infrastructure that have become basic aspects of our daily lives. Yet, these services are often only noticed when they are disrupted and when the American public expects speedy restoration. In fact, the Nation relies on "critical infrastructure" to maintain its defense, continuity of government, economic prosperity, and quality of life. The services provided by these interconnected systems are so vital that their disruption will have a debilitating impact on national security, the economy, or public health and safety.

Companies are responsible for protecting their systems, which comprise the majority of critical infrastructure. Because of this, private sector preparation and response is vital to mitigating the national impact of disasters. Government actions in response to a disaster can help or hamper private sector efforts. However, governments cannot plan to adequately respond unless the private sector helps them understand what infrastructure truly is critical.

Likewise, businesses cannot develop contingency plans without understanding how governments will respond. To maximize the Nation's preparedness, Federal, State, and local governments must join with the private sector to collaboratively develop plans to respond to major disasters. There are important initiatives in this area already underway by the Business Round Table (BRT) and Business Executives for National Security (BENS) project. We must encourage and build upon these efforts. The private sector must be an explicit partner in and fully integrated across all levels of response—Federal, State, and local.

Non-governmental organizations play essential roles in preparedness by complementing and supporting preparedness efforts. In times of crisis, NGOs—especially community groups, faith-based organizations, places of worship, and relief organizations—provide essential human faces, helping hands, compassion, and comfort to all American people, whether or not they are victims of an incident. As such, they fill an essential need in the response system in ways far beyond the capacity of the Government. Thus, their contributions must be fully integrated at all levels—Federal, State, and local.

THE ROLE OF EACH LEVEL OF GOVERNMENT IN A CULTURE OF PREPAREDNESS

Today, we operate under two guiding principles: a) that incident management should begin at the lowest jurisdictional level possible, and b) that, for most incidents, the Federal government will generally play a supporting role to State and local efforts. While these principles suffice for the vast majority of incidents, they impede the Federal response to severe catastrophes. In a catastrophic scenario that overwhelms or incapacitates local and State incident command structures, the Federal government must be prepared to assume incident command and get assistance directly to those in need until State and local authorities are reconstituted.

The National Preparedness System must also recognize the role of the Federal government for monitoring and guiding national preparedness efforts.; In particular, the system must ensure that the Federal government assesses the preparedness of localities across the country with an eye towards identifying the Federal response requirement for each. In addition, Federal, State, local, and private sector partners must agree on a system in which the Federal government responds more actively and effectively while respecting the role of State and local governments.

The new culture of preparedness must stress *partnership* among all levels of government. Local governments will continue to have responsibility for providing the immediate response capabilities for the vast majority of incidents while State governors will continue to have sovereign responsibilities to protect their residents. Yet preparedness must emphasize the shared nature of these responsibilities in a catastrophic event. State governments must work with their local jurisdictions to ensure that they have developed plans and capabilities that are appropriate for the homeland security challenges confronting them. Both State and local governments must also reach out to their citizens, private sector, and community groups to promote their preparedness efforts.

Furthermore, in the new culture of preparedness, State and local governments must continually seek to work with their neighboring jurisdictions. Building upon the successes of interstate cooperation programs such as the Emergency Management Assistance Compact (EMAC), the Federal government must take an active role in encouraging and facilitating these partnerships. Regional collaboration at the State and local levels will help the Nation to reduce overlapping or redundant capabilities as well as to minimize capability gaps. Moreover, active regional collaboration will likewise be a means for identifying and sharing homeland security lessons learned and best practices.

Finally, in our new Culture of Preparedness, all required response assets and resources of the Federal government must integrate and synchronize to ensure an effective national response to a crisis. In practical terms, this entails stepping away from the bureaucratic view of a particular department or agency's institutional interests. Instead, we must continually build preparedness partnerships across the Federal government as well as with State and local governments.

10

Military, Arms Control, and Security Aspects of Nano-Technology

The announcement of the US National Nanotechnology Initiative and its counterparts in other countries has been accompanied by expressions of concern about ethical, legal and social implications, and some allotment of funding to address them, but concerns arising from military uses of nanotechnology, presumably in the service of national security, have been largely left out of the working definition of "societal and ethical implications". From the perspective of international security and arms control analysis it appears that systematic study by scholars in the hard and social sciences has hardly begun, with only a few scholarly articles published.

This is curious, since the parallel popular discourse on nanotechnology (NT) has not failed to notice that promises made for the possibilities of NT would in practice have profound implications for military affairs as well as relations between nations and thinking about war and international security. Superweapons made possible by nanotechnology are stock items by now in science fiction, and to some extent that literature has already begun to explore the technical logic to see where NT may lead us. Military writers have also taken note of these emerging ideas, while in the USA the military enthusiastically spends one quarter to one third of all Federal nanotechnology research and development funds, and its visionary powerpoint artists portray a future of nano-enabled supersoldiers fighting on nanotech battlefields. Here we try to consider the impact of evolving and possibly disruptive military NT applications within the context of history, conflict, international security and world order. The international community seeks to avoid war through a variety of mechanisms, including military deterrence, international organizations and treaties, arms control and disarmament. These mechanisms are created and evolve in a changing technological environment. Arms control in the past has included restrictions on new or emerging military technologies. Today, emerging military NT applications and their consequences need to be analysed. We advocate preventive arms control where one can identify specific negative impacts which may be subject to feasible controls.

NEW MILITARY TECHNOLOGIES

The purpose of armed forces is to break the will of an organized opponent by violent force. Who will prevail depends to some extent on comparative recklessness. Thus, war and the preparations for it do not only go beyond civilized behaviour, but carry an inherent tendency to transcend all other rules, including the ones applying to armed conflict. Innovation in military technology can become an extension of warfare itself. Being ahead in technology provides an important advantage in armed conflict, and if the lead position is not attainable, then one should at least stay as close as possible behind.

Thus, all potential opponents have constant strong motives for military research and development and for incorporating their results into the armed forces. Secrecy and worst-case assumptions – both to some extent necessary elements of military preparation – increase these motives. Military applications of new technologies take place in a framework that is quite different from civilian ones: the bad and ugly uses are not results of accidents or criminal actions – they are prepared in an organized way on a large scale by and with the resources of the state. A special problem arises here: states have to reckon with an opponent using any means at hand. If technology allows new, more effective weapons, they might be used– even if they violate the law of warfare. In order to protect oneself, one needs to know the characteristics of the new weapon; this creates a motive to research and develop the new weapon oneself – which, in turn, creates mistrust and fear between potential opponents.

An example of this mechanism can be seen in the debate regarding biological-weapons – what constitutes legitimate defensive research, and where does forbidden development of biological-warfare agents begin? Of course, the economic capacity of the state limits its pursuit of weapons, and limitation is also possible by political decision. Self-restraint may be exercised in respect of national or international public opinion. Limits are also implied by the international law of warfare. Finally, potential opponents may agree on mutual limitations (arms control). In general, for these to be effective, there need to be reliable ways of verifying compliance.

General Aspects of War and Peace

Throughout history, improved technology has provided advantages in battle. In the 20th century, science and technology became tightly integrated with the system for waging and preparing war. Following the Second World War, military research and development (R&D) continued to expand, in particular in the USA and USSR.

The 1950s to 1970s, roughly, marked the era of "big science" – big in budget and in physical scale, while often in pursuit of control over the very small. Nuclear bombs, nuclear-driven submarines, long-range ballistic missiles, and orbiting satellites mark some of the important milestones in the qualitative and quantitative arms race of the Cold War – achieved at extremely high cost and effort. Even though the Cold War is over, military threats are still at work as instruments of geopolitical will as well as the basic mechanisms of national and international security. Nuclear deterrence is a doctrine still in effect, and thus nuclear war could still start at any time, although this may be improbable. Despite massive reductions (from a high of 65,000 in 1986), there remain about 20,000 nuclear warheads on Earth. The experience of the World Wars has led to a fundamental change in international law.

Through the centuries, states assumed a natural right to go to war – for whatever reason or purpose. With the founding of the UN and the acceptance of its Charter in 1945, maintaining international peace and security became the central imperative (Art. 1). The use of force and threat to use force in international relations were forbidden (Art. 2), with few exceptions: one is force legitimized by the UN Security Council to restore peace and security, and the other is in self-defense until the Security Council has taken its measures (Art. 51). The security mechanisms foreseen in the UN Charter were hardly implemented, and nuclear war after 1945 was not prevented by adherence to its articles, but rather by the threat of mutual annihilation.

Yet the norm established in the UN Charter has had strong effects on the international community. Wars waged since 1945 have usually been claimed to be defensive, and when such claims have been rejected the offending power has often come under collective pressure to cease or restrain its aggression. Of course, the principle of refraining from the use of force except in self-defense is severely endangered if preventive wars are being waged based on perceptions of threats, not on actual aggression.

Thus, we believe the 2003 US war against Iraq has weakened the UN and the international mechanisms of maintaining and restoring peace and security. When armed conflict occurs, regardless of whether it constitutes legitimate or illegitimate use of force according to the UN Charter, the warring parties are limited in their choice of means and methods of warfare by international humanitarian law, which consists of basic as well as specific rules, often written down in international agreements, which evolve over time. Many rules have become customary international law and are binding for all parties to a conflict; this holds, *e.g.*, for the principle of attacking only military targets or of humane treatment of combatants *hors de combat*. Some rules are only obligatory for the respective signatory parties, *e.g.*, the Additional Protocol 2 to the Geneva Conventions of 1949 on non-international armed conflict. Before introducing a new weapon, means or method of warfare, the states are obliged to check whether its employment would be prohibited by international law.

Arms Control and Disarmament

Despite the nuclear threat that loomed throughout the 1950s, limitation talks between the Cold War antagonists were unsuccessful until the experience of the Cuban missile crisis (1962) when nuclear war seemed imminent. Real progress in arms control started with the Partial Test Ban Treaty in 1963.

Important multilateral treaties that followed included the Outer Space Treaty (1967) and the Nuclear Non-Proliferation Treaty (1968). Political relations between the USA and the USSR improved enough to permit the bilateral Anti-Ballistic Missile (ABM) Treaty and SALT I (1972), later SALT II (1979). Another tense period of confrontation and impasse in bilateral arms control followed, until the Soviet approach changed under Gorbachev, leading to the INF and START I Treaties (1987/1991). Full disarmament, that is reduction to zero, was agreed for biological weapons (1972, multilateral), and chemical weapons (1993, multilateral). Nuclear test explosions (1996), and anti-personnel land mines (1997) have also been banned. These agreements have been mostly successful, despite the lack of full participation by all relevant powers, and despite some serious violations which have been detected and exposed – most notably with respect to the Biological Weapons Convention which was implemented without provisions for verification, inviting contempt. General and complete disarmament (all countries, all armaments and armed forces) has been the declared goal of the UN and was mentioned in several arms-control treaties, but this goal has not been seriously pursued in actual policy.

Arms control must be considered an unfinished project, and important gaps remain: there is no ban on nuclear weapons, there is no prohibition on space weapons (except for weapons of mass destruction deployed in space), and limitations on conventional arms and forces exist only in Europe. Recently, arms control and humanitarian law have become endangered by actions of the USA. Even before Sept. 11, 2001 the US refused to ratify the Comprehensive Test Ban Treaty and blocked the negotiations on a Verification Protocol to the Biological Weapons Convention. Recently there have been moves towards easier re-sumption of nuclear tests. In 2002, the USA abrogated the ABM Treaty. The US has also systematically sought to undermine the International Criminal Court that was instituted by the international community.

MILITARY NANOTECHNOLOGY

Nanotechnology will change many aspects of our lives. Powerful computers will be ubiquitous. With the advance of artificial intelligence, the replacement of human labor by artificial systems will accelerate. New materials will lead to higher energy efficiency. Therapeutic drugs will be designed for the individual. Along with opportunities, there are also potential risks, be it to health, the environment, social justice or privacy. Convergence of nano-scale, biomedical, information, and cognitive science and technology (NBIC) can lead to applications with profound impacts on the human condition. The 2001/2 U.S. workshop on NBIC convergence mentioned, *e.g.*, nano-implant devices, slowing down or reversing aging, direct brain-machine interfaces, human-like artificial intelligence.

These and other far-reaching concepts of manipulating the human body and mind imply risks and dangers, as well as ethical challenges, on an unprecedented scale. Containing abuse and unintended consequences will be difficult even in the civilian realm. Military NT applications pose special risks – first, because of the reparations for destructive uses and second because of secrecy. Tackling this problem calls for special efforts. In order to provide reliable information, one can look at actual military NT research and development in the USA, which is both the leader in military NT and also much more transparent about its military research and development than any other country. In addition, one can extrapolate scientific-technical advances and assess what military applications will become possible in principle.

Military NT R&D in the USA: In the USA, military research and development in nanotechnology (NT) has surged. Of the funds for the National Nanotechnology Initiative, one quarter to one third goes to the Department of Defense – in 2003, $ 243 million of $ 774 million. This is far more than any other country – the UK expenditures, for example, were stated as about $ 2.6 million in 2001. Assuming total West European funding five times as high, with similar levels respectively for Russia, China and the remaining countries that are active in military NT R&D, the US expenditure would be five times the sum of all the rest of the world. (In military R&D at large, the USA accounts for two thirds of the global total.)

U.S. work spans a wide range in the spectrum from basic research to advanced technology development – development of actual systems for deployment is still several to many years off. University research grants fund nanoscale machines, carbon nanotubes, quantum computing and magnetic nanoparticles. The Defense Advanced Projects Agency funds projects in magnetic memory, bio-computing, bio-molecular motors, sensors for chemical and biological warfare agents, and micro robots, among many others. The research laboratories of the armed services work on self-assembly of nanostructures, organic light-emitting diodes, carbon nanotubes and composites, nanomaterials for explosives and propellants as well as for armor and projectiles, and many similar topics.

In 2002, the Army selected the Massachusetts Institute of Technology to house an Institute for Soldier Nanotechnologies, with up to 150 staff to work in seven multidisciplinary research teams. Their goals include a battle suit that protects against bullets, chemical and biological agents, and stiffens on demand to act as compress or splint. Sensors are to monitor the body status. For carrying heavy loads, an exoskeleton with "muscles" from artificial molecules is envisaged.

Potential Military Applications of NT: In general, NT can lead to improvements in traditional military systems and to qualitatively new ones. Very small but highly capable computers will be used in weapons, uniforms, logistics, and communication systems. Increasingly sophisticated and discriminating sensors may become very small, and cheap enough that they can be scattered in high numbers to saturate an area, ostensibly yielding "total awareness". Guns will shoot farther, projectiles and missiles with cheap guidance systems will become smaller and more accurate. Vehicles will become lighter and more agile, with more powerful engines and greater range. Energy storage is a key problem for many military systems, and NT is often considered a key to solving it.

Autonomous vehicles (robots) for reconnaissance and communication, but also for fighting, will arrive; some of them may be very small. NT ultimately raises the prospect of even microscopic mobile robots, although macroscopic vehicles are needed for high speed or long distance travel. Sophisticated fighting robots, the successor to today's killer drones and prototype robot combat planes (UCAVs), will be enabled by advanced computers, smart materials, advanced energy and propulsion systems, and other NT-based refinements.

Similarly, NT will contribute to lowering the cost and increasing the capability of space systems, including possibly very small antisatellite weapons. Robotics will be used in logistics, production and automation of complex weapons systems. A key enabler of robotics applications will be advanced computers capable of situation assessment and action planning, for example the motion planning needed to coordinate dextrous manipulators, or to maneuver through "battlespace".

New chemical or biological warfare (CBW) agents may become possible that act selectively only against the intended targets. Nanobiotechnology is ambitious enough to propose robotized artificial microbes, which could become tools of assassination or mass murder. At the same time, nanomaterials for filtration and neutralization, and NT-based sensors and nanomedicine in general may provide new approaches to CBW defense. Advances in biocompatible materials and portable biomedical systems may allow the creation of body implants to monitor health status, release drugs or interface to the nerves and brains of fighters. Their portable computers may evolve into wearable information appliances producing an "augmented reality" which simultaneously gives the fighter access to information from the net and also gives command access to the soldier, placing her under some degree of "remote control".

The tendency toward cyborgization follows directly from such military goals and culminates in the vision of direct brain-technology interfaces, but the possibility of improving in this way on the performance of well-trained human senses and bodies, whether for fighting or for piloting or for thinking interactively, seems remote. NT can be used in enhanced versions of existing nuclear weapons incorporating improvements to safety, reliability, etc., or possibly new types of conventional explosive in the fission primary. More speculative concepts include qualitatively new weapon types such as pure-fusion explosives of arbitrarily small yield. It is hard to predict how NT advances may impact nuclear weapons production and barriers to proliferation, but we have seen substantial advances in these technologies since 1945 and further improvement seems possible.

Scenarios along these lines, of more or less visionary character, are being discussed within the military and national security establishments of the world, particularly the USA, but many of these concepts will not prove militarily effective, as has been the case through-out history. Countermeasures to NT weapons will exploit NT as well, giving rise to complicated correlations of forces and complex arsenals within which unexpected interactions can arise.

Preventive Arms Control

Preventive arms control is qualitative arms control applied to the future; it is about stopping or at least limiting dangerous military developments before they become actual, in particular weapons exploiting or based on new technologies. Limitations can be designed to intervene at the stages of development or testing, or sometimes research. Precedents include:

i) the ABM Treaty, which prohibited not only deployment, but also development of anti-ballistic missile systems that are sea-based, air-based, space-based or mobile land-based;

ii) the nuclear testing treaties, which preclude certain experiments with actual nuclear explosions; and iii), the Protocol on Blinding Laser Weapons (1995), which explicitly bans only the use of blinding lasers but led to halting their development.

Preventive arms control assesses a potential new military technology using several criteria. One group of criteria concerns dangers to arms control and the international law of warfare: will the new technology undermine existing controls, law and norms? Another set of criteria concerns stability: will the new technology destabilize the military situation, *e.g.*, by reducing reaction times? Will it lead to a technological arms race? How about proliferation, in particular to regions with high probability of conflict? Finally, one needs to consider unintended hazards to humans, society or the environment. If there are good arguments for restricting a particular technology, then one needs to take into account any positive uses – in particular in the civilian realm – and if possible devise rules that exclude the negative applications without overly restricting the positive ones. Methods for verifying compliance also have to be thought out – they must provide assurance that illegal activity would be detected, but must not be too intrusive or too burdensome.

Preliminary Assessment

When considering the various potential military NT applications under criteria of preventive arms control, one finds several that will be close to civil uses, such as small, fast, distributed computers or strong, light-weight structural materials. A few uses could help to protect against terrorism or would act mostly defensively. Examples are sensors and decontamination agents for biological weapons or improved injury care. Preventive limitation would be unrealistic or counterproductive in such areas. However, there are several potential military applications of NT and/or NBIC at large that raise serious concerns under criteria of preventive arms control. In the medium term, the most dangerous ones involve:

- New selective chemical or biological warfare agents: These would violate the existing conventions, while posing new challenges to verification; they could be used either as weapons of mass destruction or for targeted assassinations, not only by armed forces but also by terrorists.
- Autonomous fighting systems – robots and robotic vehicles on land, in water or air: They would violate the international law of warfare if they would produce superfluous injury or could not recognize non-combatants or combatants *hors de combat*. Autonomous tanks or combat aircraft considered

outside of the definitions of the Treaty on Conventional Armed Forces in Europe could undermine and endanger that treaty. Small satellites capable or attacking other satellites by direct hit or by manipulation after docking would destabilize the situation in outer space – not without consequences on Earth.

- Mini-/micro-sensors and-robots, including biological/artificial hybrids: They could be pre-deployed covertly in an opponent's territory to strike at an appointed time or on command, or to guide other weapons. If such devices are produced at low cost in large numbers, diffusion to other countries and to criminals is probable, creating the possibility of their use in asymmetric warfare or terrorist attacks.
- Body manipulation including implants: Under the imperative of combat efficiency, armed forces may more readily explore new possibilities for body manipulation than civilian society. Soldiers might voluntarily, or maybe under some pressure, accept risky or ethically questionable technologies that modify body chemistry, rewire brain, nerve and muscle, or otherwise radically alter the human organism. This could create "facts" and circumvent barriers in civilian society, preempting a thorough debate on benefits, risks, ethical aspects and needs for regulation.

MOLECULAR NANOTECHNOLOGY

Molecular nanotechnology, sometimes called molecular manufacturing, is a term given to the concept of engineered nanosystems (nanoscale machines) operating on the molecular scale. It is especially associated with the concept of a molecular assembler, a machine that can produce a desired structure or device atom-by-atom using the principles of mechanosynthesis. Manufacturing in the context of productive nanosystems is not related to, and should be clearly distinguished from, the conventional technologies used to manufacture nanomaterials such as carbon nanotubes and nanoparticles. When the term "nanotechnology" was independently coined and popularized by Eric Drexler it referred to a future manufacturing technology based on molecular machine systems. The premise was that molecular scale biological analogies of traditional machine components demonstrated molecular machines were possible: by the countless examples found in biology, it is known that sophisticated, stochastically optimised biological machines can be produced.

It is hoped that developments in nanotechnology will make possible their construction by some other means, perhaps using biomimetic principles. However, Drexler and other researchers have proposed that advanced nanotechnology, although perhaps initially implemented by biomimetic means, ultimately could be based on mechanical engineering principles, namely, a manufacturing technology based on the mechanical functionality of these components (such as gears, bearings, motors, and structural members) that would enable programmable, positional assembly to atomic specification. The physics and engineering performance of exemplar designs were analysed in Drexler's book *Nanosystems*. In general it is very difficult to assemble devices on the atomic scale, as all one has to position atoms are other atoms of comparable size and stickyness.

Chemistry and Environment

Chemical catalysis and filtration techniques are two prominent examples where nanotechnology already plays a role. The synthesis provides novel materials with tailored features and chemical properties: for example, nanoparticles with a distinct chemical surrounding (ligands), or specific optical properties. In this sense, chemistry is indeed a basic nanoscience. In a short-term perspective, chemistry will provide novel "nanomaterials" and in the long run, superior processes such as "self-assembly" will enable energy and time preserving strategies.

In a sense, all chemical synthesis can be understood in terms of nanotechnology, because of its ability to manufacture certain molecules. Thus, chemistry forms a base for nanotechnology providing tailor-made molecules, polymers, etcetera, as well as clusters and nanoparticles. Chemical catalysis benefits especially from nanoparticles, due to the extremely large surface to volume ratio. The application potential of nanoparticles in catalysis ranges from fuel cell to catalytic converters and photocatalytic devices. Catalysis is also important for the production of chemicals.

Platinum nanoparticles are now being considered in the next generation of automotive catalytic converters because the very high surface area of nanoparticles could reduce the amount of platinum required. However, some concerns have been raised due to experiments demonstrating that they will spontaneously combust if methane is mixed with the ambient air. Ongoing research at the Centre National de la Recherche Scientifique (CNRS) in France may resolve their true usefulness for catalytic applications. Nanofiltration may come to be an important application, although future research must be careful to investigate possible toxicity.

A strong influence of nanochemistry on waste-water treatment, air purification and energy storage devices is to be expected. Mechanical or chemical methods can be used for effective filtration techniques.

One class of filtration techniques is based on the use of membranes with suitable hole sizes, whereby the liquid is pressed through the membrane. Nanoporous membranes are suitable for a mechanical filtration with extremely small pores smaller than 10 nm ("nanofiltration") and may be composed of nanotubes. Nanofiltration is mainly used for the removal of ions or the separation of different fluids. On a larger scale, the membrane filtration technique is named ultrafiltration, which works down to between 10 and 100 nm.

One important field of application for ultrafiltration is medical purposes as can be found in renal dialysis. Magnetic nanoparticles offer an effective and reliable method to remove heavy metal contaminants from waste water by making use of magnetic separation techniques. Using nanoscale particles increases the efficiency to absorb the contaminants and is comparatively inexpensive compared to traditional precipitation and filtration methods. Some water-treatment devices incorporating nanotechnology are already on the market, with more in development. Low-cost nanostructured separation membranes methods have been shown to be effective in producing potable water in a recent study.

Molecular Mechanics

More complex analyses, particularly analyses that involve searching through large configuration spaces, can limit the size of system that can be effectively handled. The need to search through large configuration spaces (as when determining the native folded structure of an arbitrary protein) can be avoided by the use of relatively rigid structures (which differ from relatively floppy proteins and have few possible configurations).

The modeling of machine components in vacuum reduces the need to model solvation effects, which can also involve significant computational effort. In molecular mechanics the individual nuclei are usually treated as point masses. While quantum mechanics dictates that there must be a certain degree of positional uncertainty associated with each nucleus, this positional uncertainty is normally significantly smaller than the typical internuclear distance. Bowen and Allinger provide a good recent overview of the subject.

While the nuclei can reasonably be approximated as point masses, the electron cloud must be dealt with in quantum mechanical terms. However, if we are content to know only the positions of the nuclei and are willing to forego a detailed understanding of the electronic structure, then we can effectively eliminate the quantum mechanics.

For example, the H_2 molecule involves two nuclei. While it would be possible to solve Schrodinger's equation to determine the wave function for the electrons, if we are content simply to know the potential energy contributed by the electrons (and do not enquire about the electron distribution) then we need only know the electronic energy as a function of the distance between the nuclei.

That is, in many systems the only significant impact that the electrons have on nuclear position is to make a contribution to the potential energy E of the system. In the case of H_2, E is a simple function of the internuclear distance r. The function E(r) summarizes and replaces the more complex and more difficult to determine wave function for the electrons, as well as taking into account the inter-nuclear repulsion and the interactions between the electrons and the nuclei. The two hydrogen nuclei will adopt a position that minimizes E(r). As r becomes larger, the potential energy of the system increases and the nuclei experience a restoring force that returns them to their original distance. Similarly, as r becomes smaller and the two nuclei are pushed closer together, we also find that a restoring force pushes them farther apart, again restoring them to an equilibrium distance.

More generally, if we know the positions $r_1, r_2.... r_N$ of N nuclei, then $E(r_1, r_2.... r_N)$ gives the potential energy of the system. Knowing the potential energy as a function of the nuclear positions, we can readily determine the forces acting on the individual nuclei and therefore can compute the evolution of their position over time. The function E is a newtonian potential energy function (not quantum mechanical), despite the fact that the particular value of E at a particular point could be computed from Schrodinger's equation. That is, the potential energy E is a newtonian concept, but the particular values of E at particular points are determined by Schrodinger's equation.

While it would in principle be possible to determine E by solving Schrodinger's equation, in practice it is usual to use available experimental data and to infer the nature and shape of E by interpolation. This approach, in which empirically derived potential energy functions are created by interpolation from experimental data, has spawned a wide range of potential energy functions, many of which are sold commercially. Because the gradient of the potential energy function E defines a conservative force field F, molecular mechanics methods are also called "force field" methods.

While it is common to refer to "empirical force field" methods, the more recent use of ab initio methods to provide data points to aid in the design of the force fields makes this term somewhat inaccurate, though still widely used. The utility of molecular mechanics depends crucially on the development of accurate force fields. Good quality force fields have been developed for a fairly broad range of compounds including many compounds of interest in biochemistry.

While we will not attempt to survey the wide range of force fields that are available, one particular subset of compounds for which good quality force fields are available involve H, C, N, O,

F, Si, P, S, Cl when they are restricted to form chemically uncomplicated structures (*e.g.*, bond strain is not too great, dangling bonds are few or absent, etc.). Many atomically precise structures which should be useful in nanotechnology fall in this class and can be modeled with an accuracy adequate to determine the behaviour of molecular machines. The, given essentially arbitrary coordinates of the carbon and hydrogen atoms in a system, Brenner's potential will return the energy of the system. This permits molecular dynamical modeling of arbitrary hydrocarbon systems, including systems which use synthetic reactions involved in the synthesis of diamond.

Brenner has commented on the utility of this potential for modelling proposed molecular machine systems. Of course, the "accuracy" of the force fields depends on the application. A force field which was accurate to (say) 10 kcal/mole would be unable to correctly predict many properties of interest in biochemistry.

For example, such a force field would lead to serious errors in predicting the correct three-dimensional structure of a protein. Given the linear sequence of amino acids in a protein, the protein folding problem is to determine how it will fold in three dimensions when put in solution.

Often, the correct configuration will have an energy that differs from other (incorrect) configurations by a relatively modest amount, and so a force field of high accuracy is required. Unlike the protein folding problem, where an astronomical range of configurations of similar energy are feasible, the bearing basically has only one configuration: A bearing. While the protein has many unconstrained torsions, there are no unconstrained torsions in the bearing. To significantly change any torsion angle in the bearing would involve ripping apart bonds. Thus, the same force field which is of marginal utility in dealing with strands of floppy protein is quite adequate for solid blocks of stiff diamondoid material. Not only will small errors in the force field still result in an accurate prediction of the global minima, (which in this case will be a single large basin in the potential energy surface) but also the range of possible structures is so sharply limited that little or no computational effort need be spent comparing the energies of different configurations. Long computational runs to evaluate the statistical properties of ensembles of configurations are thus eliminated.

This style of design has been called, only half in jest, "molecular bridge building" because bridges are also designed with large safety margins. This observation, that the same force field that is inadequate for one class of structures is quite adequate for the design and modelling of a different class of structures, leads to a more general principle.

Computational experiments generally provide an answer with some error distribution. If the errors produced by the model are of a similar size to the errors that would result in incorrect device function, then the model is unreliable. On the other hand, if the errors in the model are small compared with the errors that will produce incorrect device function, then the results of the model are likely to be reliable. If a device design falls in the former category, *i.e.*, small errors in the model will produce conflicting forecasts about device function, then the conservative course of action is to reject the proposed design and keep looking. An even stronger (although somewhat more subtle) statement is possible.

The bearing illustrated in figures is simply a single bearing from a very large class of bearings. The strain in the axle and the sleeve is proportional to the diameter of the bearing. By increasing the diameter, we can reduce the strain. Thus, we can design bearings in this broad class in which the strain can be reduced to whatever level we desire. Because we are dealing with what amounts to a strained block of diamond, the fact that we can reduce strain arbitrarily means that we can design a bearing whose local structure bears as close a resemblance to an unstrained block of diamond as might be wished.

We can therefore be very confident indeed that some member of this class will perform the desired function (that of a bearing) and will work in accordance with our expectations. Given that we have developed software tools that are capable of creating and modelling most of the members of a broad class of devices, then we can investigate many individual class members. This investigation then lets us make rather confident statements about the functionality that members of this class can provide, even if there might be residual doubts about individual class members. A moments reflection will show that the class of objects which are chemically reasonably inert, relatively stiff (no free torsions), and which interact via simple repulsive forces that occur on contact; can describe a truly vast class of machines. Indeed, it is possible to design computers, robotic arms and a wide range of other devices using molecular parts drawn from this class.

MILESTONES IN NANOTECHNOLOGY

The nano-level world is an entirely different place where materials with familiar properties take on new and unfamiliar properties. At this level of scale, often referred to as the mesoscale, physical properties are subject to a combination of rules of quantum and classical physics.

Basic Definitions and Concepts

Nanotechnology is still an emerging technology and the nomenclature and classification of the materials is yet to be developed. The American National Standards Institute (ANSI) is in the process of establishing a standardized nomenclature for nanomaterials and has formed a Nanotechnology Standards Panel which first assembled in late September 2004. For now, the basic concepts in nanotechnology may be known by multiple names.

Nanoparticle

Typically, a nanoparticle is formed from a single element or a simple compound and has at least one dimension less than 100 nanometers. At this magnitude, the laws of classical physics become blurred and at sizes less than 50 nanometers, the rules of quantum physics take precedence. As opposed to classical physics, quantum physics is the special set of physical rules applicable to matter on the molecular or atomic scale. The transition from classical physics to quantum mechanics begins at approximately 50 nanometers; at this very small scale familiar materials take on new properties. For example, materials have different colors and their magnetic qualities are altered.

What is more interesting is that as the size of the particle shrinks, the ratio between mass and surface area changes and the surface area becomes proportionally much greater. It is possible for one gram of a nanomaterial to have a surface area of 1000 square meters. Because chemical reactions take place at the surface interfaces, nanoparticles are much more reactive than their bulky macro relatives. There are particular subtypes of nanoparticles.

Nanotubes

A nanotube is a cylindrical and hollow structure usually less than 100 nanometers in length, but may be much longer. Carbon nanotubes were discovered by the NEC Corporation in 1991. Nanotubes may consist of materials in addition to carbon, but the prototype for the nanotech building block remains the carbon nanotube (CNT), a hugely versatile object. The CNT is a tubular form of carbon with diameter of 1 nm and a variable length ranging from nanometers to microns. The cylindrical CNT is basically a layer of carbon atoms arranged as a sheet rolled into a tube. The CNT has special properties; it has extraordinary strength, nearly 100 times stronger than steel and is as stiff as a diamond with a tensile strength to 200 GPa. In addition, the CNT has a maximum strain that is 10% more than any other known material and a strength to weight ratio 500x more than aluminum.

The electrical properties of nanotubes make them particularly interesting; the CNT can be metallic or semiconducting depending on chirality. (Chirality is a term reflecting variation in the number of layers and the direction in which they spiral.) The nanotube has a tunable bandgap and electrical properties which may be altered by application of a magnetic field or mechanical deformation. The conductivity of a CNT is 6 orders of magnitude higher than that of copper and with a very high current carrying capacity. Interestingly, the thermal conduction of a CNT is directional; it is much greater in the axial direction versus the radial direction and it far exceeds copper's ability to retain heat with almost no thermal leakage. The tubes can carry electrical charges at twice the speed of silicon circuits. Carbon nanotubes may allow the construction of three dimensional integrated circuits, something not possible with contemporary silicon technology. All these unique properties make CNT especially valuable to the microelectronics and computer industries.

Buckyball

A buckyball, or fullerene, is named after Buckminster Fuller, a futurist and global thinker best known for the invention of the geodesic dome. The structure consists of 60 carbon atoms arranged in a sphere with a pattern of hexagons and pentagons similar to a soccer ball. The buckyball is hollow, but can be used to carry another material; the outside surface of the buckyball can also be coated. A buckyball is also a semiconductor and small enough to penetrate biomembranes ordinarily thought relatively impenetrable such as cell walls or the blood brain barrier. Given these unique properties, it is not surprising that buckyballs are source of great interest to engineers and pharmaceutical researchers. The discovery of the fullerene was important enough to earn Richard Smalley, Robert Curl and Sir Harold Kroto the 1985 Nobel Prize for chemistry.

Quantum Dot

Quantum dots are nanoscale crystals made of a few hundred atoms. Their small size allows them to be inserted into cell and they can be used to trace biological changes in the cell. Quantum dots can be made from a variety of substances and can be designed to fluoresce in almost any colour.

Although humans have always been exposed to nanoscale particles from forest fires or volcanic eruptions, the recent history of nanotechnology dates to 1959. In a December 1959 speech to the American Physical Society at the California Institute of Technology, Physicist Richard Feynman reports that the laws of physics, as he understood them, did not prohibit man from designing devices intended to move individual molecules.

The term nanotechnology was introduced by Norio Taniguchi in 1974 and taken to mean the very precise, indeed, the ultra precise, machining of materials on a molecular scale. Implied in this notion are the concepts of nanomeasurement and nanomanipulation, namely, the notion of manufacture on a molecular level. The goal of nanotechnology is described as the ability "to produce complex products on demand using simple raw materials".

The next milestone in the evolution of nanotechnology came in 1981: Binnig and Rohrer of the IBM Zurich Research Laboratory invented the scanning tunneling microscope (STM) for which they received the 1986 Nobel Prize in Physics. The STM allowed researchers to "see" materials on the atomic scale and led to the development of the atomic force microscope which allows the manipulation of nanoparticles on surfaces, i.e., nanoparticles could now be arranged to form structures.

The STM does not function like a conventional microscope. Visible light waves are too large to illuminate the details on a nanocoated surface; the STM employs a probe to feel the surface under examination and provide an image of the contours.

Five years later, in 1986 K. Eric Drexler published *Engines of Creation: The Coming Era of Nanotechnology* in which he discusses a coming change in manufacturing methods and he visualizes molecular assemblers. The molecular assembler, as proposed, is a nanoscale device, basically a machine that would assemble other machines. In theory, given the raw materials, time and the proper instructions, the assembler could manufacture a vacuum cleaner or similar object in a few hours and with a minimum of energy and virtually no waste or pollution. Contrast this method of production with the current system of top down production in which requires an enormous source of raw materials, including a source of copper and iron ore, a coal mine, etc. and then to refine and process the raw materials to derive the components of the vacuum cleaner all the while using substantial amounts of energy which produce excess heat and waste greenhouse gases.

Drexler believed that the assemblers will build with molecular precision, using only the precise amounts of resources and energy required and avoiding virtually all pollution and with no adverse environmental impacts. This technique of manufacture was described as "bottom up" manufacture as opposed to the conventional methods which are described as "top down" manufacture. He suggested that nanotechnology may even enable man to colonize solar system and approach immortality. However, Drexler saw some potential danger with uncontrolled self replication of robots. There was some fear that self replicating nanorobots might escape and embark on a rampage of self replication with widespread and uncontrolled consumption of raw materials.

This would lead to swarming waves of nanorobots forming a sort of "grey goo". This fear was found unjustified based on considerations of energy requirements for the nanorobots.

In 2000 the Clinton administration announced the National Nanotechnology Initiative (NNI) dramatically increasing the funding to the fledging industry in the United States. The initial budget for the NNI was $500 million. The developmental path of nanotechnology was not entirely smooth.

Also in 2002, Roco and Bainbridge published a report *Converging Technologies for Improving Human Performance* in which they saw the convergence of four areas of research (science, bioscience and medicine, information technology and cognitive science); the resulting new discipline will become the body of knowledge for nanotechnology. They predicted that the new technology will lead to major improvements in social outcomes, human abilities, productivity, quality of life and overall environmental improvements over the next 20 years. In early 2004, Drexler and Chris Phoenix withdrew their earlier concerns about self replicating robots, the so-called "grey goo", and instead warned that nanotechnology lends itself to the development of new weapons systems that may lead to undesirable shifts in economic and political power, even beyond the shifts occurring with globalization. Nevertheless, Drexler favored aggressive development in nanotechnology.

A 1995 study by RAND (Max Nelson and Calvin Shipbaugh) suggested that nanotechnology may not have a certain future and hinted that nanotechnology may go the way of controlled nuclear fusion, i.e. a good idea on paper but either not capable of being harnessed or simply more difficult than anticipated. The authors proposed a number of hurdles that nanotechnology must overcome in the years after 1995 to demonstrate the technology's viability: first, materials would have to be produced at the nanoscale and then processed into components. Second, the components would have to be connected and made to interface with the macroenvironment. Third, there must be the ability to control a massive number of nanodevices in a coordinated fashion. Finally, these devices would subsequently have to be powered. All but the last of these hurdles has been surpassed thus suggesting that the technology will demonstrate its viability as a discipline.

MILITARY USE OF HIGH TECHNOLOGY

While superior technology has been a decisive factor in wars in all of history, it was only in the last century that the armed forces incorporated science into their organisation in a systematic way. In particular after World War 2, rich/large/leading nations built up big centers for military research and development (R&D) and funded innovation in military industry on a large scale. Much of this was connected to nuclear weapons and their carriers, but increasingly was carried over to all other areas of warfare. Armed conflict is about breaking the will of an opponent by violent force. The law and rules of civilian society – that exclude pursuing one's will by force – no longer apply. Only the law of warfare poses some limits on how force is used; in peace time, agreed arms limitations can reduce the likelihood of war and restrict the number and quality of its tools. Success in armed conflict depends on many factors, among them technology, strategy, morale and surprise. Since highest national values may be at stake, there is an immanent tendency to circumvent the rules in order to prevail. In peace time, there is a motive to covertly compile more armaments than what arms-control agreements stipulate. This emphasises the importance of verification of compliance. In actual conduct of war, on the other hand, compliance with the international law of warfare depends on the spirit of a force; public scrutiny, experience with rule-keeping by the opponent, but also the fear of reprisal play a role. When armed conflict is raging, there is no reliance on the law of warfare; the necessity of prosecuting war criminals by international courts is only too obvious.

Since technology increasingly provides advantages in battle, all potential opponents have strong motives to stay in the lead, or at least to keep the lag small. New fields of technology make possible new ways of destruction. Military exploitation of new technology means putting the new possibilities into practice:

researching the potential, developing and testing devices. Sometimes international law or arms-control treaties impose limits– e.g. the Biological and Toxin Weapons Convention of 1972 prohibits all non-peaceful uses of biological agents and toxins, including development and testing. Offensive biological weapons are prohibited thus, whereas defensive protection (such as gas masks, vaccination) is allowed. However, in principle an opponent might break the rules covertly and achieve victory in this way. Thus, there is a strong motive to understand what such an opponent could bring to bear in order to be prepared to counter such development.

As a consequence, even a defensive-minded state can feel a need for some R&D of the forbidden offensive weapons. In such a way, scientific-technical advance has a tendency to undermine agreed limitation treaties. The only ways to contain this danger between potential opponents are 1) reliable verification of compliance with existing agreements, and 2) early conclusion of treaties for new technologies, that is preventive arms control.

A central means of securing effectiveness in combat is secrecy. Knowledge of technical details, strategies, plans, even the motivation of an opponent's armed forces makes attacking them easier, thus there is a strong motive to keep such information secret on the own side– and to gain it by espionage on the others.

There can be many additional motives for secrecy, and states differ widely how they handle it. The more secretive an armed force is, the higher is the possibility of a covert breakout: massing of weapons or personnel, introduction of qualitatively new weapons so that one side would suddenly dominate militarily. This problem becomes more urgent if new technology promises revolutionary change, as is the case with NT. Again it points at the necessity of supporting agreed limits by reliable verification, but it also emphasises the need to balance the required transparency with the (perceived) need for secrecy.

When potential military opponents prepare for the possibility of war by using new technology, small differences in technology can lead to high differences in the outcome. It is relative differences that count mostly. Shooting somewhat faster, at somewhat longer range, looking somewhat farther etc. can all mean that one's systems survive whereas the other's are destroyed.

This explains the race for the "leading edge" and the high price that the military are prepared to pay for new technology. It makes agreement on limitations more difficult. However, there are additional factors; e.g. a more defensive orientation can give more tolerance.

Mainly because of their very task – prevailing in armed conflict by selective or massive destruction – the armed forces want to prepare many of the bad and ugly uses of new technologies that civilian society will try hard to preclude. Criminal development of such prohibited uses – new poisons, eavesdropping equipment etc. – within society is severely restricted. Access to laboratories, expertise, testing grounds etc. is very difficult if one has to work clandestinely, under permanent threat of prosecution. On the other hand, in military R&D such activities are carried out in an organised manner under the protection and with the resources of the states. This sets a conceptually different framework for technology assessment and subsequent regulation.

Within societies, there is a higher authority with the monopoly of legitimate force that protects sub-state actors from attacks by others and prosecutes perpetrators. The international system, on the other hand, can still be characterised by the security dilemma. There is no overarching authority with a monopoly of force – states try to make themselves secure by their individual armed forces. Usually, strengthening the latter increases the mutual threats, leading to motives for further strengthening. If unchecked, the net outcome is decreased security of all.

There are several ways out of this security dilemma– they are mutually reinforcing. One is voluntary agreement limiting the mutual armed forces (arms control). Since the armed forces keep their task of prevailing in war, should it occur, there is an obvious friction between the motives for limitation and the motives for combat effectiveness. Nevertheless, an enlightened view of national security should lead to the preference of mutual limitations. A second alternative is restructuring of the armed forces so that combat efficiency is high in static defence of the own territory, but is low in attacking others. A third way out of the security dilemma is political détente, economic co-operation etc. so that one could not gain from an attack and it would become politically/culturally unthinkable. Finally, states could develop the United Nations to the international authority with monopoly of legitimate force similarly to the one that governments represent within states.

NANOTECHNOLOGICAL IMPROVEMENT OF EXISTING TYPES OF NUCLEAR WEAPONS

Nuclear weapon technology is characterised by two sharply contrasting demands. On the one hand, the nuclear package containing the fission and fusion materials is relatively simple and forgiving, i.e. rather more sophisticated than complicated. On the other hand, the many ancillary components required for arming the weapon, triggering the high-explosives, and initiating the neutron chain-reaction, are much more complicated. Moreover, the problems related to maintaining political control over the use of nuclear weapons, i.e. the operation of permissive action links (PALs), necessitated the development of protection systems that are meant to remain active all the way to the target, meaning that all these ancillary components and systems are submitted to very stringent requirements for security, safety, and reliable performance under severe conditions. The general solution to these problems is to favour the use of hybrid combinations of mechanical and electronic systems, which have the advantage of dramatically reducing the probability of common mode failures and decreasing sensitivity to external factors. It is this search for the maximisation of reliability and ruggedness which is driving the development and application of nanotechnology and MEMS engineering in nuclear weapons science.

To give an important example: modern nuclear weapons use insensitive high-explosives (IHE) which can only be detonated by means of a small charge of sensitive high-explosive that is held out of alignment from the main charge of IHE. Only once the warhead is armed does a MEMS bring the detonator into position with the main charge. Since the insensitive high-explosive in a nuclear weapon is usually broken down into many separate parts that are triggered by individual detonators, the use of MEMS-based detonators incorporating individual locking mechanisms are an important ingredient ensuring the use-control and one-point safety of such weapons.

Further improvements on existing nuclear weapons are stemming from the application of nanotechnology to materials engineering. New capacitors, new radiation-resistant integrated circuits, new composite materials capable to withstand high temperatures and accelerations, etc., will enable a further level of miniaturisation and a corresponding enhancement of safety and usability of nuclear weapons. Consequently, the military utility and the possibility of forward deployment, as well as the potentiality for new missions, will be increased.

Consider the concept of a "low-yield" earth penetrating warhead. The military appeal of such a weapon derives from the inherent difficulty of destroying underground targets. Only about 15 % of the energy from a surface explosion is coupled (transferred) into the ground, while shock waves are quickly attenuated when travelling through the ground. Even a few megatons surface burst will not be able to destroy a buried target at a depth or distance more than 100-200 meters away from ground zero. A radical alternative, therefore, is to design a warhead which would detonate after penetrating the ground by a few tens of meters or more. Since a free-falling or rocket-driven missile will not penetrate the surface by more than about ten meters, some kind of active penetration mechanism is required. This implies that the nuclear package and its ancillary components will have to survive extreme conditions of stress until the warhead is detonated.

Fourth-Generation Nuclear Weapons

First-and second-generation nuclear weapons are atomic and hydrogen bombs developed during the 1940s and 1950s, while third-generation weapons comprise a number of concepts developed between the 1960s and 1980s, e.g. the neutron bomb, which never found a permanent place in the military arsenals. Fourth-generation nuclear weapons are new types of nuclear explosives that can be developed in full compliance with the Comprehensive Test Ban Treaty (CTBT) using inertial confinement fusion (ICF) facilities such as the NIF in the US, and other advanced technologies which are under active development in all the major nuclear-weapon states-and in major industrial powers such as Germany and Japan.

In a nutshell, the defining technical characteristic of fourth-generation nuclear weapons is the triggering-by some advanced technology such as a superlaser, magnetic compression, antimatter, etc.-of a relatively small thermonuclear explosion in which a deuterium-tritium mixture is burnt in a device whose weight and size are not much larger than a few kilograms and litres. Since the yield of these warheads could go from a fraction of a ton to many tens of tons of high-explosive equivalent, their delivery by precision-guided munitions or other means will dramatically increase the fire-power of those who possess them-without crossing the threshold of using kiloton-to-megaton nuclear weapons, and therefore without breaking the taboo against the first-use of weapons of mass destruction. Moreover, since these new weapons will use no (or very little) fissionable materials, they will produce virtually no radioactive fallout. Their proponents will define them as "clean" nuclear weapons-and possibly draw a parallel between their battlefield use and the consequences of the expenditure of depleted uranium ammunition.

In practice, since the controlled release of thermonuclear energy in the form of laboratory scale explosions (i.e., equivalent to a few kilograms of high-explosives) at ICF facilities like NIF is likely to succeed in the next 10 to 15 years, the main arms control question is how to prevent this know-how being used to manufacture fourth-generation nuclear weapons. As we have already seen, nanotechnology and micromechanical engineering are integral parts of ICF pellet construction. But this is also the case with ICF drivers and diagnostic devices, and even more so with all the hardware that will have to be miniaturised and 'ruggedised' to the extreme in order to produce a compact, robust, and cost-effective weapon.

The potential of nanotechnology and microelectromechanical engineering in relation to the emergence of fourth-generation nuclear weapons is therefore of the utmost importance. It is likely that this discussion will be difficult, not just because of secrecy and other restrictions, but mainly because the military usefulness and usability of these weapons is likely to remain very high as long as precision-guided delivery systems dominate the battlefield. It is therefore important to realise that the technological hurdles that have to be overcome in order for laboratory scale thermonuclear explosions to be turned into weapons may be the only remaining significant barrier against the introduction and proliferation of fourth-generation nuclear weapons. For this reason alone-and there are many others, beyond the scope of this paper-very serious consideration should be given to the possibility of promoting an 'Inner Space Treaty' to prohibit the military development and application of nanotechnological devices and techniques.

Near and Long-Term Applications and Implications of Nanotechnology

Considering that nanotechnology is already an integral part of the development of modern weapons, it is important to realise that its immediate potential to improve existing weapons (either conventional or nuclear), and its short-term potential to create new weapons (either conventional or nuclear), are more than sufficient to require the immediate attention of diplomats and arms controllers.

In this perspective, the potential long-term applications of nanotechnology (and their foreseeable social and political implications) should neither be downplayed nor overemphasised. Indeed, there are potential applications such as self-replicating nano-robots ('nanobots') which may never prove to be feasible because of fundamental physical or technical obstacles. But this impossibility would not mean that the somewhat larger micro-robots of the type that are seriously considered in military laboratories could never become a reality.

In light of these extant and potential dangers and risks, every effort should be made not to repeat the error of the arms-control community with regard to missile defence. For over thirty years, that community acted on the premise that a ballistic missile defense system will never be built because it will never be sufficiently effective-only to be faced with a concerted attempt to construct such a system! If some treaty is contemplated in order to control or prohibit the development of nanotechnology, it should be drafted in such a way that all reasonable long-term applications are covered.

Moreover, it should not be forgotten that while nanotechnology mostly emphasises the *spatial* extension of matter at the scale of the nanometer (the size of a few atoms), the *time* dimension of mechanical engineering has recently reached its ultimate limit at the scale of the femtosecond (the time taken by an electron to circle an atom). It has thus become possible to generate bursts of energy in suitably packaged pulses in space and time that have critical applications in nanotechnology, and to focus pulses of particle or laser beams with extremely short durations on a few micrometer down to a few nanometer sized targets. The invention of the 'superlaser', which enabled such a feat and provided a factor of one million increase in the instantaneous power of tabletop lasers, is possibly the most significant recent advance in military technology. This increase is of the same magnitude as the factor of one million difference in energy density between chemical and nuclear energy.

MILITARY PONDERS FUTURE OF NANOTECH

While nano-sciences offer an array of potentially useful technology for the Defense Department, not all military researchers have jumped on this bandwagon. The disparity of viewpoints was on clear display at a recent lightweight materials conference, where researchers gave differing assessments of its impact.

"If you think biotech has been moving these last few years, just wait," said James Murday, chief scientist for the laboratories at the Office of Naval Research. "The electronics industry will be all nano by the end of the decade."

Other researchers contend the impact will be far less than the predictions of true believers such as Murday. "I'd be shocked if [nanotechnology] will be the thing in 10 years," noted David Stepp, chief of the materials science division of the Army Research Office. "There's always something after."

The federal government is certainly concentrating on nanotechnology. The Clinton administration's 2001 budget raised an informal "nano-scale science and technology working group" to the level of a federal initiative. The National Nanotechnology Initiative (NNI) was born, an effort that has received steady increased in research and development funding.

Federal funding for nanotechnology research and development has increased from $116 million in 1997 to an estimated $961 million in 2004. President Bush's 2005 budget request calls for an additional 2 percent increase, boosting the NNI budget to $982 million. The Defense Department is one key player in NNI, with a firm interest in developing new materials and manufacturing processes that could determine the shape of a 22nd century fighting force. The Pentagon recognizes 10 broad applications of nano-science, including ultra-small computers, low-power communications systems, bio-chemical defense suites, new targeting lasers and countermeasures and innovative materials for armor systems.

Future plans, Murday said, could include further advances, such as directed self-assembly and repair, nano-porous materials that could screen the passage of particles through a membrane and transparent ceramics and composites that could shame current efforts.

Some long-standing engineering problems may find solutions in nanotech. For example, an artificial sapphire used on the nose cones of infrared-guided missiles could be enhanced using advances in nano-science, said Larry Kabacoff, program manager for nano-structured materials for the Office of Naval Research.

If a new material can be formed, it could be an answer to a problem vexing researchers who are searching for a material tough enough to survive insect and weather damage in flight and transparent enough to allow infrared waves through without refracting them. The current systems rely on sapphires which often are damaged while in flight, Kabacoff told National Defense, and using damage-resistant diamonds is cost prohibitive.

Kabacoff's group found that a single-phase material with a structure 20 times smaller than the infrared wavelengths would allow the light to pass unaffected. The program was cut in 2003, "just as progress was being made." A small project with Raytheon still exists, which is generating data that could be used to mount an argument to resume ONR funding. Other nations also are turning their eyes towards nanotechnology, Murday noted. He called China "a major player" who is investing steadily in the emerging technology, and added that Japan is matching the United States' investment dollar-for-dollar.

"We'd just as soon be on the front end of that curve," Murday told the conference attendees.

Social, Military and Ethical Issues in Nanotechnology

Nanotechnology has become a major area of intensive research funding worldwide. The FP6 of the European Commission has set aside 1.3 billion Euro for research within this field in the period 2003-2006. Many countries-with the USA in a leading position-are strengthening their research in nanotechnology similarly. Norway has followed this international trend in science policy through a strategic cooperation between UiO, IFE, SINTEF and NTNU called FUNMAT. An annual budget of 150 million NOK is set aside for ten years in order to increase national expertise in nanotechnology. However, some critical voices like e.g. the etc.-group claim that our current knowledge is too limited to handle the risks that one may have to face.

But not only the risks are debated, also the ethics of some possible applications that may be generated are discussed. Nanotechnology travels in miniscule dimensions: one nanometer is one billionth of a meter, while e.g. a human hair is about 80,000 nanometer. Within such a scale one is in effect already below the levels of life and touching the very elements of nature. While many scientists recognise the benefits that the nanotechnology revolution could bring, some have serious concerns. This apprehension is not restricted to one field, but covers human health, environmental impacts, effects on international trade and developing countries, and the possible proliferation in armaments.

A major concern is however that we just do not know what the impacts of nanotechnology will be. It is this lack of knowledge that leads some scientists to call for a moratorium on certain aspects of nanotechnology use and research. The question one needs to confront is whether there is an urgent need for a strict and harmonized regulation of research in this field and how ethical issues related to possible applications could be explored before facts are created that may be difficult to contain or control.

The organizers have invited three international experts that shall address some of the problematic issues in their presentations. The experts are:

Dr. Jürgen Altmann, Experimental Physics III at the University of Dortmund, Germany, chair of the group "Physics and disarmament", and chair of the "Bochum Verfication-project". Dr Altmann is author of the book Military Uses of Microsystem Technologies: Dangers and Preventive Arms Control, Münster 2001. He has spoken extensively on the possible military uses of nanotechnology in various fora, among others for the Royal Society, London, working group on nanotechnology and nanoscience. He has just finished a 15-months project on preventive arms control for NT (funded by the new German Foundation for Peace Research DSF), however the book will only appear in 2-3 months. An overview can be gained from an article co-authored with Mark Gubrud. Dr Altmann has made specific proposals for precautionary action in nanotechnology development.

Prof. Vivian Weil is Director of the Center for the Study of Ethics in the Professions at the Illinois Instiute of Technology, Chicago. Dr. Weil is a Fellow of the American Association for the Advancement of Science, a member of the Governing Board of the National Institute for Engineering Ethics, and Chair of the Executive Committee of the Association for Practical and Professional Ethics. She serves on the editorial boards of various journals, including Science and Engineering Ethics and Science Communication.

She received her A.B. and M.A. from the University of Chicago and her Ph.D. in philosophy from the University of Illinois, Chicago. In 1990-1991, she directed the Ethics and Values Studies program of the National Science Foundation (NSF). Recently, she has been involved in NSF conferences to integrate ethics and societal implications in nano science and technology, as a speaker on ethics and as a member of the organizing committee of its most recent conference in December, 2003. Dr. Christoph Baumgartner, from the Interdepartmental Center for Ethics in the Sciences and

Humanities (IZEW) of the University of Tübingen, Germany. Dr. Baumgartner, born 1969, studied Chemistry and Theology in Tübingen (Germany) and acts as Academic Coordinator of the IZEW. His doctoral Thesis was about "Problems of Motivation in the context of environmental behaviour as a challenge for environmental ethics." His main areas of research are: Environmental Ethics, Problems of Motivation to Morally Responsible Behaviour, Ethical Aspects of Biopatenting, Ethical Aspects of New Technologies, especially Nanotechnology. He has especially worked with the ethical challenges in medical nanotechnology.

Bibliography

Andrew, N.: *Foundations of Nanomechanics: from Solid-state Theory to Device Applications*, Berlin, New York, 2003.

Berube, D.M.: *The Rhetoric of Nanotechnology*, Amsterdam: IOS Press, 2004.

Bhaskara Rao: *Military Conversion : Impact on Science and Technology*, Discovery, Delhi, 2003.

Bhatia, Shyam: *India's Nuclear Bomb,* Ghaziabad: Vikas Publishing House, 1979.

Burnham, John. *Total War: The Economic Theory of a War Economy.* Boston: Meador Publishing Company, 1943.

Cathy Solheim: *Military Economics: Issues, Policies, and Solutions,* Washington, D.C., Island Press, 1995.

Cochran, Thomas B. *Nuclear Weapons Databook.* Cambridge, MA: Ballinger Publishing Company, 1987.

David, J.: *Micromachines and Nanotechnology: the Amazing New World of the Ultrasmall,* Parsippany, Dillon Press, 1995.

Dunne, J. P. and Brauer, J.: *Arms Trade and Economic Development: Theory, Policy*, Routledge, London, 2004.

Friedman, G.: *The Future of War: Power, Technology and American World Dominance in the 21st Century,* N.Y., Random House, 1996.

Greider, William. *Fortress America: The American Military and the Consequences of Peace.* New York, 1998.

Gupta, Asha: *Military Rule and Democratization : Changing Perspectives*, Deep & Deep, Delhi, 2003.

Harkavy, Robert E. *The Arms Trade and International Systems.* Cambridge, Mass., 1975.

Hayles, N.K. : *Nanoculture: Implications of the New Technoscience*, Bristol, Intellect Books, 2004.

James L. *The Economic Impact of the Cold War: Sources and Readings.* New York, 1970.

Krause, Keith. *Arms and the State: Patterns of Military Production and Trade.* Cambridge, U.K., 1992.

Mary, W.: *Military Space Force: the Cultural Dimensions of Authority,* Cambridge, Belknap Press, 1985.

Nininger, Robert D. *Minerals for Atomic Energy*. New York: D. Van Nostrand Company, Inc., 1954.

Pierre, Andrew J. *The Global Politics of Arms Sales.* Princeton, N.J., 1982.

Posen, B.R.: *The Sources of Modernization Military,* Ithaca, 1984, Cornell Univ. Press.

Rollins, John: *Terrorist Capabilities for Cyberattack: Overview of Policy Issues*. Congressional Research Service, 2007.

Rosen, P.: *Societies and Military Power: India and its Armies,* Ithaca, Cornell University Press, 1996.

Samuel P. Huntington: *The Soldier and the State : The Theory and Politics of Civil-Military Relations,* Natraj Pub, Delhi, 2005.

Sherwin, Martin J. A World Destroyed: *The Atomic Bomb and the Grand Alliance*. New York: Vintage Books, 1977.

Sivard, R L.: *World Military and Social Expenditures,* World Priorities, Washington D.C, 1993.

Smith, H. A.: *Nanotechnology Infrared Optics for Astronomy Missions,* Washington, National Aeronautics and Space Administration, 2002.

Sutton, J., *Technology and Defence Market Structure,* MIT Press, Delhi, 1998.

Tomellini, R.: *Nanotechnology: Revolutionary Opportunities and Societal Implications, Workshop, Lecce,* Luxemburg: Office for Official Publications of the European Communities, 2002.

Van de Goor, L.L.P.: *Conflict and Development: The Causes of Conflict in Developing Countries,* The Netherlands Institute of International Relations, The Hague, 1994.

Weimann, Gabriel: *Terror on the Internet: The New Arena, the New Challenges*. Washington, D.C.: United States Institute of Peace, 2006.

Index

M

N

O

P

S

T

❑❑❑